Contemporary Fiction, Celebrity Culture, and the Market for Modernism

New Horizons in Contemporary Writing

In the wake of unprecedented technological and social change, contemporary literature has evolved a dazzling array of new forms that traditional modes and terms of literary criticism have struggled to keep up with. *New Horizons in Contemporary Writing* presents cutting-edge research scholarship that provides new insights into this unique period of creative and critical transformation.

Series Editors:
Martin Eve and Bryan Cheyette

Editorial Board:
Siân Adiseshiah (University of Lincoln, UK), Sara Blair (University of Michigan, USA), Peter Boxall (University of Sussex, UK), Robert Eaglestone (Royal Holloway, University of London, UK), Rita Felski (University of Virginia, USA), Rachael Gilmour (Queen Mary, University of London, UK), Caroline Levine (University of Wisconsin–Madison, USA), Roger Luckhurst (Birkbeck, University of London, UK), Adam Kelly (York University, UK), Antony Rowland (Manchester Metropolitan University, UK), John Schad (Lancester University, UK), Pamela Thurschwell (University of Sussex, UK), Ted Underwood (University of Illinois at Urbana-Champaign, USA).

Volumes in the series:
Creaturely Forms in Contemporary Literature, Dominic O'Key
Thomas Pynchon and the Digital Humanities, Erik Ketzan
Northern Irish Writing After the Troubles, Caroline Magennis
Jeanette Winterson's Narratives of Desire, Shareena Z. Hamzah-Osbourne
Transatlantic Fictions of 9/11 and the War on Terror, Susana Araújo
Life Lines: Writing Transcultural Adoption, John McLeod
South African Literature's Russian Soul, Jeanne-Marie Jackson
The Politics of Jewishness in Contemporary World Literature, Isabelle Hesse
Writing After Postcolonialism: Francophone North African Literature in Transition, Jane Hiddleston
David Mitchell's Post-Secular World, Rose Harris-Birtill
New Media and the Transformation of Postmodern American Literature, Casey Michael Henry
Postcolonialism After World Literature, Lorna Burns
Jonathan Lethem and the Galaxy of Writing, Joseph Brooker
The Contemporary Post-Apocalyptic Novel, Diletta De Cristofaro
David Foster Wallace's Toxic Sexuality, Edward Jackson
Wanderwords: Language Migration in American Literature, Maria Lauret

Forthcoming volumes:
Encyclopaedism and Totality in Contemporary Fiction, Kiron Ward

Contemporary Fiction, Celebrity Culture, and the Market for Modernism

Fictions of Celebrity

Carey Mickalites

BLOOMSBURY ACADEMIC
LONDON • NEW YORK • OXFORD • NEW DELHI • SYDNEY

BLOOMSBURY ACADEMIC
Bloomsbury Publishing Plc
50 Bedford Square, London, WC1B 3DP, UK
1385 Broadway, New York, NY 10018, USA
29 Earlsfort Terrace, Dublin 2, Ireland

BLOOMSBURY, BLOOMSBURY ACADEMIC and the Diana logo are trademarks of Bloomsbury Publishing Plc

First published in Great Britain 2022
This paperback edition published 2023

Copyright © Carey Mickalites, 2022

Carey Mickalites has asserted his right under the Copyright, Designs and Patents Act, 1988, to be identified as Author of this work.

For legal purposes the Acknowledgments on p. vi constitute an extension of this copyright page.

Cover design and illustration by Namkwan Cho

All rights reserved. No part of this publication may be reproduced or transmitted in any form or by any means, electronic or mechanical, including photocopying, recording, or any information storage or retrieval system, without prior permission in writing from the publishers.

Bloomsbury Publishing Plc does not have any control over, or responsibility for, any third-party websites referred to or in this book. All internet addresses given in this book were correct at the time of going to press. The author and publisher regret any inconvenience caused if addresses have changed or sites have ceased to exist, but can accept no responsibility for any such changes.

A catalogue record for this book is available from the British Library.

A catalog record for this book is available from the Library of Congress.

ISBN: HB: 978-1-3502-4856-4
PB: 978-1-3502-4860-1
ePDF: 978-1-3502-4857-1
eBook: 978-1-3502-4858-8

Series: New Horizons in Contemporary Writing

Typeset by Newgen KnowledgeWorks Pvt. Ltd., Chennai, India

To find out more about our authors and books visit www.bloomsbury.com and sign up for our newsletters.

Contents

Acknowledgments — vi

Introduction: Contemporary Fiction, Celebrity Culture, and the Market for Modernism — 1
1. Signature to Brand: Martin Amis's Negotiations with Literary Celebrity — 29
2. "To Invent a Literature": Ian McEwan's Commercial Modernism — 53
3. Modernism as Postcolonial Inc.: Authorizing Salman Rushdie — 79
4. What the Public Wants: Kazuo Ishiguro, Prize Culture, and the Art of Alienation — 107
5. Zadie Smith, Inauthenticity, and Multicultural Modernism — 135
6. Marginal Literary Values, or, How Eimear McBride and Anna Burns Reframe Irish Modernism — 163

Notes — 187
Bibliography — 220
Index — 235

Acknowledgments

This book has benefitted from the support of several institutions and individuals. At the University of Memphis, I thank the College of Arts and Sciences for a semester-long sabbatical and a summer research grant, and the Marcus Orr Center for the Humanities (and its former director, Sarah Potter) for a lively and supportive fellowship. Friends and colleagues in the English department have patiently listened to ideas in progress, offering much-needed motivation and affirmation: Jeff Scraba, Josh Phillips, Darryl Domingo, Gene Plunka, and, last but not least, Romy Ghanem, who regularly asked for progress reports. Gul Hos, tireless as ever, compiled the bibliography.

I'm pleased that the book found a home with Bloomsbury. I thank Ben Doyle, publisher in literature, for supporting the project from the moment of first contact, as well as the series editors, Bryan Cheyette and Martin Paul Eve, enviably prolific scholars both. And thanks to the anonymous readers solicited by Bloomsbury. Each of these individuals made the book better than it might have been. Any remaining flaws are, of course, my own.

Finally, I thank my wife, Terie Box, and my stepdaughter, Juniper, for love, laughter, and making life a joy, every single day, even during a pandemic. This book is dedicated to Terie.

An earlier version of Chapter 1 was published as "Martin Amis's Money: Negotiations with Literary Celebrity," in *Postmodern Culture* 13.1 (September 2013).

Introduction: Contemporary Fiction, Celebrity Culture, and the Market for Modernism

How does the literature of high modernism influence the writing, production, and reception of contemporary fiction? If the former historically emerged as a set of self-conscious experimental practices circulated within a field of small-scale production and came to feature as a gold standard of difficulty and aesthetic autonomy, why have so many authors returned to its famous impulse to make literature new, particularly in a field that has become dominated by mass production, a culture of celebrity, and the undeniably commodified status of literary fiction? Salman Rushdie's career was launched with a Booker Prize–winning novel about India written in an encyclopedic Joycean mode of mythologizing the peripheral nation. Following his own Booker Prize, Ian McEwan published a book that straddles the line between a dazzling Woolfian impressionism and a critique of his predecessor's alleged social elitism. Zadie Smith, a modernist stylist if there ever was one, follows her first literary success with an homage to E. M. Forster. And Eimear McBride has recently gained widespread acclaim and commercial success with a novel that radically reframes the Joycean epiphany and its centrality to a larger tradition of Irish modernism.

As these examples suggest, I attempt in this book to answer my opening questions by framing our reception of modernism squarely within the evolving market for literary values. The case studies I advance reveal a resurgent interest, since the 1980s, in the legacies of modernism from within and along the margins of mainstream literary production, in which writers variously affirm, reanimate, or refute modernist experimental aesthetics to test the horizons of possibility for contemporary fiction in the face of a market increasingly controlled by multinational corporate conglomerates and that positions the author as a brand name in an elite and competitive field. Modernism, in this context, features as an unfinished aesthetic project, a self-conscious impulse toward formal experiment, that is posited on its historical institutionalization of cultural capital that provides authors an aura of distinction in a fully commercialized literary market.

This book focuses on the careers of seven celebrity authors from Britain and Ireland whose fiction can be situated in a contemporary field that David James and Urmila Seshagiri designate as "metamodernism." For these critics, modernism from a contemporary vantage point features as both "an era" and "an aesthetic," an established historical archive and an unfinished project of experimental writing that draws on the latent possibilities of the past to reflect on contemporary social contexts and concerns. "Metamodernism," they argue, is legible in self-conscious strategies by which contemporary authors work to "extend, reanimate, and repudiate" its existing literary legacies to address new social, ethical, and political concerns.[1] Whether writers self-consciously extend modernism's will to stylistic experiment into contemporary contexts, or critically and creatively engage with modernism as an institutional and historical formation, metamodernist fictions, in this account, "demand a critical practice balanced between an attention to the textures of narrative form and an alertness to the contingencies of historical reception."[2] Metamodernism is thus a usefully malleable term for understanding how many contemporary novelists have turned to the formal and stylistic experimentation that came to define a canon of early-twentieth-century literature, a process of rethinking the aesthetic achievements of the past and their implications for social and ethical reflection in the present.

The authors I take up here similarly engage in self-reflexive metamodernist strategies, and the driving question for this book is how that particular trend is a condition of market forces that radically differ from those in which modernism's legacies took shape. What goes missing from these accounts of the contemporaneity of modernism, in other words, is a material history of the market for modernism's afterlives. One of the defining "historical contingencies of reception" for this study lies with the publishing industry itself, and authors who self-consciously extend modernism's legacies—as an archive and a style— are also literary celebrities, at once canonized and commercially successful. *Contemporary Fiction, Celebrity Culture, and the Market for Modernism* responds to this scholarly lacuna by addressing the intersections of literary form and the conditions of increasingly corporatized literary production to theorize a larger history of the market for modernism. Contemporary authors who engage with modernist modes of stylistic experiment do so within a field dominated by multinational conglomerates and a monopolistic culture of celebrity. Most of the major works of literary fiction published since the 1980s have been produced under such neoliberal commercial conditions of publicity and mainstream marketing, and authors' complicity in corporate production and promotion have prompted anxieties concerning questions of literary autonomy, in which modernism functions as a standard for the generation of disinterested symbolic values. In the contemporary field, celebrity authors can negotiate the commercial complicity of their work by appealing to modernism's ostensibly autonomous legacy, but it's a legacy that cannot be assumed; rather, as Sarah Brouillette has persuasively shown, they view this particular modernist "inheritance … as a problem in search of a solution."[3] Unlike the work of their celebrity modernist predecessors, much of which originally circulated within a small-scale field of production, contemporary literary fiction is produced by prestigious imprints owned by multinational corporations, parts of a completely commercialized field in which successful authors are compelled to negotiate the vexed problems concerning complicity and critique, authorial autonomy and selling out.

This book focuses on how a range of formally innovative and commercially successful authors negotiate these anxieties over the mutually conditioning cultural and economic value of literary fiction—itself a privileged cultural commodity—by positioning their writing in relation to modernism's legacy of aesthetic revolution and autonomy. The historical modernists were themselves adept at self-promotion, adapting mass-market forms of publicity to a small-scale field of production to cultivate new kinds of cultural celebrity. And the mid-century institutionalization and mass marketing of a canon of modernist figures and texts had the paradoxical effect of preserving its reputation for formal difficulty and autonomy. As an archive, an open-ended set of experimental aesthetic practices, and a subject of dynamic critical debate, modernism now bears out a wealth of cultural capital and provides a mark of distinction, or "literariness," in the commercial market. I argue that metamodernist fiction not only engages in extending the possibilities of mainstream literature, but that, in staking a claim to its cultural capital, it also occupies and reflects a trend in the commercial market; its commercial success, in turn, shapes the critical reception of "serious" literary fiction and the privileged identity of the author as a brand name. Joining formal analysis of texts with a materialist approach toward the field of literary production, I hope to provide something of a dialectical history of literary celebrity in the specific context of the market for modernism. The aesthetic and historical legacies of modernism are undeniably conditioned by corporate production and a culture of celebrity. Contemporary metamodernist writing and formal experiment seek to refashion the potential for mainstream literary fiction, but that very claim depends on a market in which modernism circulates as a bearer of cultural authority and as a function of the brand name distinct to a commercial literary field.

Theorizing Contemporary Modernism

While an expansive body of criticism has, over the past few decades, placed critical pressure on our old periodizing tendencies by discovering modernist aesthetic and political practices outside the historical and geographical coordinates of a Eurocentric or Anglo-American canon, a number of critics have turned specifically to how that necessarily indeterminate canon has been a subject for renewed experiment in contemporary fiction, particularly as that return to modernism has appeared in the wake of a formerly fashionable postmodernism. In addition to the model of metamodernism I enlisted above, David James has elsewhere argued that authors writing after the "politically abortive metafiction" of postmodernism have set out to reinvigorate modernism's twinned investment in self-conscious form and social commitment.[4] James is careful to delineate his approach as a diachronic one, arguing that contemporary authors' creative engagement with modernist innovation reworks its original achievements to animate "the *prospects* of the unrealised potentialities of modernist fiction" as a body of work "to be continually tested, redesigned, and remade" to address the "cultural, ethical and political demands" of the present.[5] James's work on modernism's "futures" is in productive conversation with others who have similarly pushed for the ethical valences to be found in a reworking of modernist form. Derek Attridge, for one, has been particularly influential in staking out this focus on what Tim Woods sums up as "*the ethics of form.*"[6] Attridge argues for the ethical alterity of literature, implicitly posited on a claim for aesthetic autonomy, as its own social justification: "To respond to the demand of the literary work as the demand of the other is to attend to it as a unique event whose happening is a call, a challenge, an obligation: understand me, translate my untranslatability, learn me by heart and thus learn the otherness that inhabits the heart."[7] Elsewhere Attridge identifies a potent example of this ethical alterity in the work of J. M. Coetzee, a "belated modernist" whose writing synthesizes the ethics of literary alterity with the demand that contemporary literature in a modernist mode must involve a "reworking of modernism's methods" just as the historical modernists were themselves involved in creatively reworking and destabilizing the traditions they inherited.[8] As these critical interventions into periodizing suggest, modernism's unfinished provocations, when taken up with an eye on the different social demands of the present, provide a dialogic vantage for ongoing ethical reflection.

Dialogic and differential as these arguments are, they nevertheless implicitly rest on an assumption of some degree of historical continuity, prompting us to note an important distinction within contemporary engagements with the legacies of modernism, one that lies uneasily between modernism as an institutional inheritance versus an inspiration toward formal experiment on the text's own terms. As academic critics of modernism are fully aware, the term often designates a selective body of authors and key texts making up a received canon whose historical institutionalization has helped to secure its legacy as a mark of cultural capital. Alys Moody argues that a recently revived modernist aesthetic of detachment, for example, is built on a "selective memory" of the canon, and that its contemporary prominence in mainstream fiction is metamodernist in the specific sense that "its modernism is a retrospective one, filtered through the legacy of modernism's reception in the university."[9] On this view, metamodernist fiction that invokes modernism's institutional legacy often appeals to its established cultural capital as a source of institutional and economic prestige; or, as Neil Levi puts it, a "fidelity to the institution of modernism" constitutes "a conservative affirmation" of an existing canon that relies on and sustains its "established hierarchies of evaluation."[10] This institutional reception is crucial to my understanding of a metamodernist practice of authorial self-fashioning, evident in, say, McEwan's ambivalent emulation of Woolfian impressionism or Smith's homage to E. M. Forster. These strategies signal "a bid for consecration in the market for symbolic capital," as Jeremy Rosen writes of genre fiction, that can then be leveraged toward economic gain "in a highly competitive literary marketplace."[11]

In contrast to this kind of conservative affirmation of modernism's institutionalized cultural capital, a host of contemporary writers engage in what Levi calls a "fidelity to the event of modernism" in which "the innovations of" a prior cultural moment are taken up "as events whose implications required continued investigation."[12] This model signals a metamodernist project bent on adapting the latent provocations of modernism's formal innovations to the specific social and material conditions of its contemporary moment or, to return to James and Seshagiri's useful definition, reveals a "vastly divergent" body of fiction that "incorporates and adapts, reactivates and complicates the aesthetic prerogatives of an earlier cultural moment."[13] This kind of reanimation of the latent potential within modernist innovation, that is, seeks to extend modernism's earlier transformative designs on literary institutions and marketing. But building on recent scholarship concerned with the historical institutions and material conditions in which modernism originally emerged, one of my aims here is to subject our critical accounts of metamodernism to a more dialectical history of periodization. Contemporary fiction that engages with modernism's complex legacies bears out the potential to critically reflect on pressing problems such as social inequality—one of the perennial themes of literature writ large, of course—but that potential is fundamentally posited on a heavily marketized literary culture where these questions of what modernism means play out.

Critics espousing modernism's thematic and formal relevance to contemporary literary study, that is, have significantly expanded its function as a period concept and brought to our attention how contemporary literature draws on its aesthetic legacies in the shaping of an ongoing narrative of cultural modernity. And yet, these compelling critical approaches to the thematic or social relevance of modernism to contemporary fiction are not sufficiently historicized, and overlook the material conditions in which modernism was initially disseminated, codified, and marketed, on the one hand, or how its current revitalization, as a source of cultural capital and an inspiration toward formal experiment, is conditioned by the demands of the literary market and a culture of celebrity.[14] What goes missing from this important work, in other words, is an account of the material conditions of contemporary literary production, and how the market, the universities, and other institutions of legitimation form the social structures that provide the material support for a renewal of modernist aesthetics, where modernism functions as a "brand" whose speculative value "consolidates an audience" among writers, publishers, reviewers, and critics to generate both literary prestige and financial profit.[15]

Later in this introduction I address the stark contrast between the social conditions in which modernism emerged and the conglomerate system that today delimits the experimental possibilities for contemporary writing, but I should note here that my periodizing impulse owes a debt, and perhaps an unfashionable one, to the work of the Frankfurt School and its later inflections in Fredric Jameson's critical model of postmodern cultural production. If we understand modernism in part as an impulse toward formal experiment and aesthetic autonomy that now circulates as a kind of brand distinction in the commercial field, that view has a strong twentieth-century critical lineage. Writing at mid-century, Horkheimer and Adorno famously situate modernist claims to aesthetic autonomy at the point of its historical absorption into the imminent hegemony of capitalist mass production. While this phase of autonomy could only "exist as a separate sphere in its bourgeois form," modernism nonetheless stakes out "a degree of independence from the power of the market" by its collective insistence on art's noninstrumental value, a position that "stiffened the backbone of art in its late phase against the verdict of supply and demand, heightening its resistance far beyond its actual degree of protection" and thus anticipating the way in which a dissenting refusal of the market became itself subject to a pervasive production of formulaic "consumer goods."[16] Now, this is not the end of the story of autonomy and commodity complicity for Adorno, who would go on to complicate claims for complicity as providing its own mode of resistance to commercial culture at large, as I take up in Chapter 4. But I bring up these still-provocative arguments both because they continue to echo across contemporary discourse about authorship, autonomy, and the commercialization of the literary field, and because they form a historical touchstone for Fredric Jameson's periodizing work on modernism from the vantage of late-capitalist or postmodern cultural production.

Jameson's aptly influential work on postmodernism dialectically positions it as the historical antithesis to modernism's residual claim to autonomy, and extends the Frankfurt School's critique of the culture industry into a late-capitalist phase of the financialization of cultural production in which former claims to aesthetic innovation would become integral to the market for novelty. High modernism on this view—which Jameson associates with scandalous content, social dissidence, and the niche production of experimental work—was capable of cultivating at least a "minimal aesthetic distance," a "positioning of the cultural act outside the massive Being of capital."[17] Developing these arguments over the course of the 1980s—and thus historically aligned with the structural transformations of neoliberal finance—Jameson argues that in the wake of modernism's historical institutionalization, its aesthetic legacies have become utterly normalized, its initial shock value and aspirations for social transformation having "become integrated into commodity production generally" within a postmodern mode of cultural production that "now assigns an increasingly essential structural function and position to aesthetic innovation and experimentation" as the driving forces of late capitalism.[18] Metamodernist fiction, while sometimes capable of provocative reformulations of modernist innovation in its own terms, also brings the cultural capital of the canon in line with a neoliberal drive toward innovation in all sectors of production and marketing. In the case of the fictions of celebrity that I address, innovation is measured in relation to proven marketable forms that may appeal to a desire for aesthetic autonomy but one that most often features as a privileged fiction enabled by commercial success.

Like Jameson, I ascribe in this book to a view of modernism as a historical period, distinguished by the unique material conditions in which it sought to cultivate aesthetic experiment as a mode of claiming autonomy from within capitalist modernity. Others have recently taken up this critical lineage to complicate the historical contingencies of production and reception in theorizing modernism's contemporaneity. In an important recent volume, for example, editors Michael D'Arcy and Mathias Nilges and their contributors question "endogenous" approaches to a contemporary "modernist literary tradition that is not fundamentally interrupted and conditioned by material conditions." As a counter to such approaches, the editors and contributors stress the different conditions affecting the literary output of respective historical periods, and also, more boldly, aim to recover and test the "claims of modernist aesthetic autonomy" that such studies either assume as a rightful inheritance or leave aside entirely.[19] Following Adorno and Jameson, D'Arcy and Nilges set out to complicate "modernist distinctions" between artistic production and total commodification, autonomy and market complicity, and the debates conducted within their book offer nuanced ways of accounting for how modernist claims to impersonality and autonomy "remain salient points of reference for contemporary literary production," especially considering the encroachment of neoliberal capitalism into formerly distinct fields of cultural production.[20] This kind of dialectical approach importantly seeks to materialize those modernist modes of articulating a social aesthetic, and in a clear echo of Theodor Adorno, the editors point out that a "claim to aesthetic autonomy and reflection on aesthetic medium is not just opposed to historical or social context, but dialectically involved with it" in a process that demands attention to the fact that any claim to "autonomous art necessarily integrates the experience of late capitalism and the most advanced techniques of capitalist production."[21]

Culturally consecrated and commercially successful fiction that self-consciously engages with the legacies of modernism—as an institutionalized body of cultural capital and as an inherited will toward self-legislating formal experiment—registers a particularly privileged set of strategies by which authors negotiate the problem of autonomy as a modernist legacy that also provides a distinctive literary position within the "advanced techniques" of corporate production that enable and make visible that problem in the first place. This is the commercial context in which modernism's afterlives and contemporary relevance are necessarily negotiated. Indeed, taking up a wide range of metamodernist stylists, as I do in the chapters that follow, reveals an internally conflicted field with various designs on the market for modernism. So, for example, Ian McEwan writes in a self-conscious emulation of Woolf's impressionism in an effort to refute its socially elitist trappings, but in such a way that conforms to a sophisticated literary establishment in which impressionism has become a standard mode of rendering the idiosyncrasies of middle-class consciousness. In contrast, McEwan's equally celebrated contemporary Kazuo Ishiguro echoes the disconsoling style cultivated by Kafka and Beckett in a surrealist novel that destabilizes the collective belief in the lofty and disinterested status of high art, suggesting how that value system is itself contingent upon economic exchange and commercial publicity. As a clever satire on the "economy of prestige" on which Ishiguro's celebrity depends, his comic distortion of its logics also reflects critically on the standardizing market demands for literary fiction and how those conditions have shaped his reception. As these contrastive cases suggest, fiction that self-consciously refutes or reanimates modernism's will to style occupies a commercially privileged position and reflects a sense in which modernism's institutionalized cultural capital affords a degree of distinction in the mainstream market for literary fiction.

We might frame this argument as a partial response to an open-ended call formulated by D'Arcy and Nilges, specifically that the contemporaneity of modernism "asks to be read as indicating not only the problem of how to critically engage with modernism as it is manifest at the present time, but also as pointing to classical modernism's own involvement with the problems at issue in modernism's ambiguous afterlives."[22] The authors here register an incomplete historical dialectic that compels us "to rethink modernism's discontinuous history that reaches into the present."[23] We can think through this discontinuous history and how it plays out in contemporary fiction by returning to the formation of modernism itself, conceived as an internally disparate body of works bent on transforming the possibilities of the literary field through complex negotiations with the material and commercial conditions in which it historically emerged.

Historical Modernism (Scarcity, Celebrity, Autonomy)

If a certain canon of modernism bears out a legacy of sophistication, difficulty, and cultural capital—capital that can now be said to provide both literary prestige and economic returns—that contemporary formation is in part an inheritance of its historically active role in shaping the conditions of literary production, circulation, and legitimation. In other words, to make sense of how contemporary fiction actively registers modernism's legacies of formal experiment, authorial self-fashioning, and claims to aesthetic autonomy, we need to position those impulses within and against a larger history of the concept and its earlier practitioners' conditioned and contingent designs on the social production of literary values. Literary fiction that self-consciously reflects on modernism as an aesthetic and historical inheritance manifests a problem inherent to the social conditions with which modernism came into being, namely its ambivalent and evolving relationship to transformations within the capitalist economies of cultural production.

High modernism emerged, in part, within what Pierre Bourdieu designated as a "restricted field of production." Many modernist works now considered canonical were initially published in little magazines and by small private presses and circulated among a coterie of like-minded readers eager to engage with new writing that didn't fit with mass commercial forms. On the production side of things, writers like Ford Madox Ford, Ezra Pound, and T. S. Eliot served as editors of prestigious little magazines run on subscriptions rather than advertising; Eliot for his part wrote criticism that sought to school people in how to read modern poetry, in effect creating and cultivating a sophisticated audience of readers; and Virginia and Leonard Woolf started their Hogarth Press in order to disseminate work less likely to appeal to more commercial venues.[24] Modernist literary production, according to this story, appeared to position itself and its authors outside the perceived vulgarities of commodity culture more generally, but those strategies were neither immune to nor excluded from the larger functions of industrial and consumer capitalism. Rather, they articulated a unique mode of relation to that larger set of fields.

Bourdieu's wide-ranging work on the sociology of cultural production provides a particularly apt model with which to understand, first, modernism's relative autonomy from other forms of commodity production and, second, the altered conditions of the publishing industry following the Second World War, in which modernism's aesthetic experimentation became institutionalized within the university and marketed in ways that would reap long-term economic returns. As Bourdieu puts it, "The field of production *per se* owes its structure to the opposition between the *field of restricted production* as a system producing cultural goods ... objectively destined for a public of producers of cultural goods, and the *field of large-scale cultural production*" geared toward short-term profits.[25] Even though some of the most challenging modernist works came to acquire significant economic value during their authors' own lives, that process was one that later capitalized on the small-scale networks of production that promoted the related notions of aesthetic disinterest, distinction, and autonomy. "The degree of autonomy" cultivated by modernist writers, Bourdieu argues, "is measurable by the degree to which it is capable of functioning as a specific market, generating a specifically cultural type of scarcity and value irreducible to the economic scarcity and value of the goods in question."[26] One of the lingering legacies of modernism is precisely this notion, promulgated by its original practitioners, that the experimental difficulty of their work, aimed at a small coterie of educated artists and intellectuals, marked a stubborn refusal of the encroachment of commodification.[27] But it is through modernism's cultivation of an economy of scarcity in ambivalent collusion with the emerging discourses and practices of commercial publicity that helps us better account for its historically unique creation of cultural values and literary prestige, with the author featuring as their singular expressive embodiment.

Writers like Woolf, Eliot, and Joyce participated in the creation of a "shadow economy" of scarcity with its own forms of patronage and publicity.[28] One of the most important critical touchstones for this materialist revision of modernist production is Lawrence Rainey's study of its intersections with existing institutions and marketing. Rather than the New Critics' championing of transhistorical formal aesthetics, Rainey and others have shown that modernism reflects a complex range of compromises and negotiations with the forms of commercial publicity it often appeared to oppose. Taking as an example the "tripartite production program [of] journal, limited edition and public or commercial edition," Rainey demonstrates how the limited production and careful marketing of modernist texts like *Ulysses* enacted a "strategy whereby the work of art invites and solicits its commodification, but does so in such a way that it becomes a commodity of a special sort, one that is temporarily exempted from the exigencies of immediate consumption prevalent within the larger cultural economy."[29] Others have followed Bourdieu and Rainey in stressing the value of scarcity to modernist cultural production; zoning in on the limited edition by which many high modernist texts entered a narrow field of elite circulation, for example, Aaron Jaffe writes that "these luxury commodities were designed to be scarce, to be more heard of than come across, and to redound their excess aura to the authorial name."[30] Literary modernism is at once ordinary—dependent on specific legitimating institutions and markets—and mystified by its practitioners' and publicists' careful cultivation of an economy of scarcity, and it is this constellated set of discursive and material conditions that gave rise to a distinctively modernist mode of authorial celebrity.

Modernist authorship, disseminated in restrictive venues like little magazines and private publishing and buttressed by its own self-proclaimed notions of authenticity and originality, that is, traded on the elite cultural values it helped foster, giving rise to an unexpected overlap with the large-scale commercial production of celebrities geared toward mass consumption. If so much modernist literature foregrounds its formal complexity and stylistic novelty, it does so in a way that articulates the supremacy of a unique and orchestrating authorial consciousness, an elite mode of self-fashioning that betrays a shadowy kinship with commercial forms of celebrity promotion. The crucial difference within this analogy is one of scale, and lies with the creation of what Jaffe calls the authorial "imprimatur," a textual signature carefully modeled on the scarcity of cultural commodities that then circulates as a substitute for the author as living subject, so that the signifying imprimatur of a "Joyce" or "Eliot" serves to "sanction elite, high cultural consumption in times when economies of mass cultural value predominate."[31] In such an account of modernist cultural production, the apparent autogenesis of the author famously exemplified by Joyce's Stephen Dedalus, casting himself into exile "to forge in the smithy of [his] soul the uncreated conscience of [his] race," acts as a metafictional index of the self-created author, a fetish of artistic identity that disavows a logic of celebrity self-promotion through appeals to elite values and the text as the source of authenticity and alleged resistance.

As that example suggests, modernist authorship was cultivated at the intersections of publicity and promotion from within an economy of scarcity, on the one hand, and an impulse toward formal experiment and difficulty signaled by the use of a uniquely impersonal style aimed at shoring up a distinctive authorial identity. Authorial self-effacement and the elevation of impersonal style helped mark out a modernist distinction from mass cultural celebrity. In Eliot's widely influential "Tradition and the Individual Talent," for example, he works out this tension by asserting that the mark of a truly original writer is the result of an "escape" from personality, subsuming the raw stuff of emotion into impersonal style. Such gestures at self-effacement, while a means of remaining aloof from commercial culture's fetishization of the celebrity self, also point to what Loren Glass identifies as "the contrast between [modernist authors'] stated theories of self-effacement" and their extraliterary practices of "shameless self-promotion," a tension that, Glass argues, could be tentatively resolved through the "ability to escape personality through rendering it as style."[32] And Jonathan Goldman extends this focus on style into the textual cultivation of authorial celebrity. Through a series of close readings, Goldman demonstrates how "modernist style constitutes an entirely new kind of author—as not only the art object par excellence, but also the master choreographer of the culture that contains him as such an object." Modernist style, that is, produces the idea of the author as exceptional referent, "a means of self-production within the text that accompanies, and in fact supercedes, the self-production of marketing and promotional activities."[33] This attention to style, then, contributes to a growing body of scholarship concerned with revising our understanding of modernism's relationship with emergent mass market conditions, and it also preserves something of its writers' historically unique designs on authorship, where trading in elite values within an economy of scarcity (Rainey, Jaffe) momentarily meets with a new model of textual self-fashioning that enabled the promotion of the modernist writer as an exceptional figure of high-cultural celebrity.

And underpinning all of this is an implicit logic of fetishism that governs modernist authorial celebrity, one that continues to play out as a functional myth in the contemporary market for literary fiction. Recent work on modernism that informs my discussion here adds materialist and textual dimensions to the fetishistic production of the author as Bourdieu understands it. "The struggles for the monopoly of the definition of the mode of legitimate cultural production contribute to a continual reproduction of belief in the game," he writes, amounting to an "*illusio*" that enables the generation of aesthetic value perceived as distinct from the material conditions that enable it.[34] While Goldman argues that the generative mimesis of modernist style produces the author as the unique expressive subject of celebrity, Bourdieu locates such a creation of authorship within the larger field of cultural production. "The producer of the *value of the work of art* is not the artist," he writes, "but the field of production as a universe of belief which produces the value of the work of art as a *fetish* by producing the belief in the creative power of the artist."[35] With this fetishistic belief in mind, then, Bourdieu's critical practice requires that we "take into account not only the direct producers of the work in its materiality (artist, writer, etc.), but also the ensemble of agents and institutions which participate in the production of the value of the work via the production of the belief in the value of art in general," including the "social determinations" of class, national identity, and the author's position with regard to valuing institutions and the market at large.[36] This method allows for a double focus that takes in the mutually conditioning forces of legitimating institutions and the creative work of writers; it "allows us to describe and to understand the specific labour that the writer had to accomplish, both against these determinations and thanks to them, in order to produce himself as creator, that is, as the *subject* of his own creation."[37]

Modernist authorship perceived from our contemporary historical vantage point retains a strong sense of this fetishistic disavowal, and yet its foremost figures also cultivated novel means by which to negotiate this dilemma. Stubbornly engaged in the creation of elite institutional values and proffering a model of authorship that disavowed its relations to commercial fantasies of self through appeals to impersonal disinterestedness, high modernism and its legacies of reception could be downright snobby. Sean Latham has compellingly mined this field of snobbish cultural production, arguing that "modernism has thrived on a smug sense of cultured superiority," driving home his dispute with a lasting impression of aesthetic detachment from the market by adding that "modernism's mythologized autonomy derives from the illusion of disinterestedness, from the conviction that aesthetic pleasure exists in a realm completely antithetical to the vulgar self-promotion of the marketplace."[38] For Latham and others, high modernists walked a fine line between claims to a realm of symbolic values for a small coterie and a penchant for securing lasting economic gains, which, he argues, they anxiously negotiated in their "metatextual" figures of snobs, like Joyce's Stephen Dedalus or Woolf's Lily Briscoe.[39] In his revisionary take on modernist cultural capital as a snobbish affair, Latham rightly argues that modernism was and remains a model of distinction because of a dubious claim to absolute autonomy, one in which the cultivation of restrictive values came to garner the economic returns its practitioners seemed to oppose: "They have become icons of cultural capital, which can be converted into both social prestige and material wealth," an evolution legible in the phenomenon by which "the snob reveals that the presumed isolation of modernism from the market is itself a saleable commodity."[40]

The figure of the modernist as snob—in which elitist pretensions and market anxieties coalesce—remains a curious legacy that continues to circulate within contemporary fiction and its authors' efforts to distinguish the value of their work by engaging with modernism's experimental legacies. Metamodernist fiction, following on the rise and decline of postmodern metafiction, extends those modernist strategies of authorial self-fashioning—whether through explicit engagement with the established tradition and its familiar referents or through a foregrounding of stylistic experiment and originality—but this has come to function within a competitive commercial field. The primary difference to note at this point is one of scale: the modernist economy of scarcity has given way to modernism as a sign of elite cultural capital that upholds the social prestige of publishers' imprints and their authors as brand names, a mark of distinction operative within rather than in the shadows of commercial publishing and publicity. Before addressing that shift and what it can teach us about the role of the modernist tradition in the making of contemporary celebrity, however, we need to take up the third term in my constellation of historical modernism and the market, and what remains today its most vexed legacy: the question of literary autonomy.

As a defining concept that materialist studies of modernism have questioned, the notion of artistic or aesthetic autonomy can look decidedly outmoded, if not naïve, or at best a dubious myth upholding the elitist pretensions first articulated, whether brazenly or anxiously, by the modernists themselves. That said, modernist claims to autonomy can also be conceived as a strategy of social engagement, a multifaceted effort to expand the formal possibilities of the literary field and even to alter the conditions of its production. When Virginia and Leonard Woolf established the small independent Hogarth Press, it wasn't because they were uninterested in selling books and earning a living, but rather to exercise more direct control over the aesthetic criteria for publishing her work and that of others less likely to find a more commercial outlet and a mainstream audience. In this case, and in parallel with the production of little magazines, modernists worked to yoke their interests in literary experiment to the means of production and, to a limited extent, to mutually transform the possibilities of both. Such an example reminds us that modernists were keen to create autonomous conditions for their work by developing modes of production and circulation that best suited the aesthetic ambitions of their writing. These kinds of examples of modernists working simultaneously to create markets for their work and insisting on the experimental value of the work itself attest to a strategy that Bourdieu designates as a "position to be made," or the need to "invent" a field momentarily situated "against established positions and their occupants" in an effort to reimagine the social and aesthetic horizons of literary possibility.[41]

That notion of inventing a position against existing market conditions offers a framework for a nuanced understanding of modernist autonomy, one that aimed to alter the conditions of literary production through a different kind of engagement with its marketing. Echoing Bourdieu, Andrew Goldstone convincingly revives this relative value of autonomy for the field, arguing that it operates as "a *mode of relation* between literature and the social world of its emergence," in which we find modernist writers working within a sliding and contingent "continuum" of overtly commercial and oppositional positions.[42] Aware of the social embeddedness of their work, modernists sought ways to articulate "fictions of autonomy" that might achieve real effects on the literary market they helped cultivate, but which become visible "only in and through specific relations to the market."[43] Modernist works, for instance, might internalize the images and logics of commercial advertising, ironically or not, but the relation that such a move instigates is not merely reflective of consumer culture's empirical reality but also one that foregrounds the work of mediation which, in turn, might serve the internal and self-referential laws of the work itself. The strength of this kind of reclamation of a modernist fiction of autonomy, again, lies with its emphasis on attempts at transformation; "modernist attempts to secure autonomy in fact confront and make use of the artist's and the artwork's embeddedness in social life" such that "the pursuit of autonomy leads modernist writers to take account of, and seek to transform, the social relations of their literary production."[44]

In a very real sense, modernism did create a relative mode of autonomy according to the conditions of production, publicity, and experiment that I have been charting, and this fiction was oddly preserved, as a distinctive historical legacy, by modernism's delayed entry into mainstream fields of institutionalization and marketing, the processes by which a selective body of authors and texts became ossified into a canon of social prestige. While the defining moments of modernism as a literary-historical period—whether we pinpoint it in, say, 1910 or 1922—can best be understood and contextualized according to the small-scale conditions discussed above, the experimental trademarks that became associated with Joyce or Eliot or Woolf soon entered into mutually shaping relationships with the savvy marketing practices of glossy magazines, commercial book publishers, and other forms of production meant to bring formal experiment and stylistic sophistication to bear on the creation of long- and short-term profits. This history has been well documented since the publication of Rainey's work on modernist institutions and their role in promoting modernist literature as a "special sort of commodity," and I will only briefly rehearse it here before turning to the economic transformations that now structure a consolidated and corporate literary field.

The commodification of a "presumed isolation" from the market, as Latham describes it, has been subject to a process of historical sedimentation, including the interwar redistribution of a canon of modernist texts in the form of cheap reprints and the deepening entrenchment of this selective body of works and authors to institutional status, most legibly within the expanding postwar university system.[45] The mainstreaming of modernism initially becomes legible even within the material history of little magazines, generally aimed at eschewing the seductions of advertising and popular literature, as some of those venues for elite or experimental writing began adopting mass marketing techniques to gain a wider readership. Taking to task Andreas Huyssen's now anachronistic model of a modernist "anxiety of contamination" by the mass market for cultural goods, Mark Morrison and others have shown how a diverse range of popular publishers and avant-garde writers interacted in attempts to harness "the power of mass market technologies and institutions to transform and rejuvenate contemporary culture."[46] This kind of synergy also helped reshape the field of big commercial glossies like *Vogue* and *Vanity Fair*, both of which came, by the late 1920s, to emulate modernist styles and help make them fashionable, so that the stylistic experiments of modernist writing that took shape alongside the mass market came to influence commercial publishing on both sides of the Atlantic, helping to establish a wider audience while also bringing a modernist literary ethos and stylistic savvy to bear on the form and content of those magazines.[47] What's more, difficulty, unorthodox thematic content, and an initially restricted access, it turned out, could be turned to relatively popular appeal, exemplified by Bennett Cerf's aggressive acquisition of *Ulysses* for Random House. Begun "largely as a reprint firm" focused on producing "expensive limited editions," Random House under the editorship of Cerf was able to capitalize on the curiosity and cultural cache that censorship had brought to Joyce's famous, though largely unread, novel, and closing the deal on *Ulysses* in 1932 helped turn "Random House from a relatively unknown firm into a famous house and helped to make Bennett Cerf into a celebrity."[48] Around the same time, Random House and other expanding firms began to capitalize on modernism's prestigious reputation by publishing the existing work of established figures like Joyce and Woolf in cheap reprint series.[49]

The rise and growing availability of inexpensive reprints aided (and was aided by) the institutionalization of modernism beginning in the 1930s, so that a selective body of works became the canonical preserve of an elite field accruing cultural capital. Contemporary with the "integration" of New Criticism into university English departments, its academic critics found in an experimental tradition of modernism the kinds of difficult texts to teach, write about, and debate. In the institution once known as the literature department, "aesthetic arguments" among writers and public intellectuals "intersected with professional practices in order to produce a canon of major works that still privileged autonomy, tradition, and difficulty while making modernism itself into a compelling field of study."[50] If modernist literary production exercised some genuine autonomy in its self-conscious formal construction combined with a savvy awareness of scarcity and marketing, its integration into institutionally based systematic criticism helped make that autonomy, in retrospect, a fiction in service to the generation of academic capital. One consequence of this sedimented process is that, as Latham and Rogers usefully generalize it, even as early as the late 1930s and spreading into the postwar era, "the fixation on poetic autonomy, professional critique, and the construction of a canon also worked to end the idea of modernism as an active practice."[51] Modernism became, paradoxically, an institution of the new in the process of becoming old.[52] Bringing with it the desirable challenges of formal study and solidified by the tenets of New Criticism, modernism before the New Modernist Studies was yoked into a coherent field and an era in the academy in a way that rendered it increasingly divorced from its historical and material contexts to become a widely recognized body of aesthetic features and a gold standard of literary novelty. Writers and critics from relatively privileged backgrounds and emerging into the literary establishment from elite universities—those I take up in the following chapters—inherit this legacy, one that has come since the 1980s to resonate within the trade market for fiction as a sign of materially fungible cultural capital.

I've been arguing that modernism, as a historically unique if also mutable period concept, emerged from the curious constellation of an economy of scarcity, the cultivation of a "special sort" of authorial celebrity, and a bid for cultural autonomy, and that its gradual entry into more mainstream institutions both diluted and preserved its authoritative claim to a distinctive kind of cultural capital. It is within this intersection of institutional and creative forces that we can begin to see, partially at least, the origins of a larger "discontinuous history of modernism" (D'Arcy and Nilges), one in which its legacy of cultural capital is now a prominent marker of distinction in the commercial field. One of the main arguments I advance in this book is that contemporary writers refashion mostly familiar modernist techniques that were upheld as a mark of autonomy, but that the historical force of that potential is now contingent on the value of a modernist tradition to a contemporary corporate market, where a revival of modernist innovation continues to serve in the creation of the author as celebrity subject and to disavow writers' necessary complicity in the commercial production of their work and public persona, while continuing to generate elite literary capital.

From Autonomy to the Brand Name, or, The Market for Modernism Now

Here I turn to the market for modernism in the specific context of "serious" literary fiction as a product of the corporate conglomerate system that for several decades has controlled much of the field. And it is firmly within this longish contemporary period that we witness a remarkable range of metamodernist, commercially viable fiction that self-consciously extends or critically reframes modernism's legacies—through stylistic experiment, a creative-mimetic engagement with canonical works, or a foregrounding of the formal properties of their fiction—all of which draws on the cultural capital of a selective canon in service to authorial self-fashioning. Contemporary writing that self-consciously extends or critiques modernist experiments with form and style aspires to something like the distinctiveness of the modernist signature, but that strategy now functions according to the logic of the brand name. Unlike the "shadow economy" of scarcity that structured modernist celebrity and its claims to autonomy, literary fiction is largely a product of the economic and structural changes in the publishing industry that began in the 1960s and came to shape the conditions of possibility for authors, fictional form, and the market.

This story begins with the process by which large multinational conglomerates gradually acquired formerly small- to mid-size firms. By the last decades of the twentieth century, most of the fiction industry came under control of multinational conglomerates so that "by 2001," as Claire Squires points out, "five companies (Bertelsmann, Pearson, HarperCollins, Hodder Headline, and Hachette) had just over 50 per cent of market share in the UK."[53] The gradual absorption of small- and mid-size publishing firms by "a very small number of multinational, multimedia companies" helped pave the way for a general shift to what Paul Delany calls "a postmodern literary system."[54] This shift spelled a dramatic reconfiguration among the players in the marketing of manuscripts, published novels, and future work. Since the abolition of resale price maintenance and the end of the Net Book Agreement in 1995, publishing functions within a triangle of forces: the author and agent, the publisher, and retail, with the latter exercising more power than ever before.[55] Publishers came increasingly to seek out top-selling authors as brand names, "buying a literary property rather than taking on an author," and investing large advances as a form of speculation, in effect "[gambling] with the company's money" on both the sales of a novel and that celebrity author's future work.[56]

The conglomerate finance model also freed up capital available for short-term investments in the form of authors' advances and marketing budgets, making novel writing a potentially lucrative career, but mainly for a small number of successful authors.[57] In contrast to the economy of scarcity and the role of elite institutions in carving out a unique model of modernist production and reception, "marketing can be said to be the making of contemporary writing," and authors' careers are shaped by a complex interplay of agents, editors and publishers, advertising and retail, as well as the "journalistic capital" generated within the literary press.[58] Literary fiction, in this regard, is a fully commercial product, even if its association with "quality imprints" like Jonathan Cape, Picador, and Viking—each owned by large media corporations—marks its distinction from mass market genre fiction.[59] Here we might note that despite ongoing proclamations on the impending "death of the novel," the life of the genre over the course of the 1980s and 1990s was more robust than ever, and the explosion in the availability of good fiction over the last several decades is in part a result of these structural transformations. Following the 2008 economic crisis and the ensuing recession, the commercial literary market has gone into contraction, making the imperative to repeat successful patterns all the stronger, as Crosthwaite shows; and yet, as I will argue in the case of Anna Burns and Eimear McBride, that downturn has also been accompanied by increasing visibility for small independent presses, with access to public grants and corporate support, that can invest in the promotion of marginalized experimental fiction.[60]

Clearly, then, a traditional opposition between culture and commerce has eroded, and from the modernist to the contemporary period, broadly speaking, their mutually conditioning relationship serves as a kind of protean field in which to gauge how literary value is created in constant negotiation with the market. One particular manifestation of this shifting field of literary value is its expression in the function of the author. According to some, the modernists' dependence on patrons or an economy of scarcity has been eclipsed by the "historical shift over the last century from a model of authorship dominated by the signature to one dominated by the brand name."[61] When star authors review each other's work in the literary press, go on highly publicized speaking tours, or acquire a list of major awards, they participate in a market in which economic and symbolic values interact to create synergy. Thus, "the model of the author as a brand name" is in part "a matter of the careful management of a persona which continues to be seen as the source of value" such that "the aesthetics of the signature and of the brand are successive but complementary orders" in which the cultural capital accruing to celebrity writers is necessarily "enhanced" by a commercial regime in which literary value circulates.[62] This is especially evident, for example, in the marketing campaign that made "Zadie Smith" a star figure of multicultural writing. Celebrity writers are, of course, fully conscious of these conditions of contemporary authorship, and a turn to modernism as an institutionalized body of symbolic capital and a model for experimental aesthetics is a key strategy that allows authors to negotiate an elite position for their work within the constraints of market demand.

If one of the lasting myths of modernism is that its practitioners were able to shore up some relative autonomy from more obvious forms of mass commodification, successive decades of market consolidation and contraction have prompted widespread and repeated fears that publishers would steer clear of serious literature to focus exclusively on less risky investments, as in mass market genre fiction. While this has in some cases proven true, the market for fiction that self-consciously engages with the aesthetic or historical legacies of modernism signals a strong example of serious fiction that straddles commerce and cultural capital. At least prior to the 2008 crash and the ensuing recession, serious or experimental fiction had occupied an important part of market shares. As sociologist John B. Thompson argues, serious fiction can generate longer-term profits than more strictly commercial publications; it allows companies to create and maintain a more "diversified portfolio of risk"; and, most important for my purposes, "symbolic capital matters to most large publishing corporations," both for cultural reputation and for the increased visibility, and economic returns, it can bring to authors and their publishers.[63] And the promotion of successful authors as brand names, particularly those whose names bear the marks of literary prestige, drives the formation and promotion of literary celebrity in what Dan Sinykin aptly dubs "the conglomerate era."[64]

Literary prizes also play a major role in consolidating prestige and generating literary and economic capital. The explosion of the prize phenomenon, something that didn't exist during the period of high modernism, has become increasingly important to the publishing and retail industry, the literary media, and the careers of individual novelists. A quick glance at the covers of books by the writers I address here will reveal a competitive list of awards, and there is no doubting its significance as a paratextual factor in defining an author's career and the continued legitimacy of serious literary fiction. As James English has shown at length, literary prizes have come to embody and reflect the dynamic intersection where symbolic and economic capital are reproduced in upholding "the economy of prestige."[65] Reflected and sustained by the literary prize phenomenon, this cultural economy bears out the joint production and "intraconvertibility" of symbolic and economic capital.[66] The Booker Prize serves as a striking example of the complex interplay of different forms of capital and prestige in the shaping of literary value. The fact that the Booker generally goes to works of literary fiction is important here; as Richard Todd argues, the genre itself bears highbrow distinction and "tends to exclude best-selling genre-fiction" and enters quickly into academic consecration even as the late twentieth century witnessed significantly expanded "commercial possibilities" in the marketing, sales, and distribution of these serious novels.[67] The Booker carries a cache of cultural prestige while it simultaneously influences commercial values and "exercises [as of 1996] a more substantial effect on sales patterns than any other kind of award."[68]

The mutual imbrication of aesthetic and economic value embodied by the prizes also suggests that their larger function is to affirm their own authority in the creation of those values. Commenting specifically on the Nobel, English argues that the prize operates according to "a logic of cultural *production* in its own right," one that drives an internal field of competition and that exists "to test and affirm the notion of art as a separate and superior domain, a domain of disinterested activity which gives rise to a special, nontemporal, noneconomic, but scarce and thus highly desirable form of value."[69] In short, "the prize functions as a claim to authority and an assertion of that authority— the authority, at bottom, to produce cultural value."[70] As that suggests, prizes— together with journalistic reporting, book-marketing, and other discursive features—keep the fiction of celebrity going and actually help to uphold what English calls the "collective belief" in the symbolic value of serious literature.[71] Whether we talk about the Booker, the Nobel, or other less lucrative awards, they all play an enormous role in the cultural consecration and economic viability of serious literary fiction, keeping its authors' names on the university syllabus, in the review pages of the literary press, and prominently on the shelves of our real and virtual bookshops. The utterly commercial production and circulation of books and the collective make-belief in the social and symbolic value of literary fiction are mutually conditioning features of our contemporary culture industries.

In response to conglomerate publishing and the collapsing distinctions between symbolic and economic capital reflected by prizes, writers have developed novel ways of articulating claims to literary distinction in the commercial field, most intriguingly by openly reflecting on their integration with corporate publishing. A clear example of this self-conscious mediation of authorial complicity is Martin Amis's *The Information*, which I address in Chapter 1. Putting contemporary production into stark contrast with modernism's shadowy cultural economy, Nicholas Brown argues that while the work of art is a commodity like most any other, a combination of intentionality and an insistence on the "self-legislating formal properties" of the literary or artistic work signals the potential to "suspend the logic of the commodity, legibly assert[ing] a moment of autonomy from the market."[72] Similarly concerned with questions of autonomy and market complicity, but situating his investigation squarely within the postwar structural transformations in the publishing industry, Paul Crosthwaite looks to the genre of "market metafiction"—work that openly internalizes the "market logics" of literary production—as revealing an attempt to translate the market constraints on literary form into self-conscious experiment and critical reflection. Attention to the genre, he argues, reveals a range of "inventive and resourceful ... strategies via which formally ambitious writers seek to open up spaces of manoeuvre immanent to, but not simply determined by, the market."[73]

While I find these arguments refreshing, the claims I advance here are more modest, assuming that self-conscious formal experiment and critical reflection on market complicity depend, in the first place, on the economic and social structures by which literary fiction is marketed and valued. I argue that contemporary authors engage modernism's legacies—as both institution and will to experiment—to cultivate not only new formal terrain for the novel but also as a means of claiming cultural capital and negotiating the culture of celebrity in which their work and public persona circulate. One of the legacies of modernism that this book traces is the promotion of the fetishized value of authorship itself. Reading major novels that make self-conscious claims to a place in the modernist tradition alongside paratextual phenomena such as published interviews, prizes, and promotional material, we see how metamodernist fiction, the market, and our own critical investments contribute to a fetishized belief in "the creative power of the artist." If modernist writers achieved a degree of distinction and celebrity by "turning the self into an object," to repeat Goldman's phrase, that aim has become completely contingent on the creation of branding in the conglomerate era. Brouillette identifies this as a form of "commodity fetishism" in contemporary literary production that "obfuscates the realities of the making of the product by channeling our attention toward the author as the singular creator" whereby "the circulation of the unique author's indivisible identity and style signals the distinction of the product within the market, and the value that thereby attaches to the author's name continues to be the major source of the value of the product in general, benefitting everyone within the circuit," from agents to editors, journalists to academics.[74] Focusing on literary fiction that appeals to or even interrogates a legacy of modernism, though, also "reveals an unexpectedly diverse array of strategies for negotiating changing conceptions of literary and cultural value," to tweak Sean Latham's point about the elitist anxieties of modernism, and allows us both to historicize modern literary culture more broadly and to gauge how its consecrated status—including older claims to autonomy—provides surplus value to a small and elite segment of the commercial field.[75]

From the 1980s through the time of this writing, that is, we continue to witness a notable "engagement with the stylistic, thematic, and political afterlives of the formal and intellectual ambitions of literary modernism"—in David James's ambitious phrasing—a redux suggesting that "the modernist project is unfinished"; but I want to insist that those ambitions have been simultaneous with and integral to the large-scale economic transformations in the literary field, and that they reveal a perversely logical historical outcome of modernism's uneven entry into mainstream commodity culture.[76] A host of major figures have turned, in the wake of postmodern irony and pastiche, to modes of formal experiment inspired by the methods of earlier modernists, reworking impressionistic inwardness to explore the limits to subjective self-determination under neoliberal capitalism, rewriting vast literary traditions by way of a narratorial master choreographer, or foregrounding a self-legislating formal experiment as a mark of aesthetic autonomy—and each of these demonstrates a broad impulse to, in essence, make modernism new again, sometimes by expanding the horizons of the novel as a privileged form of cultural commodity. And yet another, equally visible, pattern is one in which writers rework familiar techniques of modernist texts to demonstrate, as Jeremy Rosen writes of genre fiction, their "possession of significant quantities of cultural capital" and a deep "familiarity with the 'great books,' even if this familiarity manifests itself in a critical stance toward those books," in order to "leverage that capital to gain strategic advantages in a highly competitive literary marketplace."[77]

We should note here that the field of elite literary fiction—which I'm aligning with writers who self-consciously engage with modernism's legacies—remains a shockingly exclusive one. While it isn't a central argument in this book, it is important to note that work by women and writers of color make up only a tiny percentage of the field of commercially valued and culturally prized fiction, so that a celebrity author like Zadie Smith can be made to represent some ostensibly ethnic and hybrid authenticity in ways that belie the unrelenting and predominantly white, male, and middle-class purview of contemporary publishing and marketing.[78]

Metamodernist fiction self-consciously reflects and redeploys the accumulated cultural capital of a modernist tradition and thereby participates in the ongoing generation of literary value in the market and within complimentary institutional networks like the university system, and should thus be understood as a further reflection of the exclusive tendencies of the corporate publishing industry. Across the case studies making up this book, I identify three broad and intersecting phenomena structuring a contemporary market for metamodernist writing. Authors in the genre extend modernist modes of authorial self-fashioning as a means of disavowing commercial complicity (exemplified by Amis, McEwan, and Rushdie); foreground the self-legislating formal properties of their fiction in ways that critically reflect on market constraints (Ishiguro, Smith); and demonstrate a commitment to destabilizing a masculine Irish modernist canon from the margins of the big conglomerates (Burns and McBride). Charting across such an eclectic selection of writers, and paying close attention to the unique formal and stylistic means by which they variously reanimate or contest the institutional and aesthetic legacies of modernism, reveals a market segment for literary fiction that is one of both privilege and innovation, in which the dictum to make it new expresses the commercial conditions that enable it.

The Shape of Things to Come

Chapter 1 reads Martin Amis as a self-conscious stylist in the modernist tradition and a writer whose career indexes the historical shift from the authorial signature to the brand name, a process that is comically reflected and critically mediated in the metafictional form of some of his major novels. Amis's reflexive style pits itself against the system of speculative financial markets that became the model of corporate publishing, revealing a strategy of modernist self-fashioning which translates anxieties of authorship into a satirical position that straddles complicity and a will to autonomy. The chapter opens with the public scandal that erupted following his 1995 switch in agent and publisher, accompanied by a huge advance for *The Information*, a satire on the publishing industry. Fueled by a sense that Amis had sold out, the event itself provides a convenient entry point to the book, *in medias res*, because it suggests a powerful and lingering belief in disinterested literary values at a time when the industry had already undergone the structural transformations into a model of high finance, making it an ironic reflection of the very satire of *The Information*. Amis's redeployment of a modernist mode of authorial self-fashioning, specifically the cultivation of a signature style, serves in the construction of cultural capital and distinction while it anxiously acknowledges the increasing predominance of commercial branding as a condition of literary celebrity.

Ian McEwan's ambivalent turn to impressionist style, one of the most lasting achievements of modernist fiction, is the focus of Chapter 2, where I argue that his dual imitation and repudiation of writers like Woolf and Henry James aligns his fiction with a canonical modernist tradition even as it tries to overcome its influence. This ambivalent recirculation of a modernist brand, one that reductively rejects it as historically elitist, also sheds light on the larger market demand for a modernist referential field that has become mainstream. Rejecting a modernist legacy he sees as socially elitist, while demonstrating a commitment to impressionist style as a privileged mode of representing consciousness, McEwan's fiction exemplifies the kind of "pseudo-impressionism" recently identified by Jesse Matz, and participates in the contemporary commercialization of a once-radical mode of literary representation. McEwan's ambivalent impressionism marks the literariness of his work while answering, at the same time, to a commercial demand for fiction that can successfully translate modernism's literary capital into popular forms and celebrity authorship.

Chapter 3 turns to Salman Rushdie, one of the most celebrated and scorned novelists of the late twentieth century; and the chapter also shifts attention to the emergence, beginning in the 1980s, of commercially viable postcolonial and multicultural British fiction. Rushdie's major novels self-consciously foreground a modernist penchant for stylistic experiment and capacious formal fragmentation while, at the same time, he has consistently conspired in the aggressive marketing of his work and persona. *Midnight's Children* constructs a self-consciously fictional India in a modernist mode of creative mimesis. Like Joyce, also a writer from the colonial periphery, Rushdie casts himself as the culmination of the vast literary traditions that he reworks, a self-authorizing strategy that also plays into a corporate market demand for migratory experience and hybridity. It is in light of this critical assessment of his cultivated postcolonial authority that I take up *The Satanic Verses*, arguing that the international scandal prompted by its publication should be understood together with Rushdie's rewriting of a literary tradition—"sympathy for the devil"—that runs from Milton through James Joyce, Mikhail Bulgakov, and The Rolling Stones. Rushdie's deployment of a satanic narrator, I argue, is at once a subversive pose and an act of commercial self-promotion through which he negotiates his own complicity in a multinational market for postcolonial cultural commodities. The chapter concludes with brief readings of *The Ground beneath Her Feet*, *Fury*, and *Joseph Anton*, texts that reveal how Rushdie anxiously insists on his modernist credentials as an autonomous stylist while capitalizing, at the same time, on the persecuted genius angle of his public image.

Chapter 4 focuses on Kazuo Ishiguro's oblique fictional negotiations with the logic of prizes, specifically showing how *The Unconsoled* and *Never*

Let Me Go subject contemporary assumptions about literary values to a disconsoling modernist aesthetic. *The Unconsoled* parodies the pretensions of the contemporary culture industries and the collective belief in autonomous artistic values, defamiliarizing them in a comically excessive form reminiscent of Kafka and Beckett. The novel thus engages with Theodor Adorno's theory of the modern artwork as an "absolute commodity," an object fully embedded in the commercial production of value that nevertheless openly rejects "the illusion of being-for-society."[79] As a reflection on this paradox, *The Unconsoled* imagines a total disillusionment with a collective belief in immaterial cultural values on which the logic of prize culture depends. *Never Let Me Go* extends this anxiety-ridden paradox into a dystopian vision of a totally instrumentalized society. Focused on young clones who are taught that their creative expression would "reveal their souls," the novel imagines how that fetishization of the aesthetic can come to serve completely instrumental and exploitative ends. This dystopian revelation has eerie implications for the role of the arts and humanities under neoliberal capitalism, in which an investment in ostensibly autonomous forms of creativity serves the instrumental aims of reproducing labor for corporate profits. Ishiguro thus revitalizes modernism's emphasis on self-legislating form as a mark of literary autonomy, but in such a way that profoundly questions the immaterial value of the aesthetic in the face of prize culture and the profitable corporatization of the literary field.

Chapter 5 situates Zadie Smith in a line extending from the popular postcolonialism of Rushdie and Kureishi to the equally commercialized genre of multicultural British fiction, and argues that Smith's ongoing experiments with style—her "multicultural modernism"—signal an attempt to elude the restrictive market labels that have conditioned her reception since the celebrated reception of *White Teeth*. Instantly heralded as the poster child for multicultural authenticity on the basis of her first novel, I show how Smith also playfully exploits and critiques the familiar tropes of the genre through a carefully contrived aesthetic of inauthenticity that runs throughout her subsequent work, revealing a pattern of ironic reflection on the role that celebrated cultural commodities play in mediating identity. This productive bind comes to a head in *NW*, in which Smith adopts a modernist mode of stylistic detachment that marks a break from her fashionable brand of multicultural fiction while prompting us to reflect on the troubling relationship between social inequality and the metamodernist style of the novel as a mark of institutional and economic privilege.

Chapter 6 diverges from my foregoing focus on commercially produced metamodernist fiction, and turns to the work of Eimear McBride and Anna

Burns, authors who radically reframe a modernist Irish tradition and have only recently gained widespread recognition. McBride's debut novel, *A Girl Is a Half-Formed Thing*, has rightly been received as engaging in a critical dialogue with a modernist Irish tradition, most notably for its reworking of Joyce and Beckett, and my discussion affirms and pressures that reception in showing how its radical reframing of Joyce's modernist epiphany destabilizes its masculinist assumptions to articulate its own counterclaim to formal autonomy. Burns's *Milkman*, set during the Northern Irish Troubles, reflects the claustrophobic and protracted horrors of the period, but the novel also subjects that social content to its own pattern of finite formal digression. Those geopolitical differences make for a certain incongruity, but this comparative approach reveals the recent emergence of experimental women's writing with the power to expand and destabilize a canonical Irish modernism. Further, these novels advance a modernist claim to formal autonomy that is contingent on the unique conditions of their production. Initially published by small independent presses in the UK, and then reissued with the support of public and corporate capital, the new Irish modernism that these novels reflect also signals an emerging trend of marketing experimental writing from the margins. If this trend signals the privatization of literary production, it also points to a new historical chapter in the market for modernism, one in which genuinely experimental writing preserves its autonomy, paradoxically, in a joint enterprise between independent publishing and corporate sponsorship.

Finally, this book traces a broad narrative arc that has become apparent over the course of writing these chapters and in responding to readers' suggestions. Progressing through postmodernism, postcolonial and multicultural fiction, and the rise of a renewed commitment to formal autonomy in Irish writing, the following chapters reveal a contemporary market for modernism that continues to be reshaped by the mutually conditioning forces of institutionalized cultural capital and a will to experimental autonomy that is now fully integrated with a neoliberal model of literary production and branding.

1

Signature to Brand: Martin Amis's Negotiations with Literary Celebrity

In January 1995 Martin Amis signed on with American agent Andrew Wylie to publish *The Information* with HarperCollins, and initiated the media scandal that one paper referred to as his "greed storm."[1] The scandal resonated across multiple levels. Having broken his long-term publishing relationship with English agent Pat Kavanagh and Jonathan Cape, an imprint of Random House, UK, Amis was seen as having turned his back on the English publishing industry and, indeed, on England itself.[2] Personally, the switch put an end to the friendship with Julian Barnes, Kavanagh's husband and Amis's celebrated contemporary in British fiction. And perhaps most importantly, the deal with Wylie, to the tune of a £500,000 advance on *The Information*, signaled for readers of literary fiction a betrayal of a lofty ideal of authorship in favor of capitalist greed and glamor; Amis was a celebrity sellout.[3]

That Amis's change in agents ignited such an uproar, whether or not the move indicates a greedy complicity with the commercialization of literature, is itself telling. For one, the scandal indicates a curious moment in the transformations in the publishing industry that had been taking shape for more than two decades. By 1995, of course, most of the industry for literary fiction had come under the control of multinational conglomerates—including Bertelsmann and Time Warner at the top—resulting in a reconfiguration of the players in the marketing of manuscripts, published novels, and future work.[4] Richard Todd stresses that since the abolition of resale price maintenance following the end of the Net Book Agreement in 1995, publishing functions within a triangle of forces: the author and agent, the publisher, and retail, with the latter holding the most power.[5] Publishers acting within the multinational conglomerate system, for their part, seek out top-selling authors as brand names, "buying a literary property rather than taking on an author," and investing large advances as a form of speculation, in effect "[gambling] with the company's money" on both the sales of a novel and that celebrity author's future work.[6] Amis's "greed storm," then, gave the lie to the lingering perception in the British literary establishment that "serious" fiction occupied a relatively autonomous position from corporate production and profits. He played the game.[7] "Martin Amis" is a brand name, a celebrity, and, as one acting in seemingly obvious self-interest, was temporarily placed in the press's "shithead factfile" of sensational public outrage.[8]

I focus here on Amis's negotiations with his own celebrity status, and specifically on how his fiction reflects the ethos of corporate capitalism by satirizing and participating in its logics simultaneously. That is, how do we make sense of the scathingly satirical depiction of the Reagan-Thatcher economic policy in *Money*, for example, in light of his apparent embrace of the corporate capitalism that helped give rise to the Amis brand? In the simplest sense, Amis's novels that self-reflexively center on authorship and the publishing industry employ a cartoonish and self-conscious style to mock the commodification of literature and the vicissitudes of success in an increasingly competitive literary marketplace. But what are the effects of this satire when read together with Amis's public image and the apparent greed that came to define it? If Amis critiques the corporate publishing model and its place within the global conglomeration of capital and distribution, does he simply wind up critiquing his own authorial brand name? Certainly. As Delany has suggested regarding Amis's satire of authorial celebrity in *The Information*, his "satire cannot escape complicity with its own target."[9] While Delany is right about the limits of Amis's satire (and the same could be said about much of twentieth-century satire, such as that of Wyndham Lewis or Evelyn Waugh), I want to complicate that reading by showing how Amis's fiction mediates the market construction of Amis the authorial brand as a mark of both symbolic and economic capital.[10] In tracing his satirical treatment of authorial control and corporate publishing across *Success* (1978), *Money* (1984), and *The Information* (1995), we see that these metafictional novels participate in the production of the authorial brand precisely by folding the increasingly dominant corporate model of publishing and marketing fiction into their satire. His depictions of the commercialization of literature and the production of the author-as-celebrity in these novels are more than simply cartoonish caricatures.[11] Rather, these novels satirically reflect the corporatist economic policy that emerged during the Reagan-Thatcher era, while at the same time allegorizing Amis's own relationship with big corporate publishing, including the way his celebrity status—and the status of "literary fiction"—depends on the contingencies and volatility of speculation in the literary market. In doing so, these novels tell something of an allegorical backstory to the media scandal over Amis's advance from HarperCollins and reflect the ways in which literary value was being reformulated by the 1980s, particularly the value of the celebrity author as the embodiment of the commodification of modernist impersonality and self-styling.[12]

Amis as a case study signals both a continuation of and a rupture with modernist modes of authorial self-fashioning and the production of literary celebrity. As I argued in the introduction, literary celebrity isn't new, but the modes of its production, circulation, and economic returns have changed dramatically since the period of high modernism and its claims to a mode of relative autonomy from mass marketing. My focus is on style. Like Wilde or Joyce before him, Amis articulates a signature style in the promotion of a unique authorial identity, helping to create "the idea of the author, and therefore the celebrity, as a paradigmatic subjectivity" and a textual "object."[13] But Amis's stylistic affiliation with modernism's celebrity self-authorization is inescapably conditioned by the "historical shift over the last century from a model of authorship dominated by the signature to one dominated by the brand name."[14] Joyce's (and others') dependence on patrons or intentional scarcity has been replaced by a system in which "shrewd authors realize that it is better to get the biggest possible advance, because then the publisher will have a strong incentive to promote the book, having put a substantial sum at risk."[15] As Amis's celebrity status accrues across approximately the first half of his career, we see his fiction increasingly taking for its subject the idiosyncratic and progressively corporate means of producing the authorial brand, so that even as he redeploys a modernist mode of reflexive self-fashioning, that pattern also dramatizes and mediates the market transformations at the heart of this book, and in particular the shift from the stylistic signature to the brand name.

Finding *Success*

Critics often single out *Money* or *The Information* as exemplary of Amis's postmodern satire on social class, mindless consumerism, and authorial complicity with the shady financial markets of the Thatcher-Reagan era.[16] Central to this criticism is attention to how those novels employ structural pairings of characters, unwilling doubles that often bleed into sexual triangles, to create fictional tensions that comically reflect ideological contradictions and polarized class relations that had become especially apparent by the late 1970s.[17] More specifically, the dialogic and frictional relations between Amis's doubles raise questions about the viability of authorial control, social critique, and complicity with hyper-commercialized cultural production, exemplified by the presence of Amis's fictional surrogate in *Money* (actually named "Martin Amis"), and by the contrast between two writers, the "marooned modernist" Richard Tull and the commercially crass Gwyn Barry, in *The Information*. But the significance of Amis's doubles to his ongoing fictional engagement with the commercial production of authorial celebrity begins with *Success* (1978) and its depiction of the contradictions of social class under the new money economy leading up to Thatcher's election. *Success*, his third novel, isn't explicitly about writers or the literary marketplace, but it initiates Amis's pattern of asserting a fiction of authorial control through a signature style in the face of Britain's changing political and cultural economy. The novel's comic rendition of shifting class identities and anxieties played out by its discursive doubling of "yob" Terence and posh Gregory offers a starting point from which to trace Amis's allegorical engagement with "Amis" as an authorial brand and a major figure in contemporary fictions of literary celebrity.

The novel is made up of alternating first-person accounts, addressed to the reader, of the daily exploits of foster brothers Terence Service and Gregory Riding. Throughout the first half of the novel, Greg regales readers with his lofty old-money exploits of sex, fashion, and narcissistic charm, showering Terry's name and lower-middle-class identity with smug derision and snobbish dismissal. Terry, having been adopted by the Riders as a child after his father killed his mother and sister, limps through his episodic narratives in shame and self-loathing, ever-subservient to Greg's easy affectations of confident wealth and sneering class insularity. Excessive comic styling reduces each to categorical social types, opposites on the class spectrum, exemplified by their own self-descriptions. Terence's passages cringe with passive abjection and the bare survival of an unrecognizable "Service" class employed in pointless sales. As he says of his appearance: "I look ordinary, I look like educated lower-class middle-management, the sort of person you walk past in the street every day and never glance at or notice or recognize again," or of his job and social standing: "I do a job. That's what I do. … I was pleased when they gave it to me—I certainly didn't ever want to give it back. I am still pleased, more or less. At least I won't be a tramp, now that I've got it."[18] Greg, on the other hand, dashingly dandy and redolent of old money and new fashion, begins his days planning his outfits and recounting his elaborate exploits of the night before in cartoonish delight—"We always go to the grandest restaurants. We're always in those plush, undersea cocktail bars (we can't bear pubs). We always love spending lots of money"—before breakfasting on fresh orange juice and croissants, "[tolerating] the obsequious banter of liftman, doorman and porter," and swishing off to his posh job at an art gallery (S. 41).

These caricatures make for a fairly simple satire of 1970s class tensions. But the typological obviousness, while done for comic effect, also serves Amis's larger ironic designs on the changing conditions of economic class, changes that will inform his later self-reflexive narratives of authorial celebrity and the literary market. The novel's narrative arc traces a process of role reversal and a discursive intersection of the identities of Greg and Terry that reflects the lingering anxieties of the economic recession of the early 1970s and the "dissolution of the postwar Fair Shares consensus" that followed.[19] Briefly, Gregory gradually surfaces from his denial to reveal to readers that he's going broke: his job doesn't pay enough to live on, he can no longer afford his lavish nights out and, most importantly, his father has lost all the value of the family estate through quirky investments and charitable giving. Wallowing in debts induced by total liquidation and the outmoded ease of property owners, Greg succumbs to the paranoid recognition of money's totality: "My overdraft grows in lines of figures and print, spawning bank charges, interest payments. I can no longer read a book or even watch television without this other drama rearing up inside my mind, mangling page and screen. I cannot do anything without money leering over my shoulder" (S. 182). At the same time, following the failure of unionization coupled with rationalization (or downsizing) at the sales firm where he works, Terry gets promoted and earns increasingly higher commissions for buying and selling products that remain unknown even to him, resulting in inflated confidence and an awareness of a seismic shift in his class relations with Greg. Puffed up on disposable income, Terry "won't be scared of them [upper-class property owners] *any more*. ... They don't belong any more. What they belonged to has already disappeared; it is used up, leftovers, junk" (S. 193).

Through this comic drama of the shifting parameters of social class, the novel provides a neat satirical reflection of the increasing corporatization and financial deregulation of British society leading up to the 1980s, and it sets the stage for Amis's more complex treatment of those themes in *Money*. The Riders' financial decline is in itself rather typical of a pattern of dwindling estate values in England since the late nineteenth century. But Terence's "success" reflects the reactions following the oil crisis and recessionary cycles that defined British economics in the 1970s and that led to the embrace of a global finance system of floating exchange rates, dramatic cuts to public spending, and radical deregulation of British banking and stock markets coupled with an increasing rise in unemployment.[20] Terry's increased earnings result from the contradictions and failure of leftist unionization and the short-term shoring up of virtual capital in a free-floating exchange market. Before his good luck strikes, Terry listens to a regional union secretary at his firm who appeals to collective organization "because you want to not get fuckin' sacked," and to his boss's reply that unionization would result in several firings because they would have to pay sellers union rates (S. 100). As this comic dialogue suggests, unionization ironically favors corporate power and individual entrepreneurship, a point that is later borne out by Terry's realization that he's raking in the cash because "Veale [his boss] has already gimmicked it that I get tax relief and supplementary benefits for doing things about being Clerk (i.e., for doing things for him)" (S. 158). In his own dense way, Terry recognizes that he benefits from the effects of neoliberal deregulation and privatization that found their most notorious advocate in Margaret Thatcher. Terry's in the money while his colleagues face a rapid series of terminations.

But beyond this condensed satirical reflection of the economic contradictions of the period, I've traced *Success*'s class narrative here because it also marks the beginning of Amis's experimental negotiations with authorial identity in the face of an increasingly ubiquitous control of the media and literary industries by transnational corporate marketing. This is particularly legible in *Success*'s claims for Amis's orchestration of fictional events within the novel. Self-reflexive authorial references operate here on two distinct, ultimately conflicting, levels. First, the voices of Terry and Greg alternately point to Amis and his imaginative control over the fictional representation of shifting economic and class relations. As Terry begins to reflect on his changing financial situation, his comments on his own position have a fatalistic ring that displace the power of economic forces onto authorial control. Specifically referring to his relationship with Greg and his sister Ursula, both of whom are beginning to go mad, he says, "Things have progressed with steady certainty, with the slow cohering logic of a genre novel, or a chess combination, or a family game. Already I know how it will end—things will suddenly get much worse for two of us and never get better again—but I cannot break out" (S. 170). Of course he doesn't "break out," and Ursula commits suicide and Greg slips into poverty and madness. More importantly, this "family game" is equated with the very "genre novel" we're reading: *Success* as a nasty "condition of England" novel of the late 1970s whose diegetic structure also gestures out to the aspiring author who orchestrates its events according to Amis's sadistically "cohering logic."

Greg's voice also speaks for Amis, and does so through an increasingly impersonal style. Through Greg, we hear sly references to Amis's stylistic affectations, his rapid-fire caricatural excess of urbane postmodernist irony. In the first half of the novel, Greg's stylistic excesses expressed his big-spending confidence and smugness. Nearing the end of his decline, though, that stylistic panache only gives the lie to the protective sham of wealth. And it's during this transition that his address to readers takes on a double voice, simultaneously announcing his demise to readers and referring to Amis's stylistic orchestration of the whole thing. Disablingly claustrophobic about riding the Tube, he indulges in a triumphant fantasy of overcoming his fear in his usual style of comic-book daring: "I was looking in superb form, with my cape fanned out behind me like Superman's, wearing some crackly new snakeskin boots, my hair spruced high by an expensive haircut," to conclude the passage with his heroic emergence from "the pit of harm" to the optimistic daylight. Then comes the abrupt shift, as Greg asks: "Recognize the style (I suppose I'd better change that too now)? If you believed it, you'll believe anything" (S. 180–1). What follows is a lengthy catalogue of Greg's lies up to this point in the novel, completely undermining the rhetorical flourishes that have defined him. On a basic diegetic level, Greg's style is an expression of pompous affectation. But at the moment of this shift, hinging on attention to style, Greg's voice is less a means of expressing a character's psychological depth, and calls attention instead to Amis's intense stylistic artifice ("Recognize the style?") to suggest a fictional control—where authorial style trumps conventional realism—vying with the vastly indeterminate and unpredictable economic changes that the novel comically reflects.

Second, Amis echoes modernist literary precursors in a way that self-reflexively refers to the narrative voice masterminding the fictional reflection of real material processes in England's political economy. Also through Gregory's stylistic pomp—and Greg confesses to never having read much—Amis appropriates well-worn fragments from celebrity modernists like T. S. Eliot and Evelyn Waugh. In doing so, he signals their cultural capital to gesture toward a form of autonomy from the mass market—one in which ironic references to highbrow literacy might offer an alternative space from which to critique the sweep of commercialized culture—but which the novel's form ultimately undermines. For instance, one of Greg's more flamboyant rhetorical performances of the posh consumer opens with "April is the coolest month/ for people like myself" (89). A cheap ploy, no doubt, but the twist on Eliot's "cruellest month" (from *The Wasteland*)—and what is perhaps the most clichéd line from all of modern poetry—points in two directions at once. On the one hand, Eliot's bleak modernist social vision composed of the "fragments" of the literary tradition "shored against" the "ruins" of modernity is translated into Greg's "coolest" postmodern consumer currency and narcissistic high style.[21] The irony here, on the other hand, registers Amis's reading of modernism and his own participation, ironic though it may be, in Eliot's elitist theory of inserting one's "individual talent" into the "tradition," or literary canon. And in this modernist vein, finally, the ironically Eliotic line hints at a formalist fantasy of modernist literature's autonomy from market functions. In this light, Amis's self-conscious and comic parody of Eliot borrows from modernism's cultural capital to suggest that he, too, can claim a sophisticated space of imagined literary autonomy from which to wax ironic on the perversities of contemporary society while seeking at the same time to benefit from the market mechanisms his fiction aims to critique.

Of course the point is that Amis's satirically disdainful reflections on market society ultimately depend on the commercial conditions of contemporary literary production, in which any aura of scarcity has been elided by the stylized creation of impersonal branding. *Success*'s self-reflexive characteristics—its references to a controlling authorial figure and its appropriation of modernism's privileged cultural capital—imagine a depersonalized fiction of an author figure who orchestrates the novel's reflection of otherwise unpredictable economic changes. In other words, the novel's form reflects a reified economic society, in which characters' fates are determined by finance and fluctuating market values, making authorial control itself a fiction (operating only within the enclosed diegetic space of the novel), inextricably bound up with the market conditions it satirizes. *Success* thus introduces an important disjunction in Amis's work: the fiction points to an author figure in control of its representation of deregulated finance and economic volatility, but the novels themselves are marketed as cultural commodities in a corporate system of profits over which Amis the writer has little control. I pursue this disjunction further in what follows to show how his fiction dramatizes an ongoing attempt to negotiate the terms by which the celebrity author is a condition of transatlantic marketing. If Amis the brand is produced by the institutional networks of production, marketing, and promotion, then Amis the writer recapitalizes on that commercial mode of cultural production through the cultivation of an impersonal modernist style. This fictional engagement with the Amis brand, and its novel blend of complicity, critique, and style, comes to a head in *Money*.

Show Me the *Money*

Money (1984) logically follows *Success*, extending the earlier novel's simplicity with a more complexly layered and inflated satire on financial deregulation, economic globalization, and consumerist individualism.[22] John Self, whose name is appropriately generic and solipsistic, narrates the novel in a continuous present of excessive and self-destructive consumption often fractured by alcoholic blackouts. For Self, an English adman working in New York on a film to be called either *Good Money* or *Bad Money*, money is everything. Literally. Not only does he follow a path of insatiable commodified desire, whose appetite ranges from booze and fast food to pornography and prostitutes, but he also conflates money as a medium of exchange with the object of desire itself.[23] His desire is completely reified, a symptom of a totally commodified society whose "shady, petty dealings in high finance mirror the supposedly legitimate, grand-scale monetary dealings of Thatcherite Britain," as Patrick Brantlinger puts it.[24] Self is also the perfect dupe for the enormous financial swindle that by the end we find has been taking place throughout the novel. Lavishly living it up on credit, Self winds up criminally bankrupt and living in a London slum after a failed suicide bid.

In light of its story of excessive individual consumerism, my reading of *Money* advances two claims. First, I show how the novel yokes the imperative to endless and excessive consumption to a corporatist ethos of fast money—speculation and quick-selling—within an allegorical structure. Following Tamás Bényei's argument that the novel reflects the doubly allegorical nature of money itself—as both "the naming of something abstract" and a representation of empty serial interaction—I show how Amis's satirical allegory self-consciously rejects the conventions of literary realism in order to stress the fictive nature of speculation and virtual capital and the real material agency they exercise in global markets.[25] Second, building on this allegorical reading, I argue that Amis—who figures as a fictional version of himself in the novel—tests the limits of his own authorial celebrity against this vision of the omnipresent power of global finance and virtual markets. As such, I build on Jon Begley's observation of the novel's "precarious balance between satiric authority and a self-reflexive recognition of authorial and cultural complicity," and argue that "balance" and "complicity" are the fraught terms by which Amis critically reflects on the global publishing industry and its production of the celebrity author figure as distinct from authorial agency.[26]

John Self clearly features as a caricature of unbridled individual consumption, one that can lead to individual and national self-destruction (indeed, the subtitle of the novel is *A Suicide Note*), and his insatiable appetite for booze and fast food certainly bears this out. Shockingly funny as his endless and self-destructive consumption is, though, Self's unwitting role as a siphon for dubious finance seems, at least after 2008, more strikingly relevant to the novel's larger concern with global capital and the marriage of the credit and culture industries. Fielding Goodney cleverly directs John in this role, encouraging big credit spending with a nearly religious devotion. In response to Self's admission that he flew coach on his transatlantic trip to New York, Goodney chastises him to "pay more money, Slick. Fly in the sharp end, or supersonic. Coach kills. It's a false economy."[27] Fielding's real economy is defined by a fetishistic devotion to high finance, free-floating exchange rates, and speculation, as he tells John in a "voice full of passionate connoisseurship" of "Italian banking, liquidity preference, composition fallacy, hyperinflation, business confidence syndrome, booms and panics, US corporations," and so on (*M.* 27).

What I want to stress here, then, is Amis's emphasis that Self's insatiability is a symptom of a quick-sell economic ethos and free market deregulation, both conservative "solutions" to the economic crises of the 1970s and 1980s. Set in 1981, the novel reflects the lingering effects of the 1973 oil crisis and the failure of the Bretton Woods agreement on fixed exchange rates and the ensuing corporatist politics of deregulation and privatization that followed throughout the decade.[28] Through Self, we get a caricatured but oddly accurate sense of those complex international processes, partly because, as Amis's allegorical dupe for a booming credit economy, he rides the tide of artificially stimulated markets. Observing a "big blonde screamer" on Broadway who repeatedly shouts "'It's my money and I want it,'" Self is vaguely aware of the global links between the oil recession and reductions in public spending that came to characterize Thatcher's England and Reagan's United States:

> The city is full of these guys. ... I read in a magazine somewhere that they're chronics from the municipal madhouses. They got let out when money went wrong ten years ago. ... Now there's a good joke, a global one, cracked by money. An Arab hikes his zipper in the sheep-pen, gazes contentedly across the stall and says, "Hey, Basim. Let's hike oil." Ten years later a big whiteman windmills his arms on Broadway, for all to see. (*M.* 12)

Self's joke about reduced public spending (slashed funds for "municipal madhouses") is itself reductive, but indicates a certain awareness of the local impact of deregulated finance on the global commodities market. Indeed, in England he's both a pawn and a player in the new economy of corporate tax deferrals and reduced labor costs. As partner in the London ad agency Carburton,

Linex & Self, he's privy to the benefits and anxieties of floating corporate expenses in a booming credit economy, telling readers, "We all seem to make lots of money. ... The car is free. The car is on the house. The house is on the mortgage. The mortgage is on the firm—without interest. The interesting thing is: how long can this last? For me, that question carries an awful lot of anxiety—compound interest. It can't be legal, surely" (*M.* 78). Benefitting from corporate tax reductions and deferred interest payments, Self's reality is measured by volatile abstract values and the threat of compound interest, precisely the credit economy that allows Fielding to swindle him with little more than a rally of confidence in the future market for their film and a few quick contract-signing sessions supposedly backed by a group of domestic and foreign investors.

This comic allegory of shady finance intersects with the novel's self-reflexive allegorizing of its own literariness, and together they extend Amis's fictional negotiations with market complicity and a stylistic will to autonomy. As in much traditional allegory, characters' names in *Money* align them with social functions or moral categories, but usually with an added layer of irony. So John's London-based girlfriend who openly exchanges sexual favors for High Street fashion and expensive dinners is called Selina Street—"street seller." Always encouraging John to enjoy the high life and pornographic pleasure industries, Fielding Goodney suggests "feeling good." A washed-up, insecure, hyper-macho actor that John is forced to work with is named Lorne Guyland, who puts his "guyness" on display whenever possible. And Martina Twain, educated high-society woman and temporary love interest of John, doubles with the fictionalized "Martin Amis" as one of the novel's voices of reason; hence, "Martin-twain." Finally, as a fictional surrogate for Amis, Martina Twain lends John a copy of *Animal Farm*, perhaps the most famous twentieth-century allegory in English, in her attempt to educate him in high culture. John not only struggles to read Orwell's short novel, but thinks it's a children's book and fails to recognize it's an allegory, even trying to identify with the various animal figures (*M.* 190, 193)—a comic blindness to allegory that mirrors his swindling by Fielding (which in turn gets narrated through an extended metaphor, as we'll see). So John's misunderstanding of allegorical representation, combined with Amis's typological naming of characters, all point to *Money*'s comic allegory of high finance's virtual—or fictive—reality.

It is through its allegory of volatile finance markets that the novel engages with the production of authorial celebrity and its symbolic capital, as a cultural figure produced by those market forces yet distinct from the material existence of the writer. *Money* is a novel that is about novel writing and the commodification of the author figure, which Amis dramatizes through his own authorial presence in the novel, a fictional version of himself that plays on the split between writer and authorial brand. Amis is simultaneously a fictional character in the novel and an author-surrogate that expresses his limited control over his own circulating brand name. Martin Amis the fictional author plays the role of the high-minded artist and voice of reason, parodying the image of the writer who eschews the world of commerce, "the money conspiracy," in devotion to literature. When John asks him about his writing schedule, his reply is an arrogant description of an ascetic devotion to high culture and literary autonomy from the market:

> I get up at seven and write straight through till twelve. Twelve to one I read Russian poetry—in translation, alas. A quick lunch, then art history until three. After that it's philosophy for an hour . ... Four to five, European history, 1848 and all that. Five to six: I improve my German. And from then until dinner, well, I just relax and read whatever the hell I like. Usually Shakespeare. (*M.* 220)

Speaking with "a tone of pompous superiority rather than detached wisdom," this Amis figure seems a self-consciously constructed parody, his seriousness giving the lie to any latent fantasy of gentrified authorial detachment.[29] Or, as James Diedrick suggests, this ascetic literariness plays up to a kind of "false consciousness," the depiction of "a naïve literary modernist clinging to the fiction that he can protect his art from the influence of the marketplace."[30] And since, as we've seen, literary modernism produced its own forms of authorial celebrity, the point to stress here is that Diedrick's sense of a "naïve" modernist autonomy is a myth concealing a highly self-conscious fiction of the author's identity as a product of the market rather than autonomous from it.

This false appeal to a modernist myth of autonomy, and its implications of social privilege, supports my sense of how Amis negotiates—from within the pages of the novel—the problem of authorial control in the face of a publishing industry that is driven by economic speculation on the work of star authors. As a parody of the author figure, the fictional Amis does sometimes speak for the author of the book we're reading. When Amis's surrogate begins rewriting the film script for John's *Money*, he gives him a lecture on contemporary literature that clearly calls attention to Martin Amis's allegorical aims in the novel. First, Amis addresses the conventional relationship between author and fictional narrator, telling a distracted John Self that "the distance between author and narrator corresponds to the degree to which the author finds the narrator wicked, deluded, pitiful or ridiculous. ... This distance is partly determined by convention. In the epic or heroic frame, the author gives the protagonist everything he has, and more. The hero is a god or has godlike powers or virtues" (*M.* 229). On the other hand, when dealing with a narrator either lower on the scale of social class or simply despicable (like John Self), "the more liberties you can take with him. You can do what the hell you like to him, really. This creates an appetite for punishment. The author is not free of sadistic impulses" (*M.* 229). Note that the "heroic" treatment of the narrator echoes a "straight" reading of Joyce's *Portrait*, one that views Stephen's aesthetic theory of the artist as a godlike creator hovering behind the work, "paring his fingernails" as Joyce's own. Yet the notion of a sadistic author clearly alludes to Amis's treatment of Self, a self-consciously ironic one. The novel supports this when Amis's fictional author continues his lecture, still in self-reflexive mode, on the demise of literary realism: "We're pretty much agreed that the twentieth century is an ironic age—downward-looking. Even realism, rockbottom realism, is considered a bit grand for the twentieth century" (*M.* 231). Reminding us of the metafictional allegory we're reading, Amis yokes an appeal to modernist exceptionalism and authorial control to a sense that realism, faced with the representational crisis posed by the dominance of finance industries, is a dead game.

And yet Amis's depiction of John Self as a loutish drunken dupe from the postwar working class, positioned within the scheming world of high finance, is disingenuous at best, and poses a stark contrast to the author figure, no matter how ironically the latter is mediated within the novel. Philip Tew poses the question of "whether such parodies of the working-class or proletarian male found in these novels can be sufficiently ironic to be reduced to generic, textual, or postmodern matters, especially when articulated from positions of cultural authority, whether represented by the novel form itself or from Amis's own self-evident class-specific position"; and Amis's self-referentiality "serve[s] to evoke an authorial presence lurking in the text like some pantomime monster" and to "reestablish a privileged position based on authorial tradition and the finely calibrated nuances of the English class system."[31] Lawrence Driscoll concurs, asserting more strongly that Self "is used by Amis to somehow shake a fist at the entrepreneurial greed of a class to which Self never belonged in the first place," allowing him to assert a middle-class "high moral ground."[32] In the context of the argument I'm advancing here, I would add that this disingenuous representation of class permits Amis to disavow the middle-class privileges underpinning his authorship and, indeed, the entire enterprise of literary fiction. Even though the fictional Amis mediates the "real" writer, indulging in a self-mocking ascetic devotion to literature, he still figures in stark contrast to the unwitting John Self, in a double move that shores up the author's position of cultural authority and disavows the social privilege on which it depends. Thus, to rearticulate the arguments put forth by Tew and Driscoll, within the fictional logic of the novel Amis projects a greedy complicity with the destructive forces of corporate capitalism and finance (whether high or shady) onto a fictional figure from the lower classes, those least poised to benefit from neoliberal deregulations or the corporate-driven culture industries. We get a clear sense of this anxious disavowal in one of the most transparently autobiographical exchanges in *Money*. During their first meeting John asks Martin about his father (Kingsley), also a writer, to surmise "Bet that made it easier," to which Amis sarcastically replies, "Oh, sure. It's just like taking over the family pub" (*M*. 86). The class-based snub here signals, again, a lofty position of the author pursuing a disinterested literary enterprise, a self-conscious pose that treats any lingering will to literary autonomy with the proper degree of irony.

But while the cultural authority that Amis manages ironically to uphold is structured on real social privilege, we do well to remember that here it only functions within the self-reflexive fictional space of the novel, where the idea of the author's sadistic control becomes itself a fiction implicitly underwritten by the "money conspiracy" (*M*. 316) of a publishing industry driven in part by speculating on the value of an author's work. *Money* dramatizes this point in its climactic chess match between Amis's fictional surrogate and John Self. Having lost everything to Fielding's financial schemes and barely having escaped from the US authorities back to London where he plans to commit suicide, John calls Amis over to his flat for a final chat. Amis of course has figured out how Fielding duped John (again in reference to the author's control of his fiction), and he tries to explain the swindle over a chess match that serves as a kind of synecdoche for Fielding's swindle. Throughout the game, Amis explains Fielding's moves, his money art, a combination of paid-off actors, insurance deals, and computer hacking that left John criminally in debt. At the same time, he plays what appear to John to be oddly defensive or counter-logical moves on the board. John, totally focused on the game, "searching for blueprints, for forms and patterns" (*M*. 344), fails to follow Amis's money narrative. Then, as the absolute victim of authorial sadism, John finds himself locked in the loser's position of a *zugzwang* endgame: the player whose turn it is is forced into a suicide move. John loses the match precisely as Amis wraps up his narrative of the financial *zugzwang* that Fielding had played.[33]

As synecdoche for the larger narrative of *Money*, the chess match brings into focus the arguments I've been making about Amis and the literary marketplace, and does so around an apparent contradiction. On the one hand, as spokesperson for Amis's metafictions of the literary market, his allegorical stand-in only retrospectively grasps the abstract functions of high finance and its very real material effects. The novel thus plays with the distinction between Amis the author and his fictional surrogate, the latter a figure for the circulating authorial name. In doing so, it contrasts the fictional Amis's strict narrative control over *Money* and the celebrity author as a product of a literary market over which he has little control. But on the other hand, and following Amis's victory in the metaphorical chess match, his narrative conflates authorial control over a self-enclosed, self-referential fiction with control over market values, as he wonders aloud to John why Fielding didn't quit earlier and cut his risks, and speculates:

> Probably he was too deep into his themes and forms, his own artwork. The illusionist, the lie artist, the storyboarder—they have a helplessness. ... Why didn't he just let you walk [away from it all]? Because he was hooked. On the fiction, the art. He wanted to get to the end. We all do. (*M*. 346–7)

Like the fictional money man, Amis insinuates that his sadistic treatment of John Self follows on a devotion to "the fiction," which here means both novels and high finance. Amis's metafictional trick here withholds any authoritative answer to the problematic commodification of the literary, hinting instead at the more modest proposal that authorship is a product of the fictions, novelistic and financial, that produce the Amis brand.[34]

The Information on Celebrities

In a retrospective reflection on authorship having become a full-blown media affair by the mid-1990s, Amis describes the obligatory book tour: "Once an outrageous novelty" (like Oscar Wilde's celebrity US tour), the enterprise "is now accepted as a fact of life and a matter of professional routine. You arrive in each city and present yourself to its media; after that, in the evening, a mediated individual, you appear at the bookshop and perform."[35] The process is one in which "your personality (whatever that may be) undergoes public processing," subjecting an already fictitious sense of selfhood to further fictional mediation.[36] These personal reflections on public tours, in fact, provide a partial summary of *The Information* and its satirical reflection on the literary star system. As in *Success* and *Money*, *The Information* is composed of antithetical doubles cleverly orchestrated by authorial intrusions. But here

Amis uses that structure to reflect ironically on a nostalgic modernist ethos of authorial self-fashioning in the context of corporate production, literary branding, and his own mediated reception.

The novel centers on two forty-year-old writers: the increasingly smug Gwyn Barry who writes highly successful dribble, and the quaveringly abject Richard Tull, a failing novelist desperately clinging to a sense of literary dignity by churning out reviews of obscure biographies. While Gwyn's success on the literary market forms the focus of much of the novel's satire, it's important to note that that celebrity status is defined against Richard's pathetic grip on an obsolete ideal of modernist exceptionalism and difficulty. Whereas *Success* and *Money* cultivate a modernist mode of authorial impersonality in the vein of a Joyce or an Eliot, as a means of claiming a tenuous distinction from within the mass market for fiction, *The Information* thoroughly debunks the myth of modernist exceptionalism while introducing a note of nostalgia for modernism's historical institutions of relative autonomy.

When he isn't writing his unpublishable novels, Richard devotes part of his working time to two such outmoded institutions of modernist literary production: private publishing and little magazines. He works as poetry and fiction editor at the Tantalus Press, a private publishing house whose authors, mostly barely literate, pay their own printing costs. But whereas the reputations and cultural capital enjoyed by Joyce and other modernists depended in part on patronage, private publishing, and niche marketing, the Tantalus is merely a vanity press, a site of literary irrelevance and failure. The allure of private publishing as a foundation for future canonization is ironically suggested when the chief editor at the Tantalus, Balfour, encourages Richard to publish his work under the Tantalus imprint: "'One should remind oneself,' he says, 'that James Joyce initially favored private publication.' Then he added: 'Proust, too, by the way.'"[37] Once "a springboard to literary eminence," Richard reflects on private publishing in the conglomerate era: it "was not organized crime exactly, but it had close links with prostitution" (*I*. 53). Richard is also literary editor at a little magazine called, yes, *The Little Magazine*, a decaying holdout against publishing as prostitution. Amis's narrator knowingly reflects on the demise of little magazines and their historical survival on the margins of advertising and commercial publicity. "Born and raised in a five-story Georgian town house next to the Sloane Museum in Lincoln's Inn Fields (1935–1961)," the offices of the fictional *Little Magazine* harbor the quaint stuff of Bohemian modernism—"dusty decanters" and "tables strewn with books and learned journals"—but by the 1990s it has declined into an "increasingly nomadic and downwardly mobile" state on the outer margins of the literary establishment (*I.* 116). As something of a metaphorical modernist vagabond out of its historical time, Amis's narrator adds: "*The Little Magazine* really stood for something. It really did stand for something, in this briskly materialistic age. It stood for not paying people" (*I.* 117).

Aligned with these dead modernist institutions, Richard's writing fares no better. His unpublished novels are torturously dense and self-consciously learned, making him, as Amis's narrator puts it, "a marooned modernist" (*I.* 125). Speaking in the guise of his narrator, Amis invites readers to "take a quick look at Richard's stuff" before waxing ironic on modernism's brief historical moment. "Modernism was a brief divagation into difficulty," he writes, and Richard, its stubbornly belated loser, "didn't want to please readers." His prose uses endless layers of "unreliable narrators and author surrogates" in what read as "indistinguishable *monologues interieurs*." In other words, the narrator tells us, Richard's problem is that "he was trying to write genius novels, like Joyce. Joyce was the best yet at genius novels, and even he was a drag about half the time. Richard, arguably, was a drag *all* the time" (*I.* 125). Amis summarily mocks Richard for trying to uphold a modernist ethos of difficulty and autonomy from public demand, an effort doomed to failure. At best, he is a wicked and unknowing parody of Samuel Beckett's *The Unnamable* and other narratives of undoing: Richard's collected works can only go by names like "*unreadable*," or, as the title of his current manuscript has it, *Untitled* ("deliberately but provisionally" given that title in imitation of Joyce's *Work in Progress*) (*I.* 125, 5).[38] Passed from one agent to the next in a downward spiral through the literary publicity machine, Richard's manuscript gives readers migraines or sends them unexplainably to the hospital, usually before they get past page seven.

Amis knows of course that one can't be a modernist in the conglomerate era without being marooned, marginalized, and subject to snarky dismissal, but underlying this is a note of nostalgia for modernism's historical moment. These mocking depictions of modernism's institutional legacies carry an undertone of loss. In contrast to the implied continuity in recent theories of metamodernism, Niall Gildea and David Wylot identify another significant trend among contemporary writers and critics, one that understands modernism's apparent persistence as an attachment to its loss, a mourning for a modernism that is perhaps dead and yet will not go away.[39] There's nothing mournful about Amis's treatment of modernism's obsolescence but as a writer who is clearly concerned about the tension between stylistic singularity and market complicity, a nostalgia for modernism's marginalized institutions of autonomy clearly haunts and motivates the novel's unrelenting satire on celebrity sellouts in the contemporary commercial field.

Despite its irony, the novel's thinly veiled nostalgia for a dead legacy of modernist autonomy makes its satire on crass commercial writers and conglomerate publishing all the more palpable. In stark contrast to Richard's failure as a belated modernist, Gwyn Barry is a talentless scribbler, a temporary success story of transatlantic literary marketing, and a product of media hype: "all fax and Xerox and preselect" (*I*. 10). Amis doesn't even represent Gwyn's writing within the novel, its absence silently supporting the insistence, voiced by fictional agent Gal Aplanalp, that the public is "more interested in the writers than in the writing" (*I*. 94). As Amis's own publicity scandal suggested, the role of the literary agent has become increasingly central to the publication and marketing of novels and the circulation of authors as brand names. As agents came to play an increasingly central role in negotiating the fate and financial futures of new manuscripts, their work also aids in a cyclically shrinking number of "star authors" receiving big advances and high-yielding royalties.[40] Central to this network, celebrity authors are marketed as unique personae with very little realistic agency in the market for their books in such a way that the author figure becomes a "marker of differentiation" that "[conceals] mass production in individuation."[41]

Obviously familiar with these corporate conditions of marketing books and authors, Amis scathingly depicts it through the smug and successful Gwyn Barry, in part to distance himself from it, as we'll see. Gwyn's success is, of course, a result of a complex network of finance, agents, marketing, and distribution; or, as Richard Menke puts it, "novels [in *The Information*] feature as the excuses for radio and television appearances, newspaper profiles and gossip columns, movie deals."[42] In a publicity event combining interviews, photo sessions, and financial arrangements with Gwyn, Amis unflinchingly depicts the media creation of an authorial persona as "crucial to the promotional circuit necessary to a book's success within the market."[43] During the photo session, the financier gives a speech—"trying to get something back for his money"—about which literary magazines he would like to be associated with. All agree: one with "high standards," and the discussion moves on to market research and questions of "targeting" the book (*I*. 17–18). Gwyn also gloats to Richard about his new agent, the American Gal Aplanalp (as a clear allusion to Amis's dealings, Gwyn "controversially" switched agents), brags about the sizable advance he's getting for his incomplete manuscript, and assures Richard that Gal's list is moving "upmarket" and becoming "more literary" (*I*. 40–1).[44] Literary here means the successful marketing of a persona, or authorial fetish. As Gal advises Richard, "Writers need definition," because "the public can only keep in mind one thing per writer. Like a signature. Drunk, young, mad, fat, sick: you know. ... Ever thought about the young-fogey thing? The young fart. You wear a bowtie and a waistcoat. Would you smoke a pipe?" (*I.* 94).[45] Ever the failed modernist, Richard suggests that he get published first, and Gal quickly shifts the conversation back to publicity, suggesting that Richard begin with a journalistic piece on the "very successful novelist" Gwyn Barry by tagging along on that all-important publicity event, the American book tour.

The novel's polarized presentation of success and failure, celebrity and obscurity, forecloses any alternative mode of literary production. Despite Richard's increasingly desperate attempts to sabotage Gwyn's public image, and thus his literary authority, Gwyn remains a media darling through the novel's end, while Richard, finally resigned to his failure to write anything the public might want to read, gives up entirely and dotes on his young sons. Amis's presence as an author figure in *Money* suggests that the writer may exercise some control over fictional form, while authorial celebrity is subject to the contingencies of marketing. *The Information* makes that point even more emphatically, withholding any alternatives and reflecting instead on the wholly reified neoliberal literary industry in which market forces penetrate, even determine, the desires of writers and readers alike. And when the fiction is precisely about the commercial production of fiction, such a restricted vision of writing for the market—either to succeed or to fail—perhaps serves in its simplicity to heighten the satirical impact of the novel that never lets readers forget that Barry's celebrity status has nothing to do with talent or originality. Were this the only achievement of *The Information*, we might simply dismiss Amis for his cynical complicity with the market, as Delany does, or for an implied smugness that holds the celebrity author above the obviously uninteresting work of his fictional creation in what amounts to a clever twist on a familiar form of postmodern irony.

But it is precisely this foreclosure of alternatives in an apparently hegemonic market for fiction that I want to complicate, by asking how that limit to the novel's imagination implicates Amis and his own negotiation with the production of authorial celebrity. My reasoning here picks up on and extends Catherine Bernard's sense that Amis's "disembodied" authorial presence "may be a mere posture to mask his lack of control and self-identity," while the novel as a whole articulates a Frankfurt School immanent critique of society by reflecting its contradictions.[46] The critique is there, but it depends on Amis's juxtaposition of a nostalgia for modernist self-styling and the celebrity culture of the conglomerate era. As Amis said shortly after the publication of *The Information*, "the two writers, Richard and Gwyn, are [him]": Gwyn's mediated ego reflects Amis's own experiences of publicity and promotion, and Richard's Joycean aspirations satirically refine his creator's.[47] Richard's failure in a *post*modern literary market also underscores Amis's admiration for Joyce as a model stylist; commenting on Richard's internal struggles with writing, Amis's narrator toys with different ways of representing that interiority, and he revises Richard's thoughts several times before deciding to drop the "I": "For the interior monologue now waives the initial personal pronoun in deference to Joyce" (*I*. 5). Even though Richard is doomed to the position of a "marooned modernist"—of belatedness and failure—Amis refines that historical disjunction into the novel's nostalgic deference to modernism's lost ambitions and relative autonomy, features of its obsolescence that motivate and temper the novel's otherwise unremitting satire on postmodern media industries.

The novel associates the mediated production of the author with the contingent and ephemeral nature of celebrity, particularly Amis's own. Consider two examples. First, in a clear authorial intrusion early in the novel, Amis briefly interjects with what sounds like a self-conscious undoing of the controlling Joycean creator, "behind or beyond or above his handiwork ... paring his fingernails." The intrusion tells a story about trying to sign with a child in the park whom he thinks is deaf. Self-consciously failing to communicate with the child, he finally attempts to make the signs—"the M, the A"—and thinks to himself, "How can I ever play the omniscient, the all-knowing, when I don't know *anything*?" (*I*. 43). If modernist celebrity depended in part on the cultivation of impersonal style as a mark of relative autonomy from a larger commercial field, then Amis's self-effacing authorial voice worryingly acknowledges that in a literary market driven by speculation, star authors, and publishers' profits, the best one can do is to "play the omniscient" by ironically subscribing to the omnipresence of neoliberal literary production.

Second, Amis pits the arbitrary and ephemeral time of fame against tropes of timelessness to reference the contingent nature of celebrity. Written as an interior monologue, Richard reflects that "Gwyn's success was rather amusingly—no, in fact completely hilariously—accidental. And transitory. Above all transitory. If not in real time then, failing that, certainly in literary time. ... Or else the universe was a joke" (*I*. 80). Amis's narrator then intrudes to reflect on the speed of light and the inconceivable and growing distance between points in space. Perhaps echoing Joyce's identification of the universal in the particular, the timeless and the trivial most manifest in the "Ithaca" episode of *Ulysses*, Amis's interjection on astronomical time answers Richard's speculation about Gwyn with a comically hyperbolic reflection on his own "literary time" of transitory celebrity in the face of the universal:

> In a million millennia, the sun will be bigger. It will feel nearer. In a million millennia, if you are still reading me, you can check these words against personal experience, because the polar ice caps have melted away and Norway enjoys the climate of North Africa.
>
> Later still, the oceans will be boiling. The human story, or at any rate the terrestrial story, will be coming to an end. I don't honestly expect you to be reading me then. (*I.* 81)

As Amis jokingly projects his own literary longevity into this grand narrative of apocalyptic global warming, the novel's indictment of Gwyn's unearned success spills over into a generalized comic anxiety about authorship and immortality as products of corporate branding.

Here it's worth noting that *The Information* failed to live up to the marketing hype and sales expectations that preceded its publication. It was widely assumed that HarperCollins would not make up the advance given to Amis, despite the fact that the book was heavily promoted: from posters in the London Underground to title-bearing T-shirts for Dillons staff members, to a neon sign in Piccadilly Circus, all contributing to a picture of marketing hype that squares all too well with the novel's fictionalized treatment, and indicating in the real world how Amis had become exemplary of the author as a "web of textual meanings … constructed socially, by himself, his publisher, and his readers."[48] Not a complete failure—the book eventually enjoyed several weeks on the *Sunday Times* bestseller list—it still did not secure the profits to cover the initial advance, making it an exemplary loss-leader that publishers in the conglomerate system are willing to risk in cases of already established authors.[49] Set alongside the book's failure to meet sales expectations, the novel's fictionalized foreclosure of any alternatives to success or failure in the transatlantic corporate production of literature, Amis's identification with his author figures, and his authorial reflections on the ephemeral and contingent nature of his own celebrity status, *The Information*, as several critics have suggested, obviously resonates with Amis's own place in the star system and its arbitrary commodification of literature that the novel supposedly indicts.[50] All of this point to an irony linking the book's promotion and reception to the larger conditions for marketing literary fiction in the 1990s. And yet, neither the novel's satire nor its sales figures did anything to challenge the market, showing instead how such an open critique of those conditions can actually affirm the sway of big corporate publishing. In short, the marketing of the novel, Amis's self-reflexive complicity, and the novel's picture of winners-take-all publishing, all point to a market for literature that appears inescapable in its totality.

Conclusion

But that's precisely the point on which I want to conclude my reading of *The Information*. In an essay on Amis and the marketing of genre, Will Norman argues that Amis's

> *Night Train* reveals a disjunction between the marketing, design and institutional reception of Amis's work as literary fiction on one hand, and the author's own strategies of composition on the other. In the light of this analysis, Amis's work yields a negative critique of the category of literary fiction from within its own domain, in rendering visible the tensions and compromises necessary to its desire for legitimacy.[51]

I fully agree with this thesis. I would add, though, that this conflicted compromise and desired legitimacy betrays a nostalgic, if empty, appeal to a modernist legacy that continues to influence our belief in the legitimacy of literary fiction. The celebrity author of literary fiction is an absolute product of successful packaging and marketing, and thus serves for Amis to sweep away any residual claims literature makes to an art that is not bound by capricious and speculative corporate values. The strength of *The Information* is that it collapses any distinction between fictional representation and its mode of production under the new star system. The novel concludes by insisting that "the information" is nothing, a kind of existential abyss of a contemporary culture lacking any ontological or moral ground. But it also suggests that the novel is about the category of literary fiction as the privileged expression of neoliberal capital and creativity. Across these texts, we see Amis negotiating with a fiction of celebrity authorship that draws on nostalgia for modernism's dead legacies—stylistic self-fashioning and a dream of autonomy—driven by the cultural transformation from the signature to the brand.

Amis self-reflexively charts this larger transformation in the industry and its implications for the symbolic value of literature, simultaneously upholding a nostalgia for modernist legitimacy as an impossible ideal, now fully subordinated to commercial branding yet capable of creative formal mediation. Turning now to Ian McEwan, we see a different kind of engagement with modernism's vexed historical and aesthetic legacies. In McEwan, modernist style is at once a mark of elitist social insularity and a resource, ambivalently embraced, for its contemporary commercialization.

2

"To Invent a Literature": Ian McEwan's Commercial Modernism

Emerging on the literary scene in the 1970s, Ian McEwan carved out a distinctive style of the grotesque, a perversely probing psychological realism that featured some "incredibly distressed, fucked up people."[1] In works like *First Love, Last Rites*, *The Cement Garden*, and *The Comfort of Strangers*, McEwan developed a kind of postindustrial gothic realism that focused on decidedly amoral and sociopathic characters and earned him a reputation as a writer of "the perverse" and "the macabre," a tendency that would continue into his Cold War spy thriller *The Innocent* and his exploration of psychopathic fixation in *Enduring Love*.[2] Those early amoral experiments can be said to advance a deviant ethical aim, in that McEwan developed an "art of unease" that destabilizes rigid "moral certainties."[3] That questioning of moral norms found expression in a formal tautness and stylistic impersonality and signaled a departure from an increasingly conventional postmodern metafiction on the one hand, and a counter to what he perceived as the "overstuffed, overfurnished English novel" of tradition.[4] In his words, McEwan sought "to make strength out of a kind of ignorance" and "to invent a literature" of his own design.[5] Linking a deviant ethics to impersonal form, McEwan's early work displays a modernist impulse to make the novel new. Having earned a strong critical following with that invention, however, and coinciding with the Booker Prize–winning *Amsterdam* (1998), McEwan's writing took up a more explicit engagement with modernism's historical and formal legacies precisely as it became more mainstream. Beginning with *Atonement*, his novels have shifted away from grotesque innovation into more narrowly middle-class concerns and conventions. I trace this adoption of modernism's self-conscious reflection on form, and McEwan's critical position regarding modernism's historical legacy, to show how that move reflects specific institutional and commercial trends. This pattern is most legible in *Atonement* (2001), *Saturday* (2005), and reaches an end point in *Sweet Tooth* (2012), and in reflexively foregrounding their formal construction, these novels also question the nature of McEwan's whole project: the capacity of literary fiction—as a privileged cultural commodity—to engage in an ethical critique of the social and economic conditions that implicitly underlie its production.

Since the publication of *Amsterdam*, McEwan's major novels show an active engagement with the production of his own celebrity status and his place in the literary canon, in part by way of an "ambivalent" return to modernism.[6] From flagged allusions to "great" figures like Henry James, Virginia Woolf, and James Joyce, to his adaptation of an impressionistic mode of exploring consciousness— what Woolf called the "dark places of psychology"—into page-turning and highly marketable fiction, McEwan's novels recuperate from modernism a fictional mode that "reflects on its own formal properties," including his "emulations of modernist modes of rendering consciousness," and they self-consciously play with fluid and disruptive temporalities.[7] McEwan deploys these familiar formal techniques of high modernism while self-consciously distancing his work from an aesthetic he sees as posited on a socially elitist insularity. To some extent this affirms Derek Attridge's insistence that "modernism after modernism necessarily involves a reworking of modernism's methods," but it also indicates a double move that is crucial to understanding how McEwan occupies a contemporary literary establishment in which writers are anxiously compelled to negotiate a place within the largely institutionalized "legacies of modernism."[8] As Laura Marcus suggests, McEwan "does not attempt merely to reproduce the modernist text, nor to create a parody or pastiche of it" but rather "acknowledges the debt even as he calls attention to the necessary and inevitable distance between his own time and that of the modernist novelist."[9] Similarly, David James calls McEwan a "reluctant impressionist," a writer who is drawn to the conundrums of "perception and judgment that lay at the heart of literary impressionism" while "reasserting his own creative autonomy" through a dialectic "of inheritance and self-determination," particularly in *Atonement*.[10] For James, this self-reflexive assertion of autonomy is bound to the ethical imperative in McEwan's novels, which "reflect in noticeable ways on their own construction, while demonstrating how impressionist methods of rendering consciousness have become the expressive medium for McEwan's epistemological and ethical concerns."[11]

While I too focus on McEwan's ambivalent embrace of modernism's formal and historical legacies, I see that as key to a position-taking strategy within a mainstream market rather than a real assertion of literary autonomy. Again, modernism's established cultural capital has come to serve the market for contemporary "literary" fiction and the promotion of particular authors' work. Modernist autonomy was in part built on the assumption that "value is not measured by commercial success" in the short term but accrues to works "destined to deferred economic gratification."[12] Following its mid-century institutionalization, particularly in the university system, "modernism has thrived on a smug sense of cultured superiority ... by appealing only to a highly educated and smartly self-conscious coterie," an inheritance that helps explain why authors like McEwan would want to emulate and distance themselves from it.[13] As an author of best-selling novels, McEwan does not aspire to an autonomy that might "seek to transform" the conditions of "literary production," as Andrew Goldstone claims for the modernists.[14] And yet the allure of the idea persists, legible in stylistic imitation and strategies of authorial self-fashioning that conceal mass production in manufactured singularity and cultural sophistication.[15] It is modernism's institutionalized and relatively elite form of cultural capital, repackaged in and as literary fiction, that forms a field of reference on which authors like McEwan can capitalize in the intersecting networks of marketing, literary prizes, college reading lists, and celebrity. Approaching McEwan's ambivalent return to modernism in this light—including the way his novels since *Amsterdam* self-consciously foreground their formal and stylistic properties—sheds light on a particular trend in the market for literary fiction. Despite Marcus's claim to the contrary, McEwan's emulations of modernist modes of representation often take the form of pastiched mimesis, a model of appropriating the cultural capital of the canon to secure elite literary distinction, even as he distances his work from their influence.[16] His ambivalent negotiations with this modernist inheritance reveals its commercial viability, feeding into a demand for what Jesse Matz has recently identified as a commercialized "nostalgia for modernist prestige" expressed in an impressionist style that has become standard to much literary fiction.[17] In other words, appeals to readers' familiarity with modernism banks on its institutional prestige as part of the marketing of the author as a celebrity and brand name.

McEwan thus extends a modernist mode of authorial self-fashioning in fictions that reflexively engage modernism's legacies, but in a way that fetishistically converts its historical associations with autonomy to the production of a commercial literary brand. So while McEwan is clearly invested in the novel as a form that is uniquely poised to address contemporary social and ethical debates, his fiction is also a privileged cultural commodity and a version of metamodernism that is especially amenable to conglomerate publishing and its promotion of exclusive celebrity authors.

Atonement and the Legacies of Impressionism

My focus in this section is on *Atonement* and its marketing and reception, but it might be useful here to position the novel in the context of the Booker Prize for *Amsterdam*. McEwan's *The Comfort of Strangers* (1981) and *Black Dogs* (1992) were both short-listed for the prestigious Booker Prize, but it wasn't until *Amsterdam* that he would win that most coveted, and most media-hyped, award in British literary culture. Several commentators have suggested that the novella is an "inferior" work and that its selection for the Booker was at best a recognition of the author's cumulative body of fiction rather than of the merits of the book itself.[18] *Amsterdam* can be read as an allegorical reflection on the social role of the author as cultural producer in general and on McEwan's career in particular. Frank Kermode notes something of this limiting irony, writing that "the failure of the composer's final symphony, after we have heard so much about the process of its composition, might uncharitably be seen as an allegory of the novel it occurs in."[19] Elaborating on Kermode's suggestion and taking note of the book's own vexed position regarding the prize culture it sets out to satirize, Head offers his own waffling account, in which "the satire bleeds out into the world of literary culture, but without the force of outright condemnation"; yet, by "inviting reflection on literary prize culture and the celebrity status of the author—McEwan ensures that its 'patness' carries a loaded moral critique."[20] Lacking any conclusive condemnation, the book subtly sneers at the dubious values produced by prize culture, but what Head's sense of a "loaded moral critique" misses is how McEwan's satire fully participates, and is embedded, in the logics of prizes and their production of cultural and economic capital. *Amsterdam* was widely perceived as an inferior work, and in this light the novella itself and its reception—constitutive parts of a literary event—participate in a system of cultural consecration and condescension that paradoxically lends literary prizes their prestige.[21] McEwan's light mockery "[does] nothing to discredit the cultural prize," to adopt English's formulation, "and in fact [serves] as crucial support for it inasmuch as they help to keep aloft the collective belief or make-belief in artistic value as such, in the disinterested judgment of taste."[22]

I want to suggest that the Booker Prize for *Amsterdam* and the controversy surrounding it help account for McEwan's ensuing and pronounced engagement with the legacy of modernism. The book banks on McEwan's accumulated cultural capital—having been short-listed twice for the Booker—within the elite field of literary fiction, and it marks a shift in McEwan's oeuvre from studies in the social grotesque to best-selling novels that adopt a modernist propensity to reflect on their own carefully cultivated formal properties and stylistic signature. As he says in an interview, "I could not have written *Atonement* without first writing *Amsterdam*."[23] Following *Amsterdam*, McEwan's novels self-reflexively address the relationship between aesthetic autonomy and literary value, on the one hand, and the market for celebrity fiction on the other. *Atonement* can be read as a response to these concerns raised by the novella and its reception (or the textual and paratextual), and it demonstrates McEwan's adept commercial negotiations with the established canon of modernist innovation.

In this light, McEwan adopts a recognizably postmodern metafictional structure not only to question the ethical function of literature—as many commentators have suggested—but to claim a place, as Geoff Dyer has noted, in "the pantheon" of the literary canon by "creatively extending and hauling a defining part of the British literary tradition up to and into the twenty-first century."[24] Other critics have picked up on and qualified Dyer's comments on McEwan's "dialogic" engagement with modernism, in particular its attempts to display and undermine the influence of the impressionist style of Woolf. David James argues that the novel dramatizes McEwan's ambivalence, noting how his "quintessentially impressionist interest" in representing consciousness is in tension with his open critique, through Briony, of what McEwan perceives as modernism's insular, elitist tendencies. On this reading, McEwan "cannot entirely undermine Briony's allegiance to the Woolfian novel of consciousness— because that's precisely the kind of novel he wants for himself."[25] In a more critical vein, Richard Robinson notes that McEwan writes a mostly "pastiched Woolf style" in an effort to undermine her influence by subordinating it to a "proleptic function in an overarching moral narrative," one that necessarily "risks a reductive evaluation of modernist textuality."[26] As I will argue in this section, McEwan's ambivalent and ultimately reductive engagement with modernism's legacy, and Woolf's impressionism in particular, also lays claim to its cultural capital, even in the act of erasing its influence. *Atonement* is McEwan's most self-consciously literary novel, and it situates Woolf within a metafictional genealogy of twentieth-century British fiction in a way that wants to critically distance his own work from modernist impressionism, while demonstrating at the same time how its techniques have become mainstream, a means of authorizing McEwan as a master of the contemporary novel form. The novel's enormous critical and commercial success, in this light, attests to the marketability of a once experimental modernist style.

The self-reflexive writerly plot of *Atonement* originates with Briony's "discovery" of an impressionist aesthetic. Early in the novel, and in a kind of epiphany that will give rise to her first serious attempt at writing fiction, Briony observes "the dividing moment between" willing her finger to move and actually moving it, and thinks that something of the "mystery" of a conscious self exists in that "seamless" passage from thought to sense and back again.[27] She quickly extends this solipsistic self-consciousness to an awareness of other people, anxiously imagining an entire social world teeming with inscrutable private minds. "Did her sister also have a real self concealed behind a breaking wave," she wonders, and if so, if "everyone's claim on life" is as "intense" as her own, then "one could drown in irrelevance" (*A*. 34). At this moment of Briony's emerging self-consciousness, we get a sense of the modernist impression as an aesthetic mode of mediating thought and feeling, of representing, as Jesse Matz describes it, "a mode of experience that is neither sensuous nor rational, neither felt nor thought, but somewhere in between," and that mediates a duality of singular consciousness and universality in a style that "is personal but universal—subjective, but not therefore wholly idiosyncratic."[28] Something of this "personal but universal" power of the impression begins to take shape a moment later in *Atonement* when Briony, still contemplating her own discovery of sensuous self-consciousness, witnesses Robbie and Cecilia tussling over the Tallis family vase at the fountain, a scene that readers have already witnessed from the perspectives of the would-be lovers. First seeing their struggle as an act of aggression or romance promising a moral tale, Briony then brings her formative aesthetic sensibilities to bear on the scene and understands it as a "real" adult moment of individuals failing to grasp each other's conscious motivations. Her dawning realization of an impressionist mode that mediates the sensuous and the rational then prompts her to reimagine the scene as the source of an aesthetic of consciousness: "She could write the scene three times over, from three points of view," she thinks, none of which is inherently good or bad, for "she need only show separate minds, as alive as her own, struggling with the idea that other minds were equally alive. ... And only in a story could you enter these different minds and show how they had an equal value" (*A*. 38). Briony's discovery of sensory consciousness as the basis for fiction simultaneously marks a return to the impressionist modes of rendering consciousness associated with the likes of Henry James and Woolf, and advertises the motivation for McEwan's own novelistic enterprise, his aim "to present, obviously in a very stylized way, what it's like to be thinking."[29]

Focalized through the young Briony, this impressionist endeavor is seamlessly contained within the form of the novel's long first part. Indeed, the scene instantiates the recursive plot of the whole novel. Robbie's and Cecilia's conflicting, partial perspectives are each tinged with possessive jealousy and distrust, giving their struggle a sexual charge of erotic possibilities and compelling Cecilia to strip out of her skirt and blouse and descend into the fountain to retrieve the fractured parts of the vase and initiating Robbie's guarded sexual fantasies. Their "separate minds" are rendered through conflicting impressions that create the erotic suspense fueling their mutual attraction (before, i.e., their bond is violently torn apart by Briony's immature false impressions of Robbie). In McEwan's protracted handling of these cumulative impressions, then, we sense something of the larger aspiration of the earlier impressionists. Matz discerns this aim on the part of Ford, Conrad, and Woolf, in which "to get in the impression not just sense perception but sense that is thought, appearances that are real, suspicions that are true and parts that are whole—this was the 'total' aspiration of the Impressionist writer."[30] The conflicting impressions of Cecilia and Robbie reflect a sense of isolated consciousnesses, of "separate minds" marked by class difference, but they also serve as "parts" that generate the erotic suspense, or " 'total' aspiration," of a projected aesthetic wholeness.

If this protracted mise-en-scène foregrounds McEwan's ability to write like an impressionist, the novel also situates that modernist inheritance back into literary history by stressing, and ultimately struggling to undermine, the influence of Virginia Woolf. Five years after the fountain scene and during the 1940 blitz, Briony has crafted her experience into her first novella, "Two Figures by a Fountain," which McEwan makes clear is the result of a belated emulation of *The Waves* (1932), comprising largely of the stream-of-consciousness soliloquies of its characters and perhaps Woolf's most experimentally ambitious novel. Under the influence of Woolf, Briony comes to reject traditional "characters" and "plots" as so much "rusted machinery," so that, in McEwan's most overt reference to Woolf's techniques,

> it was thought, perception, sensations that interested her, the conscious mind as a river through time, and how to represent its onward roll. ... If only she could reproduce the clear light of a summer's morning, the sensations of a child standing at a window, the curve and dip of a swallow's flight over a pool of water. ... She had read Virginia Woolf's *The Waves* three times and thought that a great transformation was being worked in human nature itself, and that only fiction, a new kind of fiction, could capture the essence of the change. To enter a mind

and show it at work, or being worked on, and to do this within a symmetrical design—this would be an artistic triumph. (*A*. 265)

If the watery metaphors here clearly signal the influence of *The Waves*, McEwan also reworks fairly familiar Woolfian assertions that reach back to the 1910s and 1920s, when what we now call modernism was taking shape. The "transformation" to "human nature" recalls Woolf's claim that "on or about December 1910 human character changed"—referring to the first showing of postimpressionist art in London as a moment that witnessed the birth of modernism, while Briony's desire "to enter a mind and show it at work" echoes Woolf's stated aim in writing *Mrs. Dalloway* (1925): "to criticise the social system, and to show it at work, at its most intense."[31] Two significant implications can be drawn from these echoes of Woolf. First, McEwan strips the social out of Woolf's aesthetic theories, so that while Briony rightly picks up on the "new kind of fiction" that Woolf produced in the 1920s, one that aimed to "capture the essence of the change" to modern society, he reduces Briony's lessons from modernism to mere inwardness. Second, McEwan has the fictional Briony belatedly echoing these keynotes of high modernism, in 1940 and in the midst of the war that put a damper on its earlier exuberance; so part of his point is that, as Robinson notes, she is "a modernist out of time."[32]

This disjointedness in Briony's development, then, both reflects back on the impressionist aspirations she entertains in Part One—and which McEwan adapts to his own aesthetics of consciousness and sensation—and marks a key turning point in McEwan's fictional referential field of modernism's literary history. While his writing openly depends on the legacy of impressionism as a mode of rendering "the fine print of consciousness," he also feels compelled to undermine its influence, to distance his achievement from modernism both by reducing it to a simplified evasiveness and erasing it from Briony's narrative. This double move comes about in a near omission, in that Briony's impressionist debut, "Two Figures," does not materialize in *Atonement* but figures as a ghostly presence haunting Briony's literary aspirations. Her novella is rejected by "C. C."—an allusion to Cyril Connolly, editor at the then-new literary magazine *Horizon*—who both praises and chastises Briony's writing for its allegiance to Woolfian impressionism and stream-of-consciousness: "*We wondered if it owed a little too much to the techniques of Mrs. Woolf,*" the letter reads, even if "*the crystalline present moment is of course a worthy subject in itself*" that allows one to "*delve into mysteries of perception, present a stylized version of thought processes, permit the vagaries and unpredictability of the private self to be explored and so on*" (*A.* 294). The problem is that Briony's story "lacks forward movement" and narrative "backbone" (*A.* 294, 296). As Richard Robinson observes, C.C.'s letter calls attention to the process, dramatized within the form of the novel, of eliding or erasing Briony's impressionist emulation of Woolf, so that *Atonement* "pretends to be a modernist palimpsest that has undergone continual erasure."[33] The novel's intertextual coding and metafictional layering prompt us to read the impressionisms of Part One according to the advice contained in the rejection letter from C. C.

Indeed, it points to McEwan's insistence that *Atonement* performs a moral indictment of an elite modernist insularity, a criticism he advanced in a 2006 interview with David Lynn against the kind of "modernism that promoted the notion of the artist as sort of high priest who belonged to a small elite and was not going to ever have his pages dirtied and grubbied by the hoi polloi. I think it was a nonsensical view. Writers like Virginia Woolf saying 'Character is now dead,'" helped push the novel down some very fruitless impasses."[34] And specifically addressing his own surrogate author, McEwan suggests that he dramatizes Briony's act of burying "her conscience beneath her stream of consciousness" so as "to enter into a conversation with modernism and its dereliction of duty in relation to what [his fictionalized Connolly calls] the backbone of plot."[35] The rejection letter provides the intertextual coding for McEwan's fictionalized literary genealogy, and he uses it both to criticize modernism's influence while guiding readers toward that same judgment.

The dual praise and criticism that Briony receives, that is, reflects on her original aspirations, so that the novel's metafictional conceit figures prominently, on a formal level, in McEwan's anxious negotiation with the legacy of modernism. The early promise of a Woolfian mode of rendering the ineffable impressions of a singular consciousness is largely subordinated to the novel's metafictional distancing from what McEwan has deemed its elitist social detachment. If we return to the mise-en-scène of Briony's writerly narrative, we find a proleptic authorial intrusion (one that, we'll see, is not only the fictional Briony's but also McEwan's) that anticipates the terms of C. C.'s letter and bears the ghostly traces of an anxiously disavowed impressionist influence. Immediately following the scene that inspires her to write the impressionistic "Two Figures," McEwan's narrator looks ahead to reflect on Briony's career:

> Six decades later she would describe how at the age of thirteen she had written her way through a whole history of literature, beginning with the stories derived from the European tradition of folktales, through drama with a simple moral

intent, to arrive at an impartial psychological realism which she discovered for herself, one special morning during a heat wave in 1935. She would be well aware of the extent of her self-mythologizing, and she gave her account a self-mocking, or mock-heroic tone. Her fiction was known for its amorality, and like all authors pressed by a repeated question, she felt obliged to produce a story line, a plot of her development that contained the moment when she became recognizably herself. (*A.* 38–9)

This apparent endorsement of a privileged psychological realism that favors amorality resonates with McEwan's own early work, in which a macabre style and taut "story line" gained him a secure critical following. At the same time, and reflecting more immediately on the novel we're reading, Briony's path through impressionism is glaringly omitted, and underscores McEwan's act of reducing modernism to an aesthetic slogan only to bury it. The plot of Briony's becoming "recognizably herself" and achieving a self-conscious signature style "contained the moment" of her discovery of an impressionist technique even as it elides it, so the passage functions as a synecdoche for the novel's metafiction, the way it both displays and disavows McEwan's own engagement with a modernist canon in becoming "recognizably [himself]."

So while McEwan writes impressionism out of Briony's "self-mythologizing" tale, he does not entirely eliminate it from his novel. As James notes, McEwan "cannot entirely undermine Briony's allegiance to the Woolfian novel of consciousness—because that's precisely the kind of novel he wants for himself,"[36] a tension that is at the heart of McEwan's "dialogue with the structures of modernist fiction," even if *Atonement* works to subordinate Briony's impressions to its larger metafictional realist form and "forward movement."[37] We find notable traces in Part One in which a recognizably modernist impressionism gives rise to a kind of lyrical realism in echo of Woolf's flights of aesthetic fancy. When Cecilia enters Paul Marshall's room, for example, McEwan renders her vision in a mode of pure sensory immediacy that transcends the rationalist dictates of psychological realism: "The air was smooth with the scent of wax, and in the honeyed light, the gleaming surfaces of the furniture seemed to ripple and breathe. As her approach altered her angle of view, the revellers on the lid of an ancient trousseau writhed into dance steps" (*A.* 46). The stylized sensory immediacy here recalls Woolf's poetics; and this is the kind of lushly lyrical representation of sensory immediacy that Briony aspires to, emphasizing the "very stylized way" McEwan has of depicting the "vagaries of perception" interacting with consciousness.[38] At the same time, though, those stylistic effects contribute little to the narrative's "forward movement," and can be read as a deliberately "pastiched Woolf style."[39]

The novel's strategic containment of those traces of impressionist modernism, obviously signaled both by those instances of pastiche and McEwan's open references to Woolf, is especially instructive about the legacy of modernism within the commercially elite field of literary fiction. In *Atonement* McEwan would seem to want it both ways, self-consciously emulating Woolf's modernist aesthetic while rendering it outmoded, burying it beneath Briony's eventual embrace of a psychological realism that is also McEwan's signature style, all of which is folded into the novel's metafictional conceit. This process points to a comparison with Fredric Jameson's dialectical theory of realism. Defining itself in opposition to a host of other genres—such as the romance—the realist novel internalizes its other in a dialectical process: "Realism is opposed to romance only because it carries it within itself and must somehow dissolve it in order to become its antithesis," and "the novel in question must first construct the structure whose dismantling is the primary work of its narration in the first place."[40] McEwan's novel cannot do without the stylistic and formal designs that had earlier reshaped twentieth-century literature, but the (pastiched) impressions are embedded within the form of a novel that constructs and then dismantles their primacy to position his own work as modernism's literary-historical outcome and himself as its metafictional master.[41] The question, then, is whether his own developing brand of literary fiction aspires to the same transformation that Woolf and her contemporaries can be said to have achieved.

Embedded within and subordinated to the novel's metafictional realism, those emulations of a recognizable modernist aesthetic serve a specific market for fiction, in which the symbolic value of an institutionalized canon translates into a sign of literary distinction. Again, the novel "risks a reductive evaluation of modernist textuality," and McEwan's reductive pastiche and formal encoding signal a sense in which a modernist aesthetic associated with Woolf and once occupying a restricted field of cultural production becomes formulaic and commercially viable.[42] While McEwan's reduction of Woolf's technique to a form of pastiche may be a means of claiming a certain degree of autonomy from its influence (to tweak David James's argument), it also displays his possession of modernism's cultural capital, which in turn appeals to a market demand for what Jesse Matz has recently described as "pseudo-impressionism."[43] An impressionist mode of rendering consciousness has become common to much of "mainstream literary fiction," Matz argues, and a mimetic engagement with its legacy risks "trivializing" their predecessors and appropriating "an outworn aesthetic serving only to authenticate literariness."[44] This strategy, moreover, functions within a "literary establishment constituted by prestige publishers and other institutional arbiters [that] still defines successful representation in terms set by the historical impressionists" and that now signals a commercially effective mark of literary authority.[45] Taking *The Master* as an example, Matz argues that Colm Tóibín's mimetic homage to Henry James amounts to "a kind of power grab" in which "the prudishly self-evasive James authorizes Tóibín as the real Master."[46] *Atonement* embeds a formerly experimental but now familiar impressionist aesthetic within itself to authorize McEwan and justify a privileged place in a competitive, if predictable, literary market.[47] In other words, McEwan both trivializes Woolf and appeals to modernism's cultural prestige, a twinned gesture aimed at authorizing a fiction of celebrity as a constitutive factor in a system that benefits editors, publishing firms, and marketing departments, all of those operating within the market for literary fiction. Impressionism here might otherwise be just another "outworn aesthetic" (in Matz's words) in a vicious cycle of capitalist obsolescence, but it also reveals how modernism's cultural capital is a crucial ingredient in keeping "the economy of prestige" afloat.[48]

The Author as God, or, McEwan Paring His Fingernails

Atonement's doubled metafictional conclusion flaunts McEwan's self-conscious participation in cultivating authorial prestige within this economy. The primary plot of the novel concludes with a self-reflexive gesture that by 2001 had become the stale stuff of postmodernism. In the novel's first ending, Briony visits Robbie and Cecilia, promises to confess the nature of her crime and then, after leaving, decides it is time to write "a new draft" of the whole story. This is followed by the fictional authorial stamp, "BT London, 1999," which both folds back on the contents of the novel and, in a sly wink to readers, acknowledges Briony's fictionality in a way that tacitly refers to McEwan as the controlling creator behind the whole conceit. The trick elicits two implications: first, that Briony, who has written her way through an entire literary tradition to become "recognizably herself," is a fictional surrogate for McEwan's ambivalent engagement with modernism's legacy and, more important, that Ian McEwan is ontologically prior to the enclosed and self-referential fiction of the novel. McEwan capitulates to what Bourdieu calls the "charismatic ideology … which directs the gaze towards the apparent producer … and prevents us [from] asking who has created this 'creator' and the magic power of transubstantiation with which this 'creator' is endowed."[49] This magic also goes by the name of "commodity fetishism in the literary field" that, as Brouillette argues, "obfuscates the realities of the making of the product by channeling our attention toward the author as the singular creator."[50] The novel thus reflects a literary ideology that elides its production and marketing, even though it's packaged in cover blurbs and best-seller labels.

Recognizably *post*modern as this metafictional conceit may be, though, the postscript serves as a second ending that actually marks a return to a modernist technique of authorial self-fashioning, a strategy that suggests how the idealized author is an impersonal figure produced by the text that circulates in the market. There, Briony writes that, as creators of wholly fictional worlds not subject to external judgment, novelists have the "absolute power" of a god and that, upon publication of the novel after her death, "we will exist only as my inventions" (350). A likely nod to Barthes's famous pronouncement of "the death of the author," Briony's claim also begs comparison to Stephen Dedalus's theory of aesthetic impersonality in Joyce's *Portrait*: "The personality of the artist, at first a cry or a cadence or a mood and then a fluid and lambent narrative, finally refines itself out of existence, impersonalises itself, so to speak" so that, ultimately, "the artist, like the God of the creation, remains within or behind or beyond or above his handiwork, invisible, refined out of existence, indifferent, paring his fingernails."[51] Now, as we know, Stephen will never become this artist, but this aesthetic of impersonality anticipates the author of *Ulysses*, the text whose inimitable styles would become a kind of trademark for Joyce as a quintessential modernist figure who, through a trick of masterly mimesis, "is created simultaneously with the text."[52] And if Briony is the fictional bearer of McEwan's own capacity for metamodernist mimesis, even when it's subject to parody and pastiche, then she also signals the impersonality of the celebrity author figure who is simultaneously the fetishized product of his fictional creation. Briony's Joycean reference, that is, suggests that McEwan's authorship is a feature of the writing, appealing to this modernist mythology in such a way that disavows the corporate production that enables it.

Neoliberal Modernism

Saturday extends McEwan's ambivalent metamodernism, drawing on its cultural capital to reflect on literary fiction's privileged capacity to critique the social contradictions of neoliberal capitalism. Like *Atonement*, it constructs an intertextual field of allusions to "great" modern works and authors and integrates them into stylistic and formal adaptations of Henry James, James Joyce, and Virginia Woolf. The novel's setting on a single day in the life of its protagonist is clearly a nod to *Ulysses* and *Mrs. Dalloway*.[53] These metamodernist echoes, though, beg to be read with the questions the novel raises about global capitalism, uneven distribution, and the war on terror, social problems that have divided critical opinion.[54] These aesthetic and social aspects of the novel are actually two sides of the same coin. *Saturday* reflects an ideological tension that Jonathan Eburne and Rita Felski identify in contemporary modernism, one "suspended between direct political engagement and an aesthetic autonomy that remains vital for the imagining of a radically alternative future."[55] *Saturday* knowingly engages with this modernist tension between aesthetic autonomy and social commitment, but fails to imagine an escape from a sense that literary fiction, as a privileged cultural commodity, is fully embedded in the neoliberal economic conditions that McEwan wants to criticize.

The novel's alleged critique of the contradictions and constraints of neoliberal capitalism hinges on its presentation of Perowne, who is both its central consciousness and the ostensible object of the implied narrator's ethical scrutiny. McEwan's use of a continuous present in free indirect style means that we are never far from Perowne's language and consciousness, but that style harbors a degree of authorial detachment meant to expose Perowne's privileged position as a Western consumer with a limited capacity for ethical and imaginative empathy.[56] Early in the novel, for instance, as he watches a couple of nurses in the sleepy square below the high window of his lavish eighteenth-century Charlotte Street townhouse, we witness him as he "not only watches them, but watches over them, supervising their progress with the remote possessiveness of a god."[57] Later, thinking dismissively about the pessimistic liberal professors at his daughter Daisy's college, he inwardly professes an uncritical faith in Western material progress and a world in which life "for most people ... has improved," concluding that "if the present dispensation is wiped out now, the future will look back on us as gods, certainly in this city, lucky gods blessed by supermarket cornucopias, torrents of accessible information" (*Saturday* 77). When he later surveys the cornucopia on offer at the sprawling fishmongers, Perowne recalls recent findings that "even fish feel pain," a fact he feels is indicative of "the growing complication of the modern condition, the expanding circle of moral sympathy" in which "the trick ... is to be selective in your mercies" and focus only on "the close at hand" (*Saturday* 128). As Tim Gauthier has noted, passages like these hint at "the difference between Perowne's sensibility and the ethos of the novel" and allow McEwan to expose how "Perowne's musings are devoid of self-appraisal—of even the slightest consideration of complicity or responsibility."[58] For Gauthier, this exposure is part of the novel's ethical aim, a point that McEwan has affirmed, in suggesting that Perowne is a typical "fat cat contented Western man" and that, if his character is offensive, then that is because readers sense something of themselves in his failure to acknowledge his own privileged complacency.[59]

The narrator's critical perspective on Perowne is inseparable from the novel's self-reflexive questioning of the ethical value of literature itself. This question is at the heart of the debate between Perowne and his poetry-writing daughter, Daisy. While Perowne is an avid consumer of music and art, he has little patience for imaginative literature. Prodded by Daisy, he reluctantly submits to a program of reading canonical works by Tolstoy, Flaubert, and James down to the magic realists, who elicit his particularly scathing dismissal. The rationalist surgeon is impatient with stories that feature characters who grow wings or survive falls from high-flying airplanes (allusions to Garcia Marquez and Rushdie, respectively), not to mention a novel in which a "visionary saw through a pub window his parents as they had been some weeks after his conception, discussing the possibility of aborting him"—referring of course to McEwan's own *The Child in Time*. Perowne can only feel that this fascination with "the supernatural was the recourse of an insufficient imagination, a dereliction of duty, a childish evasion of the difficulties and wonders of the real" (*Saturday* 66). When he complains to Daisy she reproves him for his own lack of imagination with the full force of Dickensian caricature—"You Gradgrind. It's literature, not physics!"—and when she insists "that people can't 'live' without stories," he quietly replies that "he is living proof" that one can (*Saturday* 67).

In pitting the poet-aesthete against the neurosurgeon, the novel does not merely adopt some one-sided championing of a Romantic belief in the consoling power of a literary imagination, or even an enlightened synthesis of the arts and sciences. While the novel tempts us to read Perowne's impatience with literature as a sweeping critique of his imaginative limits, McEwan is careful to avoid precisely that kind of straightforward "self-congratulation," as Brouillette puts it;[60] such passages are not without their irony, but they raise a larger question about literature's noninstrumental cultural value, even if readers of literary fiction already take that value for granted. In other words, in *Saturday* we find these positions held in suspense, forming a productive tension through which McEwan explores questions about the ethical value of novels, like *Saturday* itself, that critique the excesses of global capitalism from the position of corporate commodities that depend on its structures of social privilege and inequality.

If McEwan avoids an easy affirmation of the social and ethical value of his own enterprise, his references to the modern literary canon—understood as a body of cultural values irreducible to the merely instrumental—dramatize the compromised critical position that *Saturday* occupies. Specifically, the intertextual allusions in *Saturday* create a hermeneutic field that exists just beyond Perowne's consciousness and from which McEwan critically displays Perowne's limited ethical imagination. For example, in a self-referential nod to the novel's own method of free indirect style and limited perspectivism, the narrator subtly mocks Perowne for his inability to appreciate the exacting formal demands of Henry James, modern master of rendering the complexities of consciousness in slowly penetrating prose. Pressed by Daisy to read James, of whom she is a keen student, Perowne predictably finds him tedious, preferring the rational cognitive psychology of William to the perspectival subjectivism of his "fussy brother." As Perowne reflects on his daughter's deep appreciation for James's novels, McEwan's own free indirect style renders his consciousness in a way that imitates that of the master and winks at knowing readers from a position of critical detachment. McEwan alludes to *What Maisie Knew* when Perowne thinks, "What Daisy knows!" before the rationalist surgeon indulges in a dismissive reflection on precisely that novel, "the one about the little girl suffering from her parents' vile divorce" that left him "exhausted" as "poor Maisie soon vanished behind a cloud of words" (*Saturday* 56). His reverie concludes with the realist's stern pronouncement on another famous James title: "What's an adult to conclude or feel about Daisy Miller's [his daughter's "namesake"] predictable decline? That the world can be unkind? It's not enough" (*Saturday* 56). If Perowne has a problem, it is that he has no patience for the noninstrumental, symbolic value of the aesthetic. But again, this critical perspective depends on the narrator's sly detachment from Perowne and McEwan's appeals to readers in the know. The metonymic link between "what Daisy knows" and these Jamesian novels is at best on the perimeter of Perowne's consciousness, an implicit nod to readers who value the formal difficulty of James and can feel a smug satisfaction in recognizing the allusions. These impatient and vague meditations, operating on a level above or beyond Perowne's reckoning, appeal to readers' familiarity with the crystalline formal autonomy James is known for, enlisting their sympathy in the novel's subtle critique of its protagonist's fixation on plot—even if it eludes his interest—and his limited imagination.

McEwan's stylistic echoes position Perowne as the object of a dense web of modernist intertextual reference outside his consciousness; he is the object, as Mark Currie observes, of "the unknowable conditions in which his fiction life is embedded."[61] This impersonal narrative technique is even more remarkable in *Saturday*'s undisguised relationship to Woolf's *Mrs. Dalloway*. Other critics have explored *Saturday*'s parallel explorations of war, technological and material progress, and the temporal flux of consciousness subject to the "myriad impressions" of modern life.[62] We might also note, though, how McEwan rewrites Woolf's representation of the everyday experience of shopping, adapting the novelty of her impressions of the market to the rationalizing dictates of the neoliberal age. We can start with the latter. In a high pitch of anxiety following his threatening encounter with Baxter and his frustrating squash game with Jay Strauss, and on his way to Marylebone's High Street to do his shopping, Perowne finds himself further annoyed by the sight of Arab women in burkhas, a material sign of Muslim gender politics that prompts his angry reflections on the hypocrisies of Western liberals. Inwardly goaded by the subordination of Muslim women, a system eliciting a "distaste" in Perowne that is downright "visceral," he's equally skeptical about liberal "relativists" who might see their garments as "sacred, traditional, a stand against the fripperies of Western consumerism" (*Saturday* 124). Bothered, in fact, by the vast complexity of world politics beyond his control, Perowne suspects that he's projecting his anxiety onto the burkha-wearing women, that they are merely "veils for his irritation," and, finally arriving safely at the High Street he thinks, "It's time to go shopping." At this point he is able to dispel his frustration by attending to the pleasurable promises held out by the lush display of secular consumer goods. Reflecting on Marylebone's "contentment," Perowne takes in the bustling scene and thinks:

> Such prosperity, whole emporia dedicated to cheeses, ribbons, Shaker furniture, is protection of a sort. This commercial wellbeing is robust and will defend itself to the last. It isn't rationalism that will overcome the religious zealots, but ordinary shopping and all that it entails—jobs for a start, and peace, and some commitment to realisable pleasures, the promise of appetites sated in this world, not the next. Rather shop than pray. (*Saturday* 127)

The pleasures of "ordinary shopping" provide Perowne with a private moment of secular grace, in which he can dispel dispiriting thoughts about migration and terrorism, both results of a global capitalist system in which his own "prosperity" is implicated. If this is retail therapy, it's a form of indulgence posited on a fetishistic disavowal of the exploitative and uneven economic conditions that make Perowne's pleasure "realisable."

On a thematic level the passage echoes Clarissa Dalloway's shopping spree. Like McEwan, Woolf subtly suggests how Clarissa's consciousness is partly structured on a capacity to disavow social inequality and unnerving class difference. On her way to buy the flowers for the party she's to host that evening, Clarissa's feelings are in a state of flux, and she is particularly wracked by guilt over her snobbish distaste for her daughter's tutor, the self-righteous, lower-middle-class German, Doris Kilman. Ambivalently conscious of her class prejudice and the accidents of birth that account for one's social position, Clarissa inwardly notes of Miss Kilman that "it was not her one hated but the idea of her," and that "with another throw of the dice, had the black been uppermost and not the white, she would have loved Miss Kilman! But not in this world," all of which builds to a crescendo of mixed snobbery and liberal guilt in which "self-hatred" and "self-love" are inextricably mixed.[63] Then, pushing through the doors of Miss Pym's familiar flower shop, she thinks, "Nonsense, nonsense," indulges in the synaesthetic lushness of "delphiniums, sweet peas, bunches of lilac" and proceeds to move "from jar to jar" of flowers so that the pleasurable sensory immediacy of the moment is felt like "a wave which she let flow over her and surmount that hatred, that monster, surmount it all."[64] Clarissa's pleasurable indulgence in shopping allows her to disavow her social guilt under a wave of sensory pleasure and material prosperity. On a thematic level, then, McEwan rewrites Clarissa Dalloway's shopping scene in a way that similarly exposes Perowne's capacity to indulge in a fetishistic disavowal of the contradictory material conditions that structure his privileged position.

On the level of style, though, McEwan's echo of Woolf withholds the latter's sensually experimental impressionism, reducing it to a form of anachronistic pastiche that privileges realist rationality. As Jennifer Wicke has argued, Woolf's impressionism gave lyrical literary expression to the novelty of a market culture in which the sensory appeal of an increasingly commodity-saturated experience seemed to eclipse nineteenth-century market rationality. Free indirect style rendering an ephemeral consciousness gives modernist expression to the ways in which "the market has come to defy description, in that it is no longer equitable with realist or entirely rationalist modes of representation."[65] I would add that Woolf's impressions of the market foreground the irrationality of commodity fetishism—what Marx called the "material relations between persons and social relations between things"—to paradoxically achieve a degree of aesthetic autonomy in a style that remains irreducible to realism and its cousin, bourgeois instrumental reason.[66] McEwan's echo twists Woolf's impressions of an irrational market into a conventional realism that takes for granted—much like Perowne— the material prosperity it merely catalogs. Finally, the impersonality borne out by McEwan's narrator, formerly a trait of modernist aesthetic autonomy, creates the fiction of omniscience, disingenuously positing McEwan and his novel as above the unethical complicity in contemporary capitalism that they assign to the all-too-human Perowne. In other words, McEwan's pastiched allusion to Woolf's shopping scene reproduces, on the level of style, the social conditions of neoliberal capitalist privilege that his novel ostensibly aims to critique. This gesture not only "severely circumscribes the modernist project," as Marco Roth has suggested, but compromises the novel's critical reflection on precisely the field of economic production in which it, as a privileged cultural commodity, is embedded.[67]

As that suggests, *Saturday*'s intertextual engagements with canonical modernist texts, while appealing to the relative aesthetic autonomy those works achieve on a stylistic level, also implicate the novel in the critique it levels at Perowne. If *Saturday* enlists a belief in the irreducible symbolic value of the literary canon—even if it relinquishes that belief—in order to expose the fetishistic disavowal of its protagonist's privilege, then in translating those values into best-selling fiction, it also risks a similar disavowal of the economic conditions of its own production and marketability. In this sense, *Saturday* exemplifies a compromised tendency within the contemporary creative industries more generally, in that the critical position it adopts is, in Brouillette's words, "marketable, consumable, and often articulated in a way that anticipates their suitability to what they contest."[68] Through free indirect style and authorial detachment, McEwan targets Perowne's privileged complacency, and yet the novel participates in a literary system that converts a pose of critical detachment into material capital so that it remains entirely suitable to a field of literary production that privileges successful authors like McEwan. The socially critical ambitions of elite literary fiction are already compromised by a position that allows it to translate privileged access to symbolic goods into unevenly distributed economic capital.

This is the cultural contradiction at the heart of the novel, and it takes us from McEwan's ambivalent position with regard to modernism's legacy to the more immediate problem that *Saturday* self-consciously negotiates: literary fiction's claim to engage critically with the social conditions of its own production. This problem comes to a head, without any easy resolution, in the novel's thrillingly plotted but unimaginative climax. Having felt slighted by the socially superior Perowne earlier in the day, Baxter enters the Perowne home and interrupts the family celebration, presumably to exact revenge. First holding Rosalind at knifepoint and then threatening to rape Daisy, he hesitates when he notices that Daisy, whom he has ordered to undress, is pregnant; and when he notices her newly published book of poems, he asks her to read something aloud. Following a cue from her poet-grandfather, John Grammaticus, Daisy instead recites Mathew Arnold's "Dover Beach." Soothed by what he takes to be her uniquely captivating talent for verse, Baxter lets his guard down and Perowne and son eventually overpower him and send him to the hospital with a serious head injury, safely restoring order to the bourgeois home. I suspect that readers know this passage, and probably the criticism it's generated, but I rehearse it to emphasize its irony. Any reading that addresses the novel's social ethics has to question whether Daisy's recitation of "Dover Beach"—which has the effect of calming Baxter, the disenfranchised barbarian at the gate of the cultured Perowne home—is an endorsement of literature's transformative potential.[69]

My sense is that the novel appeals to an Arnoldian ethos of cultural uplift in order to dismiss it, while simultaneously resigning McEwan's project to a similarly narrow class interest. Writing during a time of volatile class antagonisms, Arnold's critical project aimed "to replace," in Chris Baldick's words, "the current dogmatic and explicit forms of ideological expression with the implicit and intuitive properties of literary sensibility."[70] As John Guillory adds, "the Arnoldian representation of literary culture ... was always appropriated in the schools as a means of enforcing the cultural distinction of the bourgeoisie."[71] The climactic scene in *Saturday* dramatizes this transformative potential expressly to deny it, similarly reasserting the bourgeois distinction shared by Perowne and McEwan. Baxter's apparently genuine pleasure in the experience of the aesthetic for its own sake is followed by his elimination, as a class threat, and a resolution in the form of the family's return to their private reunion. So while the climax and resolution might lament class polarization and the failures of the welfare state, they still leave the former intact, neutralized, and devoid of any imagined alternative;[72] Baxter is expelled from the bourgeois sphere of aesthetic enjoyment (to which he doesn't have proper access in the first place) and power remains in the hands of those already firmly in possession of cultural and economic capital.

As Brouillette concludes in her stunning reading of cultural consumption in the novel, *Saturday* "checks its own aspirations by avoiding any complacent sense of art's obvious social value."[73] *Saturday* is resigned to its "damaged but eloquent" expression of this, and the novel thus folds back on itself, urging us to consider in what ways it, too, is implicated in the structures of contemporary capitalism that it simultaneously aims to critique. McEwan's critical perspective on Perowne is not to be dismissed—he is a privileged fat cat—and we shouldn't ignore the author's persistent assertion that the novel is a medium for ethical debate.[74] But McEwan's commitment to a realism that can only deny Baxter access to institutionalized aesthetic values necessarily points to the limit of his imaginative enterprise, so that this novel's climax not only questions an ostensibly autonomous social value of literature but also shows McEwan's aesthetic to be strictly an expression of those in the possession of the symbolic capital of a literary education.[75] The novel's penultimate formal resolution implicitly confesses to the "damaged" capacity of literary fiction, at least in its realist mode, to alter the social relations of its production and consumption.

This resignation to the economic forces that underwrite and compromise literary fiction's capacity for social critique is perhaps symptomatic of the market for modernist prestige in the contemporary commercial field. And yet, while I have tried to show that McEwan's vexed engagement with modernism has been a key strategy in his bid for literary celebrity, especially in *Atonement* and *Saturday*, the pattern also points to a larger implication about the social production of literary fiction, one that requires a qualification of Bourdieu's influential sociology of "the market for symbolic goods." "There is an economy of cultural goods," Bourdieu writes, "but it has a specific logic"; and cultural production within a "restricted economy"—such as that of high modernism— can "obey an economic logic without obeying narrowly economic interests."[76] Over the longer term—exemplified by the institutionalization of modernism as a privileged bearer of relatively autonomous symbolic value—these cultural objects can become "a two-faced reality, a commodity and a symbolic object: their specifically cultural value and their commercial value remain relatively independent although the economic sanction may come to reinforce their cultural consecration."[77] The commerce in contemporary fiction registers a reversal; economic sanction has primacy. *Saturday* alludes to the forms and figures of modernist prestige, but in a realist mode that subordinates their techniques to an easy pastiche that smooths its convertibility to book sales. Now, the economic sanction accounts for modernism's privileged institutional value and the celebrity status of writers like McEwan. Modernism, or at least its elite variants, has been recommodified in the mass market for literary fiction and celebrity authors who appeal to an elite liberal audience with privileged access to education and "culture" in a tautology of a neoliberal status quo. McEwan's novels are the expression of a fully commercialized consecration of a formerly autonomous literary field.

Sweet Tooth: Operation Branding

Published in 2012 by Jonathan Cape in the UK and in 2013 by Doubleday in the United States—both Random House imprints—*Sweet Tooth* marks a clear departure from McEwan's previous ambivalent appeals to modernist prestige. A departure, but also a return: the novel reworks previous successes with form and genre, particularly recalling the Cold War spy thriller, *The Innocent* (short-listed for the Booker), but shifts the fictional time and place of intrigue from a noirishly divided 1950s Berlin to a tale of domestic spying in 1970s England. There is a likely explanation for this in the logics of the literary market. Since the introduction of the Amazon Kindle in 2007, conglomerate publishing has faced reduced profit margins and increased pressure to avoid risky investments in novels that are, well, novel in style or form.[78] More broadly, the global recession after 2008 added pressure across all sectors to stick with proven formulae, constricting publishing to a focus on star authors and predictable forms.[79] With its integration of the spy-thriller genre and metafictional form, and written by a celebrity author, *Sweet Tooth* seems ready-made for these restricted market conditions.

The plot centers around "Operation Sweet Tooth," in which Serena Frome, recent university graduate and voracious reader of contemporary novels, stumbles her way into a newly formed branch of the MI5 and becomes embroiled in a drama in which, to quote from the back cover of the first US paperback edition, "England's legendary intelligence agency is determined to manipulate the cultural conversation by funding writers whose politics align with those of the government." After Serena crosses the line and has a long affair with her professional charge, novelist Thomas Haley, a thrilling plot of personal and political secrecy and suspense unfolds, leading to the deft, if familiar, metafictional twist at the end when we learn that the novel we've been reading is Haley's own, and that he has turned the tables and made the mission and his life with Serena the stuff of a fiction fully subject to his control. Now, my added plot summary is about as reductive as any to be found on the back cover of a best-selling novel, and arguably less compelling, but that's the point. The novel's cleverly thrilling plot, that is, is something of a red herring, and its metafictional structure recalls that of *Atonement* and coyly reminds readers of that novel's role in securing McEwan's celebrity status. No longer concerned with referencing modernist prestige, but writing novels that continue to be as tightly plotted and clever as ever, *Sweet Tooth* is a perfect example of recent fiction that has come to serve a self-perpetuating system of authorial branding.

Sweet Tooth banks on our knowledge of McEwan's oeuvre and its established place in the contemporary literary market, and does so through a mocking rehearsal of his career. Indeed, the novel contains an undisguised reference to McEwan's own highly successful metafictional debut. Recall that *Atonement* dissolves Briony into a purely fictional construction that refers to McEwan as both controlling author and product of celebrity culture. When Serena surreptitiously reads a draft of Tom's novel, she is dismayed when she reaches the last page and discovers, in McEwan's unabashed wink to readers, the same trick: "the story I was reading was actually the one the woman [in the text] was writing," and she recoils from this "fictional trick" that she feels breaks the "unwritten contract with the reader" in which "no single element of an imagined world or any of its characters should be allowed to dissolve on authorial whim."[80] Tom's story both recalls *Atonement*'s dissolving of Briony, flaunting an assumed familiarity with that novel, and anticipates the metafictional frame at the end of *Sweet Tooth*, in which Tom has become "the woman" writing the novel from Serena's point of view. Formally, *Sweet Tooth* is an adaptation of *Atonement*, only set in a different period and featuring a different cast of characters.

Before returning to the novel's internal or diegetic participation in its own commodification, let me judge the book by its cover. Published in the UK by Jonathan Cape, prestigious Random House imprint, the cover of *Sweet Tooth* featured merely a photo of a young, slim, attractive blond woman peering over her shoulder at a man far behind her in what appears to be a Tube station, along with the title and author's name. Going on to hit the best-seller list within a year, the first US edition, published by Nan Talese/Doubleday (a US Random House imprint), displayed a different photo—still a young, attractive woman—but with the added tagline: "Author of *Atonement*." The reference to McEwan's most successful title promotes this one and, in turn, expands the market for McEwan's backlist. As sales figures continued to rise, the first US paperback, brought out by Anchor Books, went one better and featured the title in a stylized red stamp design reminiscent of Cold War bureaucracy and, more importantly, the tagline at the top, "The new bestseller by the Booker prize-winning author of *Atonement*." This text enacts a logic of cumulative cultural and economic value. Informing consumers that it's a best-seller by a Booker-winning author, it ambiguously conflates the prize-winning *Amsterdam* with the more favorably received and well-known *Atonement*, the elision serving to create the most hype for a new novel, all centered on the name of the award-winning, best-selling author. Now, this is pretty standard marketing practice, but the novel's internal fictional references to McEwan's previous work, even if that work is parodied, folds out to encompass the field in which the book has been marketed, so that they form mutual parts of a network engaged in promoting a self-referential authorial brand.

Read in the light of this network of literary branding, the plot of *Sweet Tooth* also plays with anxieties about authorial control and originality in the context of hyper-commercial publishing, ultimately resolving them by affirming the free market as a site of authorial legitimation. During the early planning stages of operation Sweet Tooth, Nutting, one of its key architects, insists that the authors who receive support "have to feel free" to write what they want, in the hopes that they will produce work that aligns with anti-communist Cold War Western values. But he also imagines a plan that might mitigate risk, saying somewhat enigmatically that in the case of Tom Haley, "sooner or later one of our own is going to be chairing this new Booker Prize committee," and thus suggesting a form of covert governmental control over the ostensibly independent fields of producing and judging literary talent (*ST* 116). This jokey reference to the newly formed Booker is, of course, a nod to its dubious role in conferring "authentic" literary value and canonization and might be read as a light parody of McEwan's own reception of the prize for *Amsterdam*. But this fictional reference to the Booker also anticipates the marketing strategy that advertised the book on the basis of established authorial celebrity. The fictionalized insinuation of some kind of nefarious coercion going on behind the scenes hints at similar outcries of scandal, itself a crucial factor in garnering attention and accumulating prestige in contemporary prize culture, so that McEwan's fiction interacts with the book's marketing campaign to generate the symbolic and economic capital necessary to promoting the novel.[81]

In this sense, the Cold War struggle that the novel dramatizes between the author's freedom of expression and externally controlling forces metaphorically resonates with contemporary cultural concerns about the production and consecration of literary values—and a belief in the author as the singular bearer of those values—within the "free" market for fiction. Set during the early formation of the Booker, the novel is also set at the time when the publishing industry began to shift to the structure of multinational corporate conglomerates. With this history of the corporatization of literary publishing and the market promotion of celebrity authors in mind, it becomes particularly telling when we learn at the end of the novel that Tom Haley has successfully turned those externally controlling forces to his advantage, knowingly using the system to assert his own control over the conditions of funding and legitimation that underwrite his production. As an author surrogate for McEwan, Tom's trick suggests that rather than being subject to external ideological forces, or a product of impersonal market constraints, authors are autonomous agents exercising their originality in the free market. Operation *Sweet Tooth*, then, is a codebook that demonstrates how McEwan openly participates in a marketing strategy of authorial branding, one that dispels any attendant anxieties about the commodification of literature, paradoxically, by affirming the authorial brand as a mark of distinction and impersonal agency circulating within the free market.

***

Throughout this chapter I have tried to show that McEwan's ambivalent return to modernist aesthetics and strategies of authorial self-fashioning is inseparable from his move into a mainstream market for literary fiction. And while novels like *Atonement* and *Saturday* simultaneously display and disavow their debts to a modernist legacy, which itself amounts to a modernist effort to overcome influence, we need to read that bid for literary autonomy as part of a larger narrative in which McEwan's appeals to readers' familiarity with the symbolic capital and reified institutional authority of modernist prestige constitutes a strategy of celebrity self-promotion. McEwan's return to modernist aesthetics and formal self-reflection, then, is less a matter of making literature new than it is an expression of modernism becoming ordinary, its cultural capital a source of prestigious affirmation that is in turn readily convertible to the economic success of literary fiction. If modernist fiction is known for stylistic experimentation and a reflection on its own formal properties—both aimed at cultivating a market for relative literary autonomy and noninstrumental values—it is also a historical product of the institutional construction of taste, and a bearer of elite cultural value. The paradox, or logical conclusion, that McEwan's fiction demonstrates is that an institutionalized modernism is more marketable than ever, its residual association with relative autonomy fully amenable to the production of best-sellers. Contrary to Martin Amis's postmodern proclamation of the death of modernism, McEwan self-consciously claims some of its residual cultural prestige, albeit in a curious process of resuscitating it only to kill it off again. His recent work's confidence in a cultural economy of self-promotion suggests what is perhaps the most fully ironic realization of what the modernists were up to in the first place, in that an aesthetic autonomy with designs on altering the social structures of literary production has given way to a different fiction of autonomy, that of the self-referential commercial brand.

3

Modernism as Postcolonial Inc.: Authorizing Salman Rushdie

In an introduction written for the twenty-fifth anniversary edition of *Midnight's Children*, Salman Rushdie tells a mock-heroic story about how he prepared to write the novel that would go on to win the Booker Prize in 1981. Inspired to write a novel set in his homeland, he had traveled to and "drunk deeply from the well of India" on the £700 advance he received for his first novel, *Grimus*. But on his return to London the future celebrity of postcolonial fiction was faced with the unsexy problem of being broke, so he took up part-time work writing ad copy for Ogilvy and Mather.[1] After devoting his creative energies to the world of advertising, Rushdie tells us:

> On Friday nights I would come home to Kentish Town from the agency's offices near Waterloo Bridge, take a hot bath, wash the week's commerce away, and emerge—or so I told myself—as a novelist. As I look back, I feel a touch of pride at my younger self's dedication to literature, which gave him the strength of mind to resist the blandishments of the enemies of promise. The sirens of ad-land sang sweetly and seductively, but I thought of Odysseus lashing himself to the mast of his ship, and somehow stayed on course. (*MC* x–xi)

Looking back from the perspective of 2005, after *Midnight's Children* had not only won the Booker but also the unprecedented "Best of the Booker" in 1993, Rushdie is of course indulging in a bit of comic self-mythologizing, striking an ironic pose of modernist literary autonomy. The pronoun and tense slippages point to an authorial persona in the making, a figure prior to the celebrity author, who could stoically resist the siren songs of the mass market. And that's the joke. The irony of this wry little portrait of the artist as a younger man gestures toward precisely what it seems to disavow: its image of the autonomous author follows on the cultural and commercial consecration of "Rushdie" as the master figure of experimental postcolonial fiction. As an ironic fiction, that is, Rushdie's image of authorial autonomy is itself fully contingent on the market for literary celebrity.

As an equally celebrated and vilified figure in the field of postcolonial fiction, Rushdie exemplifies the multinational branding of stylistic innovation formerly associated with a modernist will to aesthetic autonomy. In his comic distortion of ancient myth and epic form—from East and West—his dexterous deployment of multiple stylistic modes, his innovative blending of surrealist and naturalist visions, and above all his emulation of an international repertoire of authorial predecessors, Rushdie came to reanimate the spirit of high modernism and bring it to bear on an emergent postcolonial literature.[2] Others have similarly argued that his fiction bears out the "legacies of modernism" in contemporary literature.[3] In particular, Rushdie's encyclopedic formal experiment, creative mimesis, and mixing of styles have garnered frequent comparisons to that master modernist, James Joyce. Laura Marcus, for one, argues that "the coexistence of a multiplicity of styles and languages in Joyce's fiction has also been engaged, in diverse ways, by postcolonial writing," especially Rushdie's, and she notes that both authors write in the English language, that of the colonizer, in order to remake it for their own aesthetic and subversive purposes.[4] As that comparison suggests, Rushdie's writing can be slotted into a cosmopolitan modernist tradition. Rebecca Walkowitz aligns Rushdie with Joyce as cosmopolitan writers who deploy what she calls a "mix-up as a literary as well as a cultural style" that throws racist stereotypes into question, thereby refusing nationalism and exclusionary forms of belonging.[5] Jean Kane also emphasizes Rushdie's modernist cosmopolitanism, comparing him to, well, Joyce, for their shared "rejection of national predecessors" and an investment in a modern European tradition, arguing that Rushdie is a "metropolitan" writer whose work imagines "transnational identities" that belie the kinds of binary structures that have been imposed on it, especially in the wake of the infamous *fatwa*.[6] And while not concerned with the cosmopolitan or with modernism per se, Robert Eaglestone makes the very modernist claim that "Rushdie has irrevocably changed the shape of the novel in English. This is not simply because of his success as a writer" though, because, Eaglestone tells us, "literary prizes don't mean all that much. Rather, it is because his work has shaped two generations of writing and criticism and still continues to influence the novel's development."[7]

Very well. But while I agree that Rushdie openly positions his work within modernism's legacies, founded on creative mimesis and a formal transformation of existing traditions, such affirmative claims ignore the economic conditions that underwrite the success of his particular brand of "postcolonial modernism," including his ongoing articulation of an ostensibly subversive authorial persona within the competitive multinational literary market. Reading Rushdie's modernist style as a mode of cultural politics aimed at disruption and transnationalism, that is, elides his participation in the cultural and material conditions of contemporary literature and the institutional reproduction of a belief in self-affirming literary values that depend on the production and circulation of global commodities and capital. In other words, these uncritical and self-affirming accounts of Rushdie's progressive cosmopolitan style or transnational authorial identity participate in the reproduction of cultural capital that lies at the intersection of celebrated literary fiction and its academic consecration, while ignoring the role of multinational corporate publishing, marketing campaigns, prominent reviews and, of course, commercially sponsored prizes, all constitutive of a self-affirming belief in literature's symbolic value within the contemporary "economy of prestige."[8]

So without denying the importance of Rushdie's adaptation of modernist strategies of stylistic excess or comic critiques of colonialism and the nation, I situate them within an expanding literary market for postcolonial cultural commodities where authorial self-promotion affirms a privileged position in the field. A sizable body of materialist criticism on postcolonial literature in general, and on Rushdie's prized place within it, has emerged over the past couple of decades, and here I want to build on that work by showing how Rushdie's fiction extends a modernist project of authorial self-fashioning to articulate a position in the field of popular postcolonial fiction, a fully commodified field whose circulation and consecration depend on and reproduce the globalized conditions of Western corporate capitalism. Aijaz Ahmad, for instance, has criticized the "postmodern" cosmopolitanism of writers like Rushdie for their celebration of the privileged "pleasures of ... unbelonging," a point that Timothy Brennan has extended in identifying Rushdie as a "convenient" cosmopolitan, a writer whose contributions to the international expansion of "English" literature are also fully "conditioned" by Western "book markets."[9] And others have amply contributed to this critical assessment of Rushdie's prized status within the postcolonial culture industry. Arguing that Rushdie benefits from the production and circulation of "the postcolonial exotic" in a Western market bent on "prizing otherness," Graham Huggan has shown that such Booker Prize–winning authors "are assimilated into the mainstream" and that the anti-imperial sentiment expressed in their fiction is also a product of "imperial market forces" in which the postcolonial functions "as a sales tag for the international commodity culture of late (twentieth-century) capitalism." Socially privileged writers like Rushdie, who are "adept at manipulating the commercial codes" of this market system thus "risk becoming complicit" with it.[10] Sarah Brouillette also takes up the issue of complicity, arguing that Rushdie's ongoing "pursuit of self-authorization" as a subversive writer "derives its meaning and force from the same field of production with which it takes issue."[11] Noting that Rushdie's career arc is "uniquely analogous to the literary marketplace ... defined by the processes of transnational corporate concentration," Brouillette demonstrates how Rushdie is a "paradigmatic figure" among postcolonial writers who enjoy what Leela Gandhi calls the "'win-win' situation" of "simultaneous privilege and dissent," and that his work reveals "a tension between self-articulation and its market constraints" which together shape the author's public persona as a globally circulating commodity.[12]

Drawing on these materialist assessments, my focus in this chapter is on how Rushdie's major novels, which are fundamentally about issues of authorship, set out to establish and uphold an elite authorial subjectivity in the market for postcolonial literature, one in which a return to the stylistic self-fashioning of modernism has proven especially effective. Echoing Bourdieu, Pascale Casanova observes that multinational "publishing giants" have absorbed a formerly autonomous field of avant-garde literary production to create "a new source of literary legitimacy through the diffusion of writing that mimics the style of the modern novel," often recycling "all the familiar devices of exoticism" to create the "appearance of literariness."[13] I want to extend this important critical work at the intersections of postcolonial fiction and the multinational publishing industry, and argue that Rushdie's fiction engages with modernism's legacy—through overt allusions, stylistic experiment, and formal self-reflexivity—in order to mark its literariness and to authorize Rushdie as a global celebrity posing as a subversive writer. Rushdie's work circulates in a now global market for commodified novelty and simulated authenticity, and it indexes the commercialization of modernism in a popular postcolonial style. More specifically, his major novels dramatize a central ideological contradiction within the field: Rushdie constructs a subversive authorial pose as a claim to aesthetic autonomy in a way that reflects the author's privileged position in a neocolonial literary market.

Writing India, Authorizing Rushdie

In the sprawling comic epic that is *Midnight's Children*, Rushdie adopts a pose of Indian authenticity, embodied by his narrator Saleem Sinai, to mythologize the new nation and to authorize himself as a leading Anglo-Indian writer in an expanding market for postcolonial fiction.[14] While the novel was immediately deemed a seminal text in the "writing back to empire" genre, and greeted by publishers, academics, and the press with laudatory claims that it put a literary India "on the map" of an expanding field of English fiction, Rushdie's reception of the Booker Prize in 1981 and the novel's stellar commercial success thereafter indicate that we should contextualize that reception in light of the social conditions of promotion, and here I want to show that the novel's vast metafictional conceit adapts a modernist mode of authorial self-fashioning in a way that flirts with a cosmopolitan market for elite and exoticized fiction.

In a statement that has become something of a slogan for Rushdie's method and a mantra for postcolonial literary studies, he wrote in "Imaginary Homelands" that his "physical alienation from India" compelled him to reclaim something of the nation lost to him through emigration, but that in the face of such an impossibility "we will ... create fictions, not actual cities or villages, but invisible ones, imaginary homelands, Indias of the mind."[15] This fiction of the nation is indeed central to the novel's method and plot, a point that the narrator Saleem Sinai stresses when he projects back to his prenatal existence and the final countdown to the departure of the Raj, a moment that ushers in "a new myth to celebrate," a new nation that, despite its "five thousand years of history ... was nevertheless quite imaginary ... a country which would never exist except by the efforts of a phenomenal collective will ... India, the new myth—a collective fiction in which anything was possible."[16] India in both of these statements is an "imagined community," not bounded by physical borders but a discursive construction in "constant flux" which, as Bill Ashcroft writes, is key to the postcolonial diaspora, the idea of the nation as "a discourse in process" in which "place is just as much constructed as identity itself."[17]

And while this emphasis on the discursivity of the lost land of identity is constitutive of the postcolonial project, its ambivalent mixing and diasporic remaking, Rushdie also exploits the nation as myth, signaling a metafictional claim to author "India" as "the new myth" of postcolonial literary invention.[18] All of this is of course governed by the novel's central conceit, namely, the 1,001 midnight's children whose fates metaphorically reflect the fate of the nation, as Prime Minister Nehru's letter to the infant Saleem says. This governing metaphor also allows Rushdie to subject the historical and political events of modern India to self-consciously literary designs. The novel foregrounds its highly stylized fictionality to articulate Rushdie's own creative authority in the literary market, in part, by making nationalism and the nation "appear only in refracted form, transformed and reinterpreted in literary terms."[19] Or, as Saleem later tells us, "reality can have metaphorical content; that does not make it any less real," and in reference to Rushdie's riff on Scheherazade and the *Tales of the Arabian Nights*, those 1,001 "midnight's children can be made to represent many things, according to your point of view; they can be seen as the last throw of everything antiquated and regressive in our myth-ridden nation, whose defeat was entirely desirable in the context of a modernizing, twentieth-century economy; or as the true hope of freedom" (*MC* 230). Saleem's aside here encompasses the plot and tenor of the novel, in which the midnight's children represent an internally conflicted myth of national optimism in the face of India's struggle to enter the global stage of economic modernity in the wake of colonial history; and it signals Rushdie's effort to bring a "myth-ridden" national idea into literary modernity.

Echoing a modernist will to aesthetic autonomy, the novel makes such a claim by mythologizing itself. Rushdie self-reflexively foregrounds the novel's aesthetic shaping, making its formal design and imaginative conceits central to its subject matter in a way that supports Brennan's apt description of the story as an "allegory of narrative composition."[20] Early in his narrative Saleem foreshadows his own bodily dissolution at the novel's end and speaks for Rushdie's literary method, saying that he contains "six hundred and thirty million particles of anonymous, and necessarily oblivious, dust" (*MC* 36), the population of India itself and a literalization or myth of its impossible totality that over the course of the novel swells out from his family's history into that of intersecting Hindu, Muslim, and Christian cultures, the legacy of colonialism in the sectarian post-partition state, all within a sprawling and digressive postmodern pastiche juxtaposing Indian mythologies and exoticist imagery with Superman comics and the epic romances of Bombay talkies. This self-generating and excessive narrative form is of course comically yoked together under the grand trope of Saleem's central role in his own story, in which "to understand just one life, you have to swallow the world" (*MC* 121). This "passive-literal" mode, however, always points to Saleem's authorial role, his writing a fantasy of India that, I will argue shortly, signals Rushdie's metropolitan claims on India in a bid for international literary fame. Of his telepathic powers, or his discovery of "telecommunications" at the age of nine, Saleem describes his voyeuristic impulses in a narrative aside, suggesting that entering the consciousness of the "multitudinous" nation is a fantasy in service to the novel's own fictional creation:

> Because the feeling that had come upon me that I was somehow creating a world; that the thoughts I jumped inside were *mine*, that the bodies I occupied

acted at my command; that, as current affairs, arts, sports, the whole rich variety of a first-class radio station poured into me, I was somehow *making them happen* ... which is to say, I had entered into the illusion of the artist, and thought of the multitudinous realties of the land as the raw unshaped material of my gift. (*MC* 199)

Saleem's telepathic gift metaphorically mediates Rushdie's comments on the novel's own authoritative capacity for creating illusions by subjecting the "raw material" of history to endless narrative reshaping.

Saleem's comments on the anarchic shape of the novel we're reading lend credit to the way that Rushdie's playfully mimetic use of eastern literary and mythological traditions acts as a self-authorizing strategy earlier perfected by modernists, especially by Joyce in *Ulysses* and *Finnegans Wake*. On the one hand *Midnight's Children* draws excessively on ancient epic traditions, mixing Hindu, Muslim, and Christian mythologies into its digressive and densely allusive fabric to provide a degree of "structural integrity," as Roger Y. Clark has shown at length.[21] Thus Saleem's act of writing his story at breakneck speed is comically modeled on *The Arabian Nights*, and the novel as a whole is populated by names of mythic proportion, from Shiva to Aadam to Sinai, all folded into a formal "mythic cycle" that begins in an Edenic Kashmir, proceeds through a series of religious and secular falls from grace, and ends on an ambiguous note of redemption.[22] That said, Rushdie subjects those allusions and formal borrowings to parody, so that the novel dramatizes something of a modernist will to autonomy by appropriating and comically distorting myth, symbol, and traditional epic form. The novel engages in a subversive metafictional critique of Indian nationalist fiction as a subgenre of Third World literature, parodying familiar mythologies and satirically presenting them "to a naïve reading public," as Timothy Brennan argues, in order "to suggest the living presence of India's mythical past, not as 'vital tradition' but as false consciousness," all of which is aimed at overcoming "Indian nationalist fiction" and its "solemn attachment to folklore."[23] Consider, for example, Saleem's memory of his childhood friend Cyrus, transformed by his mother into Lord Khusro, "India's richest guru." According to the leaflet advertising this new guru, Cyrus/Khusro's origins lay "in the dark Midnights of CELESTIAL SPACE in a time before Time ... the sphere of Blessed KHUSROVAND" whose inhabitants could "SAW THROUGH steel, and could BEND GIRDERS with TEETH." Drawing elements of Hindu and Parsee mysticism and the "nationalist hysteria" associated with the Muslim League into a mockery of religious "charlatanism," the whole enterprise is subjected to playful parody when Saleem realizes that it's modeled on "the most potent of all modern myths—the legend of the coming of the superman" (*MC* 309). If the novel's cleverly mimetic refashioning of multiple eastern myths and epic traditions makes for a dazzling display of cultural authority, Rushdie's clever distortions of those forms, most effectively realized in this kind of intercultural leveling of sacred and popular mythologies, also disrupts Indian writing in English and its reverence for traditional mythology, a body of literature that he repudiated as "dated," "dainty," and "delicate."[24]

Through its parody and mimetic mixing of ancient and modern, sacred and commercial, the novel also participates in a modernist mode of authorial self-creation, so that "Rushdie" becomes a culminating figure of the tradition he subverts.[25] Rushdie rehashes a clichéd modernist slogan, distorting the old so as to make it new. But rather than taking up, say, T. S. Eliot's call for reverently writing oneself into the "tradition" so as to alter it ever so slightly with his own "individual talent," Rushdie deploys the more radical Joycean mode of comic and subversive mimesis exemplified by the "Oxen of the Sun" chapter of *Ulysses*. Joyce's chapter is thematically concerned with the progressive development of conception, gestation, and birth—supported by its setting in a maternity ward during a difficult labor—but better known for the way it works through a whole history of English literary styles in mock-mimetic mode, a self-authorizing strategy that "subordinates these conventional styles" to the creation of the author as "master choreographer" of his material, as Goldman argues.[26] Like the author of *Ulysses*, Rushdie writes a highly self-reflexive novel that advances Joyce's modernist mode of appropriative and subversive mimesis to imaginatively authorize himself as the master of an emergent postcolonial style.

And yet this comparison on the grounds of mimetic self-authorization also points to a crucial difference between modernism and its contemporary legacies, one that is central to this book, and finds in Rushdie a particularly pronounced manifestation of a popular and commercially viable postcolonial fiction. Published by the prestigious Jonathan Cape, a UK imprint of the multinational Random House, and marketed as a "big book" that inside reviewers claimed put literary India on the map of English fiction, Rushdie's first major success was produced within a system of mass production and celebrity culture in which short-term sales far outstripped the symbolic capital of the experimental modernism that the novel extends into the late twentieth century. When we read Rushdie's self-authorizing strategies within the novel with a critical awareness of the market reception that quickly consecrated him as the new representative figure of literary India, we see a perfect manifestation of the fetishistic production of the author as producer that Bourdieu describes: "The producer of the *value of the work of art* is not the artist but the field of production as a universe of belief which produces the value of the work of art as a *fetish* by producing the belief in the creative power of the artist." A modernist writer like Joyce or a postmodern one like Rushdie can play this game through self-reflexive strategies that call attention to the author "as the *subject* of his own creation" and disavow the commercial and institutional structures on which that belief in autonomy and literary consecration depend, even at a time when "the boundary has never been so blurred between the experimental work and the *bestseller*."[27]

Rushdie's postcolonial modernism, in this light, reveals how a formerly subversive mimetic style has proven to be a particularly valuable mode of postcolonial literary authorization. *Midnight's Children* produces a literary India as textual commodity, and authorizes Rushdie as its representative figure, while at the same time it conceals that mode of production in a pose of modernist autonomy. Here we might recall Casanova's observations on the role of the "commercial pole" of production in generating international literary capital. As she argues, experimental contemporary fiction that aspires to the status of "world literature" often "mimics" the consecrated and familiar forms of its modernist predecessors—especially when it's marked with the "familiar devices of exoticism."[28] In the process, authors can lay claim to literary and cultural authenticity in a way that both reveals and deflects from the novel's status as a mass-produced global commodity. But I would also add that the mimetic faculty of *Midnight's Children* is contingent upon and reveals the multinational corporate conditions of producing literary values: it weds "India" as a set of contents—including the legacies of colonialism and a history that remains largely peripheral or mystical to Western readers—to a modernist mode of forging authorial distinction within the expanding global market for English literature that enables such a move.

It is with this in mind that we might reconsider the important materialist critiques that have been leveled at Rushdie's prized reception and his own participation in the market for postcolonial celebrity. Folding the violent and internally conflicted attempts to define the emerging nation within its comic epic deflation of the bonds of nationalism and exclusive demands on identity, *Midnight's Children* identifies Rushdie as both "being from 'there,'" in Brennan's terms, and bearing "a mark of distinction in a world supposedly exempt from national belonging."[29] That simultaneously displaced and distinctive identification also plays into the sociological conditions that consecrate postcolonial literature as an "exotic" commodity form produced by and for Western markets. Graham Huggan has been particularly insistent on this point, showing how *Midnight's*

Children offers a prominent example of the trend. Heartily and comically populated with genies, fakirs, snake charmers, and witches, the novel is replete with the "semiotic markers of Orientalism"; and yet, Huggan adds, Rushdie knowingly "exhibits" such stereotypes in an effort to critique a Western penchant for consuming them, an enterprise from which it cannot however escape complicity.[30] Brouillette provides a usefully nuanced explanation of the tension that haunts and conditions this strategic mode of positioning, one that is inherent to any bid for distinction within the contemporary conditions of literary production. "If an author's attempt at self-definition does manifest itself as hints of a nostalgia for an autonomous past," she writes in an echo of Bourdieu and Casanova, "that nostalgia rapidly gives way to a will to be reconciled with a global market for cultural products that is dominated by concentration within transnational media firms."[31] As I expect is clear by now, I align my own reading with these differing materialist approaches, but I'm not convinced that Rushdie's novel offers a viable critique of the conditions in which it's implicated. Rather, following Brouillette's account of a twinned nostalgia and complicity, *Midnight's Children* reanimates a modernist formal self-reflexivity to assert a residual belief in a fiction of literary autonomy and to contain or mask its necessary accommodation of Western liberal expectations for highbrow "exotic" fiction.

This tension is tacitly and playfully legible in Saleem's role as a narrator, through which Rushdie strikes a postmodern pose of authenticity that mediates something of his own transnational and privileged claims on India as a literary subject, which, in turn, helps constitute the author as a celebrity object. Kane notes Rushdie's "metropolitan posture as an 'Indian' writer," arguing that in Saleem he "attempts to absorb the author's 'outsider' status into an indigenous protagonist" in order to "[resolve] the anxiety of identity through an 'authentic,' spiritually syncretic Indian agent."[32] We might put this more explicitly and say that Saleem functions as a fabricated pose of authenticity, and that this pose translates an "anxiety of Indianness" common to Indian fiction in English into a highly mediated and self-reflexively stylized narrative mode through which Rushdie can assert a transnational position of authority in the market for postcolonial identities. Rushdie's operative metonymic conceit, for one, indicates a self-reflexive play on this tension between globalization and regional identity, such as when Saleem claims of himself that "to understand just one life you have to swallow the world [of a vastly heterogenous India]," before going on to note that "to remain an individual in the midst of the teeming multitudes one must make oneself grotesque" (*MC* 121). This latter statement comically qualifies the former, suggesting both the impossibility of Rushdie's entire metaphoric frame and hinting at the grotesque need to accommodate market demands for exoticism. Born of a Hindu woman and secretly fathered by the departing English colonial Methwold, then raised in a wealthy Muslim family and claiming to be "well up in Hindu stories" (*MC* 170), Saleem does bear out the syncretism that Kane identifies, but as a comically excessive pose, one that reflects Rushdie's authorship and erudition and hints that the novel, like Saleem, is a product of colonialism claiming to speak for the Indian masses by folding them into its middle-class liberal vision.

In this regard it is important to note that Rushdie's self-reflexive pose of authenticity is also predicated on a fetishistic disavowal of labor. Consider, for example, Saleem's curious relationship with Padma. Referred to as the lotus goddess with reference to the great Hindu Earth Mother, Padma is also "The One Who Possesses Dung," and her bodily bigness and illiteracy, not to mention her references to Saleem's "writing-shiting," comically equate her name with excessive earthiness and the poor Indian masses (*MC* 20). She features as one of the novel's few representatives of the laboring lower classes, and Saleem claims that he needs her to keep his story "grounded": "How to dispense with Padma," he desperately asks in her absence, "How give up her ignorance and superstition, necessary counterweights to my miracle-laden omniscience? How to do without her paradoxical earthiness of spirit, which keeps—kept!—my feet on the ground?" (*MC* 170). And yet he later concedes that the truth of his fabulous narrative (and implicitly of Rushdie's) depends on her gullible acceptance of it: "Because in autobiography, as in all literature, what actually happened is less important than what the author can manage to persuade his audience to believe" (*MC* 310). As Brennan rightly observes, Padma's "advice is hardly ever followed, but it ostensibly tempers the shameful cosmopolitanism that would otherwise make the writing inauthentic," while Saleem is mostly concerned with "imposing his vision on others."[33] Saleem's disingenuous dependence on Padma, that is, points to the problem of Third World or neocolonial labor in order to dissolve it beneath the novel's formal and stylistic ostentation.[34] In this sense, if the novel claims to speak *for* the Indian masses, implied in Saleem's need to convince Padma, then it really speaks *to* its middle-class metropolitan readers in the same kind of authoritative imposition Rushdie's narrator desires. Like the novel's metaphor of pickling, Saleem's "chutnification of history" equating writing with labor (*MC* 529), we should be wary of such tropes; as Neil Lazarus argues, "writers and intellectuals … must beware the inclination to construe their distinctive and restricted forms of practice as paradigmatic of social practice in general."[35] The novel privileges its own stylistic savvy and formal self-reflexivity over the realities of Third World labor, and can only provide an imaginary resolution to the material conditions of uneven economic development.[36] As such, the novel authorizes Rushdie according to a particularly restricted metropolitan vision, one that playfully obscures the residual conditions of colonial capitalism—including the neocolonial structures that underwrite institutions like the Booker—in which his celebrated brand of postcolonial fiction is fully implicated.[37]

Through its postmodern pose of Indian authenticity, *Midnight's Children* fed into the easy terms of reception that came to greet it, in part because of, rather than despite, its formal difficulty. Its early reception in Anglo-American circles, for instance, was marked by praise for its originality and experimentalism, denationalized terms of consecration that nevertheless became seamlessly intertwined with market slogans claiming that in Rushdie India had found its "literary voice."[38] Rushdie transforms a modernist mode of self-fashioning into a postmodern pose of authenticity in an effort to negotiate a distinctive identity within a multinational literary market. And this highly stylized and self-reflexively mediated pose on the part of a privileged metropolitan writer mimics not only a canonical kind of modernist experiment, but does so in a way that reflects the conditions by which international consecration and commercial success have become inseparable facets of contemporary literary production, especially in the field of postcolonial fiction.[39]

Sympathy for the Devil

We might read *The Satanic Verses* as a particularly profane and playfully anxious response to this tension between complicity and critique, in which the Booker-winning and commercially successful writer strikes a subversive authorial pose in order to critique the neocolonial structures of capitalist concentration and the commodified exoticism on which that success depends. Even more than *Midnight's Children*, Rushdie's fourth novel enlists a modernist project of formal and stylistic experiment and cultural dissent in this overt critical gesture, and it does so through its multilevel performance of sympathy for the devil. Drawing extensively on the satanic sympathies within a literary tradition that includes Milton, Blake, and Bulgakov, and riffing on a host of canonical figures of antiestablishment modernism, notably Joyce and Genet, *The Satanic Verses* is a work of postcolonial modernism that, as Neil ten Kortenaar argues, "isn't a direct confirmation of a literary tradition but rather an attempt to subvert it and then thoroughly to reconstitute it with [Rushdie] as an integral part."[40] But there's the rub: as a literary commodity *The Satanic Verses* capitalizes on a privileged position in the network of global capital and concentrated multinational media industries that it claims to denounce. As Liam Connell notes, the novel transforms the "protest against the internationalisation of capital into an accommodation with or valorisation of capital in other forms," namely, I would add, the form of elite literary fiction produced and marketed by Western conglomerates like Viking-Penguin. This inescapable contradiction, then, is a central condition of the novel. Read in these terms, Rushdie orchestrates a range of self-reflexive sympathies for the devil, from the novel's satanic narrator to its subversive author figures, as a self-promotional strategy that aims at once to authorize Rushdie as an anti-imperial writer and to disavow the neocolonial capitalist conditions that produce the author as a public persona and global brand. In other words, the novel dramatizes an anxious attempt to forge a transgressive aesthetic, one which cannot escape the commercial conditions of capitalist concentration that dominate the field and that enable Rushdie's satanic pose in the first place, and it appeals to a subversive fiction of literary autonomy as an imaginative resolution to the real material contradictions structuring the field.

This performative disavowal becomes remarkably apparent when we read the novel in light of Rushdie's own self-promotional moves prior to its publication. Rushdie had worked with the British agent Deborah Rogers and editor Liz Calder, who had overseen the publication of *Grimus* and *Midnight's Children* by Victor Gollancz and Jonathan Cape, respectively, both prestigious independent presses at the time. When Calder moved to Bloomsbury, expecting to take Rushdie's next novel with her, he instead hired Andrew Wylie—"the Jackal"—the agent who has long had a reputation for luring authors with unusually generous advances. Under the direction of Wylie, the manuscript was circulated among bidders from the elite international presses, first sold to German and Italian publishers and then sparking a competition between Knopf and Viking-Penguin that drove up the book's market value and Rushdie's advance, the latter reaching $850,000. All of this was made possible by the publishers' extensive international influence, including the capacity to publish simultaneously in the UK and the United States.[41] This backstory exemplifies Wernick's observation that contemporary authorship can't escape the nets of capitalist promotion, and poses an illustrative conflict with Rushdie's fictional satire on global corporate culture within such a nicely financed novel. And in terms of literary politics, it shows how Rushdie's postcolonial modernism serves corporate branding; so while Neil Lazarus has identified a postcolonial revival of modernism that "resists" accommodation, "refuses integration, resolution, consolation," the work of opposition that emerges within *The Satanic Verses* needs to be understood in terms of the novel's integration with the economics of literary capital.[42]

The novel's overtly satirical and aptly mediated take on 1980s neocolonial commercialism centers largely on Saladin Chamcha's sycophantic role as a "colonial mimic man."[43] His complicitous role in the mediated postmodern production of racial metamorphosis in the *Aliens Show* represents a particularly bad kind of hybridity. Having already established himself in advertising as the "Man of a Thousand Voices and a Voice," and able to impersonate a range of accents for a global market in order to sell everything from "garlic-flavoured crisps" to carpets to baked beans, Chamcha gets his "big break" with the *Aliens Show*, a computer-simulated sitcom featuring a host of, well, aliens: freakish mutations of animal, vegetable, and mineral origin all acting as thinly veiled stereotypes exemplified by "a team of Venusian hip-hoppers and subway spray-painters and soul-brothers who called themselves the Alien Nation" (*SV* 62). At the center of this simulated cast are Chamcha and Mimi Mamoulian, famous for their "protean" ability to change voices and whose images, too, are "processed through machines" to become constantly mutating "simulations" primed for global distribution to "America, Eurovision, the world" (*SV* 63). As Jean Kane argues, Rushdie's mockery of these computer-generated images of ethnic hybridity "acts as a disguise as well as a revelation of typified otherness" and "an anxious displacement of the indiscriminate, grotesque appropriation that characterizes the first-world media and marketplace." For Kane, moreover, this is the point of the novel's critique of a fetishistic commodification of race: "Rushdie connects the simulated images of Western commercial media with a loop of racialized labor and consumption."[44] Rushdie, himself a former ad-writer in London, takes neoliberal corporate capitalism to task in these passages for its monstrous exploitation of ethnic otherness. And yet we might add that Chamcha's sycophantic submission to the world of commercialized stereotypes—his willingness to act as a "colonial mimic man"—can be understood as a means of negotiating accusations that Rushdie had already been pandering to expanding literary markets hungry for the "postcolonial exotic" by raising the commodified specter of a bad hybridity and stretching it to a comically caricatured form in order to distance his work from it.

Rushdie's sympathetic portrayal of a defiant satanic cult of Black and Asian Britons—in the novel's surrealist take on the South London riots—would seem to provide a critical counterpoint to the commercial spectacle of "typified otherness" reproduced as commodity fetish in the *Aliens Show*.[45] Following Saladin's "hard fall" from a state of assimilated grace (*SV* 167), his punitive transformation into a goatish devil figure slides from a metaphor of the nightmarish projection of racist perception in the Western literary tradition into an image of collective reclamation and resistance. Thus Chamcha's own devilish dreams leak into the community of migrants subjected to Thatcher-era xenophobia to explode into a force for a resistant collective identity:

> Asian retailers and manufacturers of button-badges sweatshirts posters understood the power of the dream, and then all of a sudden he was everywhere, on the chests of young girls and in the windows protected against bricks by metal grilles, he was a defiance and a warning. Sympathy for the devil: a new lease of life for an old tune. The kids in the Street started wearing rubber devil-horns on their heads. ... The symbol of the Goatman, his fist raised in might, began to crop up on banners at political demonstrations, Save the Six, Free the Four, Eat the Heinz Fifty-Seven. *Pleasechu meechu*, the radios sang, *hopeyu guessma nayym*. (*SV* 295)

In Chamcha's metamorphosis into a devilish goat-figure Rushdie draws on a wide-ranging literary tradition, alluding to Satan's fall in *Paradise Lost*, Gregor Samsa's transformation in "The Metamorphosis," the hallucinogenic scenes taking place in the Nighttown episode of *Ulysses*, and Mick Jagger's crooning, all of which the novel refashions into a surrealist critique of 1980s neocolonial Britain. These intertextual allusions crystallize in the conflicting collective perceptions of Chamcha as a satanic target of what the police authorities see as a "growing devil-cult among young blacks," a "Satanist revival," on the one hand, and, for the Black British community, "a hero" and "an image white society has rejected for so long that we can really take it ... occupy it, inhabit it, reclaim it and make it our own" (*SV* 295–6). While Saladin wants no part in this public use of his image, the collective aim to translate "insults into strengths"—as Rushdie claimed to be one of his intentions—is meant to evoke sympathy for a devilish defiance toward Thatcher-era neocolonialism.[46]

But as the novel also makes clear, such an attempt to "inhabit" the imposition of a monstrously racist image in a way that turns it into an act of collective resistance is itself subject to capitalist appropriation and reproduction. In the passage I cite above, for example, the discourse of political resistance slides easily into the signifying register of advertising. And even more tellingly, just as Chamcha's beastly body is perceived in the mediated form of a "horror video *mutey*"—in a grotesque realization of his previous role on *The Aliens Show*—his horns are later mass produced "as novelty items" signifying "racial protest" while simultaneously dramatizing how "monstrosity" as a performance of resistance "simply re-enters capital circulation" in other endlessly reproducible forms (*SV* 363).[47] If the novel invokes sympathy for the racially marginalized and economically exploited migrant community as a counter to a corporate construction of easily managed stereotypes, it also anxiously dramatizes the fact that commercial media industries capitalize on their alleged antithesis, and the hyper-simulated style of *The Satanic Verses* is thus part of "the dilemma of the novel itself."[48]

Another way of stating this problem is to note that Rushdie's ostensibly sympathetic portrayal of deviltry as resistance easily slides into parody and pastiche, such that his creative experiments with style in the market for postcolonial modernism also reflects the author's privileged detachment from the violently disenfranchised community he claims to represent. The surrealistically rendered scenes at Club Hot Wax, for instance, privilege style over viable anti-colonial politics, figured in the presiding radical representative of London's anti-racist migrant collective, Pinkwalla, described as an "East-India-man from the West Indies" and a seven-foot-tall "white black" albino. Pinkwalla is "monstrous," a caricature who raps, chants, and rants against the Thatcher-era rebirth of colonialist and anti-immigrant public sentiment: "*Now-mi-feel-indignation-when-dem-talk-immigration-when-dem-make-insinuation-we-no-part-a-de-nation*," and leads the angrily chanting crowd in a ritual burning of Thatcher's effigy (*SV* 301–2). Brennan rightly notes that Pinkwalla's performance smacks of a "parody of 'dub' poetry" that is "misplaced and self-revealing," suggesting Rushdie's cultural distance from the radical Black forms of cultural expression the novel appropriates.[49]

It seems, though, that Rushdie is aware of the limits to this twinned sympathy and parody as the contradictory conditions of the novel's critical aims. When the goatish and disenchanted Chamcha advises Mimi, his former colleague in the ad world, that the corrupt film producer "bad boy" Billy Battuta is exploiting her, she comes back at him with an erudite rationalization that clearly reflects on the novel's aims and influences. "I am an intelligent female," she says. "I have read *Finnegans Wake* and am conversant with postmodernist critiques of the West, e.g. that we have here a society capable only of pastiche. … I am fully aware of Billy boy's rep. Don't teach me about exploitation" (*SV* 270). Speaking within a novel that rewrites Joyce's modernist dream-text in Gibreel's delusional dreams of angelic power, and that provides a postmodern critique of the exploitative nature of Western capitalism, Mimi's savvy response is suggestive on several levels. It not only reflects Rushdie's own critical aims but seems also to comically deflate the possibility that either a modernist sensibility or a postmodern critique of Western capitalism can effectively counter the exploitative demands of the corporate culture industries. Mimi's knowing participation in her own exploitation, exercised from a position of relative privilege, obliquely reflects on Rushdie's literary exploitation of those he claims to represent. So even though the novel claims a position of subversive authority through its sympathy for the racially and economically oppressed, and leverages that against the neoliberal conditions of cultural production, its postcolonial critique of multinational capital is part of its self-promotional strategy and ultimately amenable to those same corporate culture industries.

But Rushdie also works to disavow this commercial complicity on the level of form by invoking the unique power of literary creation as an imaginary resolution to that problem. The most compelling strategy Rushdie deploys in this sense is his use of a satanic narrator who slides in and out of the novel, vying for control over its characters and events. The satanic voice first makes itself known in the novel's literally and literarily explosive opening scene. As Gibreel and Saladin tumble to earth from the exploded Bostan in the comic retelling of Satan's fall from heaven, and just before the hapless Indian actors land miraculously on the English shore, the narrator announces his controlling presence as a creative force with obvious hints at the author's devious intentions:

> I know the truth, obviously. I watched the whole thing. As to omnipresence and -potence, I'm making no claims at present, but I can manage this much, I hope. Chamcha wished it and Farishta did what was willed.
>
> Which was the miracle worker?
>
> Of what type—angelic, satanic—was Farishta's song?
>
> Who am I?
>
> Let's put it this way: who has the best tunes? (*SV* 10)

Satan, of course. At the beginning of the novel, then, we're introduced to the satanic narrator who both mediates Rushdie in a performance of authorial control and expresses the novel's subversive pose. Claiming responsibility for the protagonists' fall from the exploded plane and the ensuing metamorphoses they experience, the satanic narrator speaks comically for Rushdie, the celebrated author behind the whole performance, in terms that dictate his major themes and reflect on their role in the novel we're reading. "Higher Powers had taken an interest" in the fates of Saladin and Gibreel, he tells us later, "and such Powers

(I am, of course, speaking of myself) have a mischievous, almost a wanton attitude to tumbling flies." Then, in emphasis of Rushdie's familiar assertions on postcolonial hybridity as the source of novelty, he adds, "Mutations are to be expected. ... Not much of a price to pay for survival, for being reborn, for becoming new" (*SV* 137). Later in the novel the devilish narrator again speaks for Rushdie in dictating the terms by which the novel should be read: "We are not obliged to explain Our nature to you. ... Whether We be multiform, plural, representing the union-by-hybridization of such opposites as *Oopar* and *Neechay*" (*SV* 329). Through this voice and image of authorial "dissent" (*SV* 95), Rushdie can both make a claim for the subversive power of postcolonial fiction and, at the same time, engage in a rather stagey strategy of self-promotion.

These gestures of self-promotion and authorial control in tandem with Rushdie's ostensibly subversive literary pose are further buttressed by the symbolic capital the novel draws from a host of famous predecessors in the literature of dissent. As is well known, *The Satanic Verses* alludes to and riffs on a vast literary tradition, from Milton's *Paradise Lost* to Blake's *Marriage of Heaven and Hell*, not to mention Rushdie's obvious sympathy with Joyce's Stephen Dedalus and his Miltonic boast of "*non serviam*," his artistic refusal to serve church or state. What has gone relatively unnoticed in this context, though, is Rushdie's borrowing from Mikhail Bulgakov's *The Master and Margarita*, itself such a subversive masterpiece of experimental Russian modernism that it couldn't be published in the author's lifetime. Bulgakov's dazzling novel is set in 1930s Moscow, where the devil Woland shows up with a sympathetically hellish entourage to wreak havoc on those who refuse to believe in either God or Satan. Within its satirical exposure of political hypocrisy, the novel's hero is the Master, author of a suppressed book telling an alternative story about Pontius Pilate and the trial and crucifixion of Jesus. Fragments of that work of historical fiction intersect with the present-day story of Bulgakov's novel, and provide a kind of metafictional reflection of the very real forces of censorship and suppression he faced. My interest here, though, lies with the diegesis of the novel, in that Woland's mission while in Moscow is to reunite the Master with Margarita, his lover and muse, and to rekindle the author's faith in his own powers of literary creation. And while Rushdie similarly makes use of a devilish creator devoted to the freedom of literary expression, drawn directly from Bulgakov, this is also where his aesthetic veers from that source of inspiration; Woland remains a character within the diegesis of *The Master*, whereas the satanic interjections appearing in Rushdie's novel act more like authorial intrusions, collapsing the distance between the real author, character, and reader to produce a text that self-reflexively dictates the terms in which it is to be read. This creative adaptation positions Rushdie as an inheritor of a fully consecrated tradition of subversive literature, with its established wealth of symbolic capital, in a gesture that lends cultural authority to his own writing.

The novel's blasphemous dream sequence depicting the eponymous satanic verses incident also signals Rushdie's effort to straddle blatant self-promotion and a subversive fictional pose. Mediated through the delusional dreams of Gibreel, Rushdie rewrites the episode in a way that openly challenges the authority of God, the angel, and of course the Prophet, subordinating each to the novel's own capacity for mimetic refashioning. The Prophet is first introduced by the satanic narrator in Gibreel's dream and in the form of an aside that again alludes to Rushdie's purposeful assertion of a subversive aesthetic: "To will is to disagree; not to submit; to dissent. I know; devil talk. Shaitan interrupting Gibreel" (*SV* 95). Rushdie may claim that his use of "Mahound, the devil's synonym," is a strategy of "turning insults into strengths"—adopting an old Western epithet as an act of resistant reclamation—but the whole enterprise, we should note, exploits blasphemy as a decidedly scandalous mode of authorial self-creation, claiming a lofty position for its author among the likes of D. H. Lawrence and James Joyce, and anticipating his defensive appeals to literature's autonomy that he would later take up in the face of the *fatwa*.

Critics have wrestled over the import of this complex formal strategy. Alex Knönagel argues that the satanic figure who parodies God in his appearance to Gibreel implies "the devil not only as the narrator of the whole novel but also as the origin of the mysterious revelations in the Mahound dreams."[50] While compelling, the problem with this neat formulation is that it's too neat. Thus Brennan suggests that the novel "projects itself as a rival Quran with Rushdie as its Prophet and the devil as its supernatural voice," but then qualifies this to wonder if "perhaps it is not the devil but only what the parasitical self-servers within the Faith call the devil by invoking God 'to justify the unjustifiable.'"[51] Channeling these vexed interpretations, Roger Clark argues that "this [satanic] voice does not need to have a clear function" and that "its obscurity increases the level of uncertainty and insinuation in the text—all of which coincides with Satan's traditional mode of operating."[52] Indeed, undecidability is key here, in that it at once reflects the way Satan operates—intending evil and sometimes doing good, in the Faustian sense—and provides the discursive mediation within the novel that alludes to Rushdie as an authority over his canonical source texts.

Invoking a kind of devilishly uncertain authorial control in this way also allows Rushdie to imaginatively deflect from his own self-promotional strategies—both within the novel and in his aggressive publishing maneuvers—by projecting them onto a fictionalized and monomaniacal Mahound. The novel repeatedly stresses that the would-be Prophet is first and foremost a businessman serving a God who in turn figures as "a manipulative manager."[53] While the devil may narrate the verses by taking possession of Gibreel's dreams, that is, the episodes concerning the historical Muhammad not only emphasize his talents as a merchant, but also show his reception of the verses to be a projection of his own materialistic desires (*SV* 94, 95, 376). This is underscored by Rushdie's refashioning of his source material, and specifically the suggestion that Mahound's momentary compromise to allow the three goddesses to remain as intercessors makes good business sense: it would not only win souls but also maintain the flow of revenue into Jahilia in the form of travelers' offerings. Featuring as "a materialistic entrepreneur," as Clark notes, Rushdie's depiction of "Mahound is *profit*-motivated rather than *prophet*-motivated."[54] Blasphemous as this may be, it is also mediated by Gibreel's delusional dream in a way that gestures to Rushdie's authorial enterprise. Here Rushdie projects his own acts of corporate promotion onto the fictionalized treatment of a monomaniacal Mahound and the corporate hierarchy of faith.

Salman the scribe and Baal the poet add another minor dimension to this drama of writerly transgression, and they figure as author-surrogates who beget Rushdie as their imaginative "offspring."[55] Although he is Persian, Salman is clearly the author's namesake: "Trust an immigrant not to play the game," the narrator tells us, and in a comic inversion of the Booker Prize winner he laments the dearth of "public honours" bestowed on him for his writing (*SV* 378). Charged with transcribing Mahound's dream-recitations, Salman comes to question their authority specifically because of their resemblance to the modern corporate logic that the novel's mocking distortions protest:

> Salman the Persian got to wondering what manner of God this was that sounded so much like a businessman. This was when he had the idea that destroyed his faith, because he recalled that of course Mahound himself had been a businessman, and a damned successful one at that, a person to whom organization and rules came naturally, so how excessively convenient it was that he should have come up with such a very businesslike archangel, who handed down the management decisions of this highly corporate, if non-corporeal, God. (*SV* 376)

Salman's devious mistranscriptions of prophecy can be read as a projection of Rushdie's blasphemous act of gratuitous self-articulation, a metafictional analog to what Rushdie does with the historical satanic verses. As Neil ten Kortenaar nicely puts it, "Rushdie never just blasphemes; he always proclaims, 'Hey! This is me blaspheming here!'"[56] Moreover, the fictional Salman reiterates the work Rushdie wants us to believe he is doing, and this indictment of the accurately non-corporeal presence of the multinational corporate world appeals to liberal readers who are in on the book's obvious satire, even if they disregard its role in creating an authorial brand.

The story of Baal offers an equally telling analogy with Rushdie's subversive self-promotion. Having "abdicated all public platforms" in the face of Mahound's power and his own diminished reputation, the satirical poet Baal, in an echo of what earlier in the novel befell Chamcha in London, begins "to create chimeras of form, lionheaded goatbodied serpenttailed impossibilities whose shapes felt obliged to change the moment they were set" (*SV* 382). Forced into living reclusively behind "The Curtain," he convinces the whores to mimic the twelve wives of Mahound, an idea that prompts the Madam to say, "It is very dangerous ... but it could be damn good for business" (*SV* 393). Baal's transgressive collusion with the whores ends when Mahound discovers it and sentences him to death, prompting his final words of protest: "Whores and writers, Mahound. We are the people you can't forgive," and Mahound's reply: "Writers and whores. I see no difference here" (*SV* 405). Baal's story seems to be a self-reflexively comic admission that transgression can be damn good for the business of creating a fiction of celebrity. But note, too, that this gesture comes with a kind of internal, fictional disclaimer: his conviction is refracted through the delusional dreams of Gibreel and projected into a distant time and place, easily subject to the kind of fabulism the book indulges in. Moreover, the charge of writerly prostitution comes from a Mahound whose authority the novel has already undermined. Baal's transgression and his fate, then, cleverly contain the tension between "self-articulation" and the market, to paraphrase Brouillette, so that Rushdie's scandalously commercial aesthetic is at once displayed and displaced.

And yet we might also take Mahound's words at face value: sentencing Baal to death for his profitable blasphemy not only eerily anticipates the political reactions that would soon come to define the novel, but the pronouncement of writing as prostitution also implicates Rushdie's bid for celebrity, notoriety, and continuing commercial success. Pitted against Mahound's corporate claims to monopoly power, Rushdie's fictional subversives supplement his own self-promotional satanic pose and crystallize what is perhaps the definitive bind of the novel. As Andrew Wernick argues, self-promotion has become a necessary supplement to contemporary authorship, a strategy that is "not so much supplied as demanded" within the corporate and competitive literary market.[57] Channeling a modernist mode of parody and pastiche, and leveling it against the commodity fetishism of corporate capital, Rushdie's act of literary blasphemy functions as a self-promotional move to meet that demand, producing a public image of the author that is every bit as fetishized as Chamcha's sycophantic performances. And Rushdie, at the time of *The Satanic Verses*, is clearly well aware of these conditions. The novel courts religious scandal through blasphemy and claims opposition to neoliberal and neocolonial cultural production. These authorizing gestures exemplify a particular kind of "commodity fetishism in the literary field" that Brouillette describes: the writer's apparent "resistance" to "valorization" by capital "is precisely what makes [his] work valuable."[58] Staking a self-promotional claim to a subversive authorial image, Rushdie invokes a sympathy for the devil that deflects from the neocolonial conditions of cultural production that enable that pose.

Rushdie's Interminable Sentence

In the face of the notorious *fatwa* Rushdie's commercial pose as a subversive postcolonial author became increasingly constrained and dubiously defensive. Responding to the very real threat on his life, Rushdie's writing and other public statements since 1989 repeat an interminable sentence, regularly reacting to those who have demonized him and *The Satanic Verses* in terms that appeal to Western rationality, the right of free speech, and above all a claim for the autonomy of literature as his privileged medium of expression. Rushdie launched his first defensive appeal for the disinterested value of literature in the article "In Good Faith," which originally appeared in the *Independent*. "At the center of the storm," he writes, "stands a novel ... that aspires to the condition of literature," and, after reiterating his intentions to create a work celebrating "hybridity, impurity," and the like, he goes on to insist that "we must return for a moment to the actually existing book"—rather than becoming distracted by the media maelstrom of religious reactionaries—and then claims artistic allegiance with that gold standard of transgressive aesthetic autonomy, saying, "I am a modern, and a modern*ist*."[59]

These pronouncements are fairly unsurprising on two levels. For one, an appeal on the grounds of aesthetic autonomy, especially when it's deemed blasphemous, makes sense given the real threat facing the author and everyone else involved in the publication and dissemination of the book. At the same time, though, Rushdie's rhetoric appeals to a fetishistic fiction that big books can claim some undeniably autonomous symbolic value, while implicitly ignoring the equally important role of commercialized institutions—from publishers and the multinational media corporations that own them down to university professors churning out celebratory articles in their own quest for promotion. The veiled tension between the novel's commodified status and its author's claims to distinctive literary values would continue to reverberate throughout Rushdie's public defenses of the novel. When Penguin repeatedly delayed bringing out a paperback edition due to ongoing attacks on booksellers and others involved in its production and marketing, Rushdie often shuttled between defending the artistic autonomy and cultural value of the novel, on the one hand, and disavowing any commercial motivation on the other. In an interview for *Newsweek* in 1990, for instance, he claims that "the commercial reason is the least important" factor in his desire for paperback publication and that "this book should be studied" in universities because of the controversy it sparked. Repeating the issue in a subsequent interview, Rushdie asserts that the novel needs to "be studied in colleges" in order for it to "receive the judgement of posterity."[60] Rushdie's bid for posterity here is not only an unusually self-affirming (and premature) insistence on his own canonicity, but it also registers, in order to anxiously disavow, the dependence of the contemporary canon on the corporate literary market prior to its academic consecration.[61]

These uneasy negotiations with posterity and notoriety over the course of the Rushdie Affair are centrally concerned with a loss of control over interpretations of his notorious novel and his public persona, and points to a dominant theme in much of Rushdie's subsequent writing. This posturing is evident, in all its paranoia, in *Fury* (2002), as Brouillette has shown, but that novel is flanked by two major works that specifically call on Rushdie's modernist credentials as a mark of literary authority: the rock-anthem novel *The Ground beneath Her Feet* and the memoir of the *fatwa* era, *Joseph Anton*.[62] I want to conclude this chapter by tracing this repetitive pattern of self-defense and to show, specifically, how Rushdie's continuing claim to a legacy of modernism has become a self-affirming farce.

Since *The Satanic Verses* Rushdie has frequently been read as a postcolonial modernist, most often in comparison with Joyce, and in the case of *The Ground beneath Her Feet* we see this identification playing out according to a logic of the pop-culture franchise, in which the novel and its mainstream market reception create a feedback loop unquestioningly affirming Rushdie as an heir to the modernist canon. Filled with allusions to and echoes of the likes of Conrad, Eliot, and Joyce, the novel also revives a modernist "mythic method" by adapting the tale of Orpheus to an epic of rock stars and cultural globalization. And while some reviewers noted the book's predictability, excessive digressions, or overly baroque style, others gushed about its modernist credentials.[63] Writing for *Time* magazine in words that would find their way onto the back cover of the Picador paperback, Paul Gray says the novel is packed with "enough literary echoes—of Joyce, Yeats, Frost, Dante, oh hell, of nearly everybody—to keep graduate students on the prowl through these pages for years."[64] Echoing Joyce's own pronouncements on the future of *Ulysses*—that it would "keep the professors busy for 100 years"—Gray's words would also be echoed by other reviewers proffering Joycean praise. So while Anna Mundow says the novel "proves its author to be one of the most seductive Joycean heirs," Will Blythe was even more seduced, writing that "to engage in *The Ground Beneath Her Feet* must be what it felt like to read *Ulysses* in 1922, when novels were still the hottest mind-altering narcotic on the street."[65] If we note that in 1922 *Ulysses* appeared only in limited editions and was quickly suppressed, and thus was not exactly being widely read on the street, we might further note that all of this praise is gross hyperbole, insisting on Rushdie's modernist credentials and participating in a self-affirming loop that largely serves to affirm established literary values and to sustain the sales of novels, magazines, and the author-function itself.

These uncritical assessments, moreover, are also grossly prepared for by the novel itself. While Vina and Ormus are the protagonists, Umeed Merchant, the photographer-narrator, most closely resembles Rushdie, and it is through this character that Rushdie both comments on his own career—Merchant comes to love India most when he translates it into a form of aesthetic distance, for example—and pilfers indiscriminately from a cache of well-known modernist texts. Regarding the latter, Rushdie at one point creates a strange, even unpalatable composite of Conradian and Joycean echoes. Sent to get photographic evidence of a vast agribusiness swindle receiving state support, Umeed (also known as Rai) recounts a journey into the Indian hinterlands in a thinly veiled appropriation of *Heart of Darkness*, repeating Conrad's colonialist imaginary but without the latter's critical self-reflections when he describes how the "unchartedness of rural India" makes him feel "as the earth's early navigators must have done."[66] He is soon captured by a gang of bandits, stripped of his photographic equipment, and tied up in the presence of the hanging corpse of his predecessor. When he realizes that the dead man likely has photographic film of the site secreted in his boot heel, he struggles to free himself, steals the unprocessed film that later helps him make a name for himself, and the theft is told through another, glaringly literary one, as we read:

> His feet swung not far from my revolted nose and yes I wondered about the heels of his boots yes when I got the ropes off I made myself approach him yes in spite of his pong like the end of the world and the biting insects yes and the rawness of my throat and my eyes sore from bulging as I puked I took hold of his heels one after the other yes I twisted the left heel it came up empty but the right heel did the right thing the film just plopped down in my hand yes ... and I could feel his body all perfume and my heart was going like mad and I made my escape with Piloo's fate and my own golden future in my hand yes and to hell with everything I said yes because it might as well be me as another so yes I will yes I did yes. (*GBF* 244)

The passage directly echoes Molly Bloom's stream-of-consciousness soliloquy that concludes *Ulysses*, perhaps the best-known passage from Joyce's book. But why? It might be tempting to read this in line with Susan Stanford Friedman's claim that "postcolonial modernisms create distinctive aesthetic styles" and "creative adaptations" of precursor texts to "articulate the particular modernities of their position" in a planetary field.[67] But Rushdie's blatant adaptation of Joyce lacks a creative dimension insofar as it doesn't add to the form or content of his novel. In fact, the passage here twists Joyce's literary celebration of love into something downright obscene. It reads, then, as an obvious gimmick. Other rewritings of familiar modernist works abound in *Ground*, but this seems to me an outstanding instance of how Rushdie can parade this kind of gimmick in a way that plays into the press and other institutions of literary reception that eagerly await easy appeals to modernism's clichéd symbolic capital.

These modernist gimmicks and their joint participation with the literary press in marketing a belief in Rushdie's continued cultural authority, odd as all that may be, even more oddly deflect from the book's central concern with celebrity and its thinly veiled allegory of its author's celebrated and scorned public persona. Vina Apsara, the pop-icon protagonist sharing a stage with Ormus Cama, becomes subject to conflicting global media interpretations after her death. The dead pop star as mediated icon means that "*we can invent her in our own image,*" muses the narrator, and "there's no escape from the war of meanings" (*GBF* 485). Those multiple meanings replay the Rushdie Affair: Vina's life is at once celebrated in the West for its "liberating force" and denounced by "Islamist women" claiming that "this madness about a single immoral female reveals the moral bankruptcy and coming annihilation of the decadent and godless West" (*GBF* 483). As an analogue for Rushdie adapted for the digital age, Vina's image is subject to the same splintered interpretations in the massive media "feedback loop" that the celebrity author both descries and benefits from. As Brouillette argues, Rushdie "uses his work to reference his own biography in a way that can only encourage the collapsing of distinctions between self and text," a strategic elision that affirms his celebrity persona and is perhaps best exemplified by his public collaborations with U2 and his cameo appearance in *Bridget Jones*.[68] *The Ground beneath Her Feet* shows all too clearly how Rushdie has become entirely comfortable and complicit with a literary culture in which the symbolic capital of canonical modernism, the commercial conditions of postcolonial fiction, and the reproduction of a spectacle of the authorial self create an effective market synergy.

Little surprise, then, that Vina's otherwise unexpected death occurs on Valentine's Day, 1989, the date on which Khomeini pronounced the *fatwa*. Rushdie translates the Ayatollah's death sentence into his own interminable sentence, replaying its drama across an endlessly reiterated pattern of fictional and nonfictional variations in a way that links *The Ground beneath Her Feet* and the later memoir, *Joseph Anton*, according to an exaggerated collapse of self and text. As she slips into the violently gaping fissure of the Mexican ground during an earthquake, the novel's devastating opening chapter not only introduces the theme of ontological ungrounding ironically summoned by the title, but it also reiterates, in the fashion of a film franchise, a theme from Rushdie's most famous novel, specifically recalling the first line of *The Satanic Verses* when Gibreel, plummeting to earth, proclaims, "To be born again ... first you have to die" (*SV* 3). Vina of course gets reborn throughout the novel as the objectified simulacra of postmodern media culture, and yet the autobiographical significance of the date of her death anticipates Rushdie's attempt to translate the death of his private life under the public demonization of his persona into a premature birth within the pantheon of modernist masters in the memoir. In *Joseph Anton*, that is, Rushdie writes of the years he spent under British and American police protection as master trope for his own death and ongoing authorial rebirth. Written in a lofty third person, the book of course suggests the author's objectification and loss of control over his public persona following the hypermediated scandal and its attendant gossip, but the rhetorical ploy can also be read as a concession and contribution to the production of Rushdie as a brand name.

This finds support in what are essentially the two predominant and oddly intersecting threads that structure the narrative. On the one hand the memoir is typical of the genre: it indulges in the perpetuation of gossip about Rushdie's friends and enemies, replete with mud-slinging at the latter, including several of his ex-wives, and filled in with self-affirming incidents of sexual prowess. All that celebrity self-regard, on the other hand, is coupled with repeated mantras about the sanctified autonomy of "great" literature and its hallowed status as a form of artistic free speech, with Rushdie's own at center stage. For one, his choice of pseudonym, he tells us, derives from Joseph Conrad and Anton Chekhov, making this a story about the author as textual subject already slotted into the canon of modern European writers. And it is this latter move that takes Rushdie's readers full circle in understanding his career-long engagement with modernism as providing a set of experimental formal and stylistic designs that he has adapted to the market for postcolonial fiction, commercial success, and cultural celebrity. Recalling the early days of the debate over censorship of *The Satanic Verses*, Rushdie strikes a defense for free speech on the grounds of "quality," implicitly excluding the work of writers who might not fit the bill (including those he had criticized in reviews), and shamelessly aligning his own novel with the once-beleaguered works of his modernist predecessors, writing, for example, that "he hoped for, he often felt he needed, a more particular defense like the quality defense made in the case of other assaulted books, *Lady Chatterley's Lover*, *Ulysses*, *Lolita*."[69] He appeals, in other words, to what Zoe Heller paraphrases as the "extra-special rights of serious, or *important*, fiction," in a move that strikes readers with "the lordly nonchalance with which Rushdie places himself alongside Lawrence, Joyce, and Nabokov."[70] Since *Midnight's Children*, and especially following its unparalleled success, Rushdie has always toyed with the textual production of authorship. With *Joseph Anton* his career-long adaptation of modernist celebrity and authorial self-fashioning has reached an ironically logical conclusion, presented in the form of a self-aggrandizing book that struggles to wrest control of Rushdie's public persona by turning himself, again, into a textual object.

Rushdie's early work undeniably demonstrated a renewal of modernism's energy, its mythic-mimetic inventiveness, and self-styling creation of the idea of modern authorship; and its successful marketing and cultural consecration helped make his fiction central to the widening horizons for literary fiction coming out of England. And yet his work also demonstrates how the reproductive force of modernist style has become a convenient mode for global marketing, especially in the context of an expanding demand for literary commodities inscribed with the pleasures of postcolonial hybridity. Rushdie's postcolonial modernism, we can now see, has always been a fundamentally commercial enterprise, one that synergistically interacts with the affirmative work of academics, booksellers, and prestigious prizes. Despite its radical appearances—whether in terms of surrealistic style or political content—Rushdie's work might be understood in contrast to the kinds of postcolonial modernism Neil Lazarus surveys; for Lazarus, "there might be a *modernist writing after the canonisation of modernism*—a writing … that resists the accommodationism of what has been canonised as modernism and that does what at least *some* modernist work has done from the outset: namely, says 'no'; refuses integration, resolution, consolation."[71] It is telling that Rushdie does not feature in Lazarus's study of a literature of postcolonial modernist resistance; in fact, Lazarus is concerned to write against the institutional conditions, largely represented by the literary-critical establishment, that have resulted in Rushdie being figured as *the* singular "author in the postcolonial literary canon."[72] Rushdie's subversive pose, partly posited on a modernist legacy, necessarily participates in a promotional system that continues to shape a restrictive and marketable brand of postcolonial fiction, conditions that have also shaped the careers of Kazuo Ishiguro and Zadie Smith, the subjects of Chapters 4 and 5.[73]

4

What the Public Wants: Kazuo Ishiguro, Prize Culture, and the Art of Alienation

In an interview following the Booker Prize for *The Remains of the Day*, Kazuo Ishiguro credited two related phenomena for his sudden success: the prize itself and Salman Rushdie's fame, the latter taken as a sign of a book market hungry for multicultural authors and their work. "There definitely was this atmosphere where people were looking for this young, exotic—although exotic may be a somewhat unkind word—writer with an international flavor," he says, adding that "I was very fortunate to have come along at exactly the right time." Extending this characteristic modesty, he notes that the 1981 Booker for *Midnight's Children* "was a really symbolic moment and then everyone was suddenly looking for other Rushdies."[1] Ishiguro's claim points to an ostensibly expanding field for multicultural literary fiction beginning in the early 1980s, and his modesty suggests that the widespread critical and popular acclaim that greeted his third novel came conveniently predetermined by a diversifying publishing industry even as it hints at the Booker's dubious promotion of multicultural writers, or what Graham Huggan identifies as marketing the "postcolonial exotic" and "prizing otherness."[2]

Indeed, this logic confirms some of the general critical reception of Ishiguro's work. Readers had found in *A Pale View of Hills* and *An Artist of the Floating World* evidence of a "Japanese" writer whose style of psychological suppression as a response to geopolitical trauma is somehow inherent to the author's ethnic identity. This kind of ready-made Orientalism at once disregards the fact that Ishiguro had been raised and educated in England from the age of five, and provides a neat authorial platform for difference in a changing market for British literary fiction. Similarly compelled to label his work according to dominant contemporary trends, numerous critics have slotted Ishiguro into an alternately postcolonial or postmodern frame, reading his first-person narrators' tragic disavowal of the impact of imperialism, the world wars, and decolonization as an ongoing impulse to construct national allegories around those singular and traumatized figures. These kinds of categorical reception are by no means wholly misguided—several of his novels do concern colonial trauma and the unreliable memory of figures on the margins of historical events, the stuff of postcolonial and postmodern historiography.[3] But as a set of interpretive labels, they also work as a "containment strategy," in Lawrence Driscoll's terms, that can "obscure all other considerations," namely the problems of class and alienation that are central to *The Remains of the Day* and that run through many of his subsequent novels.[4]

While the essentialism that partly greeted his early work is at best questionable, it is undeniable that the number of prestigious literary prizes awarded to Ishiguro has accounted for his canonization and celebrity. Having been awarded the Nobel Prize for literature in 2017, Ishiguro's membership in what Pascale Casanova calls "the world republic of letters" is more secure than ever. If one criterion for that status is that an author's work expresses universal humanist values, then the rhetorical flourish of the prize announcement certainly rose to meet that demand. As Sara Danius proclaimed on behalf of the prize committee, Ishiguro is a writer "who, in novels of great emotional force, has uncovered the abyss beneath our illusory sense of connection with the world." At the same time, Ishiguro's fiction has been described as a modernist feat of making it new, a reworking of canonical classics to achieve a kind of pure aesthetic originality: "If you mix Jane Austen and Kafka you have Ishiguro's work," Danius continues, before adding that he has "developed an aesthetic universe all his own."[5] Without denying the validity of these claims, or Ishiguro's merit, we might note that this public rhetoric pronounces on two distinct categories at once: claiming for his work a kind of aesthetic purity on the one hand, and valuing it for its universal moral depth on the other. These claims, at odds on the surface, easily coexist in the sphere of prestigious prizes, and it is a logic bound up with the "founding language" of the Nobel's criteria: prize recipients "must have 'conferred the greatest good upon mankind'"—to carry out the "moral burden" of humanitarian work—while simultaneously achieving recognition for aesthetic "purity" and "artistic value."[6] As James English argues, this apparently dual logic ultimately serves the larger function of such prizes themselves: "to test and affirm the notion of art as a separate and superior domain, a domain of disinterested activity which gives rise to a special, nontemporal, noneconomic, but scarce and thus highly desirable form of value," which circulates back into the prize's "claim to authority and an assertion of that authority."[7] Read in these terms, Ishiguro's Nobel and the rhetoric supporting the event both register the internally conflicted demands for aesthetic distinction and social morality, and prop up the institution's authority to assert a form of cultural value that depends on a fiction of the author as its singular producer and bearer.

If Ishiguro's unquestionably prized position in the field means that his writing and its reception are inseparable from those contradictions, it also points to another tension that I explore in this chapter, namely that between his appeal to what the public wants and the unremittingly disconsoling work his fiction carries out. All of Ishiguro's novels, we might say, are fundamentally concerned with stripping away illusions about professionalism and ethical commitments in order to reveal the alienating conditions of bureaucratic capitalist modernity. In other words, his novels may expose a moral "abyss beneath our illusory sense of connection with the world," but they do so in ways that question the pervasive economic instrumentalism that has come to condition cultural values, including, as I will argue, the value of his novels as prized and privileged literary commodities. Like Driscoll, I also want to emphasize that the terms of Ishiguro's critical reception, as well as those of big prize institutions like the Nobel, work both to shore up and affirm their own cultural authority and to obscure a fundamental sense in which Ishiguro's fiction, resolutely mainstream and remarkably readable, also reflects the conditions of an alienating neoliberal cultural economy, conditions which delimit and enable the literary values that have accrued to his own work and its widely favorable reception.

I focus on this tension between the formal and thematic preoccupations of Ishiguro's novels, on the one hand, and his prized reception among both academics and the broader reading public on the other. Ishiguro, that is, clearly appeals to what the public wants, even as his work critically reflects on the dehumanizing forces of modern bureaucratic organization, the professionalization and commodification of all cultural values, and an alienating devotion to instrumental labor, at times leveling this critique at the conditions of cultural celebrity that underwrite his success. Reading Ishiguro both within and against the grain of a postmodern culture industry, I argue that his fiction revives a particularly disconsolate modernist aesthetic. As Neil Lazarus usefully suggests, "'disconsolation' is … the central aesthetic *effect* of Ishiguro's fiction," registering as it does a necessarily failed "yearning for fellowship or collectivity."[8] Like Kafka or Beckett, Ishiguro's narrative aesthetic is driven by a disconsoling social affect that nevertheless seems oddly poised to meet the demands of neoliberal cultural production, literary prizes, and the notion of the author as an international celebrity signifier. So while *The Remains of the Day* remains his most celebrated work, a reception that was buttressed not only by the Booker, but also by the 1993 James Ivory film (starring Emma Thompson and Anthony Hopkins no less), I begin with what amounts to his surrealistic send-up of that success as it focuses on cultural celebrity, *The Unconsoled*, before considering the inhuman theme and style of *Never Let Me Go*. These major works reveal a pattern in which Ishiguro's disconsolate aesthetic engages with the logics of prize culture and prestige from within a restrictive and marketable literary field. If Amis, McEwan, and Rushdie disavow the social privilege in which their work and cultural capital are implicated, Ishiguro's writing and reception signal a different kind of contradiction. Commercially successful and critically acclaimed, his work also articulates an ironic and defamiliarizing distance, a position from which to question some of the most reified liberal assumptions and blind spots about the institutionalized value of the literary. Extending a modernist mode of impersonality, "disconsolation," and inhuman aesthetics, Ishiguro participates in the cultivation of his own celebrity, but in a way that critically engages with the neoliberal conditions that confer it.

What the Public Wants

Before turning to *The Unconsoled*, let me briefly flesh out some context for that novel's critically comic response to the conditions of cultural prizes and Ishiguro's particular place within them. The story begins, then, with the reception that greeted *The Remains of the Day* and the way that that reception has compelled Ishiguro to comment publicly on his intentions in the novel. Much of the academic criticism that followed the novel's Booker Prize and mainstream success slotted it into either a form of postmodern historiography or, more oddly, a postcolonial model, the latter of which makes some sense with regard to the neo-imperial discourse that surfaced during the Thatcher era in which the novel was written. To be sure, this postmodern and postcolonial critical spectrum makes a certain sense, but it also implicitly fits the novel into critical approaches that tended to dominate academic discourse around the time of the novel's publication, thereby shoring up the cultural capital of the criticism itself. Contributing to a strange form of discursive synergy in the creation of cultural values, Ishiguro has argued with much of the academic reception of his first major success. So he comments, for example, "that people have a tendency to say that *The Remains of the Day* is a book about a certain historical period in England or that it is about the fall of the British empire" or, alternatively, that "some people thought it was about the Suez Crisis or it was about British appeasement of Nazi Germany" while insisting that its historical setting and political implications are subordinate to its "metaphorical" exploration of a life wasted by work, the instrumentalization of individual identity, and emotional repression.[9] More specifically, Ishiguro insists that we consider Stevens, as butler, to be a "good metaphor for the relationship of very ordinary small people to power."[10]

Even more telling is the context in which Ishiguro has been compelled to defend his authorial and social intentions, specifically the imperative within the industry to engage in book tours and other forms of public promotion. In a 1989 interview with Suanne Kelman immediately following his reception of the Booker Prize, Ishiguro reflected directly on the nature of publicity and the publishing industry in terms that would come to anticipate his ongoing negotiation with his work and its reception. "I do interviews because this is the way publishing has got, now, and that all seems to be part and parcel of my job," he states. "But I don't feel an overwhelming need to go around talking about my books" and telling people how they should be read. As he elaborates near the end of the interview, "publicity is good for literature in that it sells books," but at the same time it creates a risky condition in which the work of "doing promotion" might negatively "affect the way writers write" and turn a particularly successful one into "a professional conference-attender."[11] This resistance, however, soon shifted over the years following the Booker event, and Ishiguro has become inescapably caught up in the promotional scene and interview circuit. Most tellingly, he seems compelled to discuss again and again *The Remains of the Day*—his most talked-about work—as a kind of touchstone both for the content of his subsequent books and as the foundation for his authorial platform. In terms of sheer numbers, consider the fact that in the 2008 publication of *Conversations with Kazuo Ishiguro*, select interviews edited by well-known Ishiguro scholars Brian Shaffer and Cynthia Wong, the Booker Prize–winning novel comes up more than any other Ishiguro title, often featuring as a kind of interpretive lens or starting point for discussing his later books. This momentum is also registered in the content of Ishiguro's comments on his own work and, in response to the kinds of academic readings I noted above, he has conceded to the "overwhelming need" to discuss what his books are about.

While this points to a tension between Ishiguro's stated intentions and the novel's reception, the twinned canonical and prized status of *The Remains of the Day* also implies a further point of ambivalence, and even contradiction. The author's insistence that the novel is fundamentally critical of the alienated subjectivity of instrumentalized labor, as I've suggested, resonates with the rise of neoliberalism and its attendant ideological and economic forces, such as Thatcher's and Blair's famous dismissals of the relevance of social class, the declining support for the public good, and the increasing centrality of finance markets and speculative, immaterial values in Britain's economy. Yet the novel's and its author's continuing marketability, and a public discourse that keeps it in circulation, all implicate the book as a commodity in the neoliberal conditions it questions. The novel's prized position in the field, and Ishiguro's participation in upholding its visibility and relevance to his career arc, necessarily contribute to this set of cultural contradictions in ways that are similar to, say, Rushdie's problematic position in postcolonial literary production. My aim here is not to dispute any particular kind of interpretation, nor to advance some dubious claim for authorial intention. Rather, I want to highlight what I see as a productive tension between the kinds of interpretive labels that have come to mediate a privileged positioning of the book and Ishiguro's reactions to them, a tension that has helped shape his subsequent work and public persona. If *The Remains of the Day* indicts a narrow professionalism by linking it to a totally reified subjectivity, then it not only resonates with the economic and cultural conditions of its late-twentieth-century present, but also opens up a conflict with the terms of its ensuing success. More to the point, its success in the worlds of academia and literary-prize frenzy, of interviews and the production of an author's public persona, forms the material and immaterial field that then comes to jar with the content of the novel, and all of this forms the social field that produces Ishiguro the celebrity author and embodiment of literary professionalism. In other words, Ishiguro's ongoing engagement with the contradictory public demands made of cultural producers, alongside his attempts to assert a sense of literary autonomy on the level of form, has defined his career in ways that also reveal the contradictions within the literary field.

Cultural Celebrity and Modernist Disconsolation

The Unconsoled (1995) engages in a comically surreal response to this vexed condition, and the novel at once hollows out a collective belief in disinterested aesthetic values while implicitly asking whether literary fiction might effectively mediate the cultural and economic conditions of its production and circulation. What makes this intervention interesting, though, is the way the novel deploys a disorienting modernist aesthetic to uncover a pervasive sense of social alienation driving both a collective belief in purely aesthetic values and the culture of celebrity. The novel marks a double departure from the psychological realism of Ishiguro's previous books: it presents a diegetic world charged with surrealist distortions of time and space while its content comically reflects on the mutually constitutive creation of symbolic and economic values embodied by contemporary cultural celebrities. Ryder, whose name aptly condenses "writer" and "rider"—the latter being a set of conditions a performer demands—is an internationally acclaimed concert pianist who arrives at an unnamed European city to give a performance and a lecture meant to redeem its "unconsoled" citizens from an also unidentified collective malaise. Clearly bearing the influence of Kafka's *The Trial*, those climactic events never happen. Instead, we witness a tediously somnolent series of missed opportunities, misunderstandings, and dubious memories as he is whisked around the town's strangely surrealist setting in failed attempts to meet the vaguely articulated demands of his public. Indeed, the novel's digressive plotting and spatio-temporal distortions prompted some harsh dismissals from initial reviewers. Ned Rorem called it "boring" and "static," a novel "heading nowhere except back into itself."[12] Writing in the *Guardian*, James Wood concedes to the novel's originality, but in a snidely backhanded manner, saying it "has the virtue of being unlike anything else; it invents its own category of badness."[13] Dismissing the novel in similar terms, James Walton goes so far as to speak for the public at large, writing that "for months now, there have been rumours that [Ishiguro] has followed up *The Remains of the Day*—1989 Booker Prize-winner, international bestseller, major motion picture—with 'a stinker.'"[14] Whether or not the book is categorically bad, boring, or a downright stinker, all of these reactions express disappointment with Ishiguro's departure from a recognizable realist style, one that had come to be associated, as Walton's words make clear, with work that is amenable to commercially sponsored prizes, best-seller status, and the movies. Deliberately departing from that previous mode, *The Unconsoled* presents what Ishiguro has called "a landscape of the imagination," a fictive diegesis stripped of documentary references to historical or geographical specificity.[15]

As Ishiguro has indicated, this departure was an attempt to overcome the terms of his work's reception—including assertions of the "Japanese" tone of his writing and an exaggerated search for documentary historicism—and the novel marks a striking return to a defamiliarizing modernist aesthetic.[16] Ishiguro has specifically acknowledged the influence of Beckett and, especially, Kafka. In an attempt to write in counterpoint to his reception as a realist, Ishiguro says in a 1995 interview with Maya Jaggi, "Kafka is an obvious model once you move away from straight social or psychological realism."[17] Diegetically removed from any singularly identifiable place, the novel also distorts its temporal and spatial coordinates to stretch the bounds of mimesis according to its own internal fictive rules. In the opening chapter Ryder conducts what seems like a twenty-minute conversation with Gustav, the hotel porter, during what would otherwise be a short elevator ride. He is repeatedly driven for miles to remote places outside the city but can instantly return to the café or hotel from which he started out. Desperately struggling to find his way on foot to the concert hall where he's to give his climactic performance, he encounters a brick wall pointlessly blocking an entire street. A small critical industry has emerged, and most critics favorably disposed to Ishiguro's experiment note the novel's formal and "stylistic evocation of Kafka."[18] Robert Lemon takes a two-pronged approach; he demonstrates how the novel "combines two modes of narration associated with Kafka—the circumscribed perspective of the first-person narratives found in his shorter fiction and the endless detours and diversions experienced by the third-person protagonists of the novels—to produce a hybrid Kafkan text," and then teases out Ishiguro's departures from "diegetic convention" so that his comparison reveals "the different modes of narrative alienation and consolation offered by modernist and postmodernist fiction."[19] While Lemon is largely concerned with tracing the thematic and structural Kafka effects in *The Unconsoled*, others have suggestively brought the discussion to bear on questions of historicity and the legacy of modernism. Addressing the modernist mode Ishiguro deploys, Pierre François identifies the style of "oneiric realism," distinct from both magic realism and a strict adherence to literal dreaming, to argue that the novel counters postmodernism by staging a return to modernist depth and an appeal to communally shared aesthetic values.[20] Implicitly noting what Natalie Reitano calls the "eviscerated world of Ishiguro's novel," Cynthia Quarrie not only acknowledges the Kafkaesque but also places *The Unconsoled* within a larger historical context of literary modernism.[21] Reading the novel as a drama of traumatic rupture and failed filiation, Quarrie argues that Ryder's inability to console his public with music evokes a kind of literary orphanhood, or what she calls "the condition of coming after modernism."[22] What these otherwise disparate critical accounts agree on, then, is that *The Unconsoled* develops a surrealist and disconsolate mode of Kafkaesque high modernism in response to a generalized postmodern condition of alienation.

What these Kafkaesque responses overlook, though, is how the novel's digressive, distorting, and surrealist form mediates a real-world content concerned with authorial professionalism, prizes, and celebrity culture. Noting this content, Wai-chew Sim rightly reads it in service to Ishiguro's "burlesque of expert-celebrity culture"—in which Ishiguro circulates as a prominent figure—but doesn't ask how the novel's defamiliarizing modernist form reshapes those references to its own aesthetic laws.[23] In this light we might return to one of the earliest reviews. Writing in the *London Review of Books* in 1995, acclaimed novelist Amit Chaudhuri complained that *The Unconsoled* is a "strangely ahistorical book" lacking "any discernable cultural, social or historical determinants (surely fatal to any novel)," and goes on to argue that "what is unKafkaesque about Ishiguro's Kafkaesque novel is its refusal to allow its allegory to be engaged, in any lively way, with the social shape of our age."[24] Then, on the next page, Chaudhuri suggests that the novel merely enacts "a sort of revenge on the increasingly intractable and Kafkaesque world of publishers and the publishing market."[25] Chaudhuri's simultaneously keen-eyed and contradictory comments are telling, and might be taken as a sort of prompt for my reading of Ishiguro's modernist distortions of the market for literary and cultural celebrity. For one, he seems to forget that Kafka's own allegories often depart from strict mimesis; but perhaps the larger problem lies with the reviewer's implied expectation that a writer should somehow replicate the work of predecessors in order, paradoxically, to engage with its own historical moment. Moreover, Chaudhuri's claim that Ishiguro takes revenge on "the publishing market" and its demands for publicity, while certainly not wrong, is a bit snarky coming from another prized author, for one thing, and it also disavows his own acknowledgment that Ishiguro's spoof on those conditions is inextricably part of what constitutes "the social shape of our age." Finally, Chaudhuri's review is itself part of the same publicity machine, wherein the authorial name and the reviewer's claim participate in a synergistic fashion with the novel's mediated reception, all taking part in the network of publicity where literary and economic capital are negotiated and reproduced. *The Unconsoled* is a particularly pronounced fiction of celebrity, a privileged cultural commodity that is simultaneously engaged in the same publicity game it sets out to critique. While the novel's circulation is of course inseparable from that postmodern system of promotion and publicity, I hope to show that Ishiguro also deploys a belated modernist refashioning of that social content by subjecting it to the novel's own disorienting formal logic, a strategy that forces us to rethink what literary autonomy might mean in the face of its absolute commodification.

Let me first take up the easier part of this equation, specifically how *The Unconsoled* internalizes and parodies, on the level of content, the culture of prizes, public promotion, and celebrity branding. While the marketing regimes that structure contemporary creative economies are often subordinated to the novel's more prevalent concern with a groundless belief in disinterested aesthetic values, they do come in for Ishiguro's knowing parody. Pierre François argues, somewhat convincingly, that the diegetic world of the novel "encompasses all the activities we associate with the modern way of life, [yet] it departs from our expectations of urban modernity in one important respect: it substitutes artistic achievements for economic determinants. It is not the money-man who can arguably soothe collective anxieties but the artist."[26] Indeed, it is the artist to whom Ishiguro's fictional city turns for some kind of consolation for their unidentified malaise, but the novel also insists in subtle but telling ways that the social value of the aesthetic is contingent on the support of commercial institutions. Citizens of this city are proud of their locally managed Jürgen Flemming Prize, and they eagerly anticipate the upcoming visit by the Stuttgart Nagel Foundation Orchestra—the latter comically equating hardware sales and symphonic sophistication. The cultural values of high art are everywhere contingent on these kinds of institutional support, comically suggested as Mr. Hoffmann, the hotel manager, repeatedly pleads with Ryder to peruse his wife's "albums," clippings of mass media articles that document Ryder's career arc and that amounts to a familiar form of celebrity worship, one that is just as importantly meant to display Mrs. Hoffmann's cultural attainments.

Recall that, following the acclaim that greeted *The Remains of the Day*, Ishiguro stated that doing interviews had become part of the job of being a writer, but he would soon lament the fact that he found himself "doing very little except publicity," expressing a concern about the pressures of literary celebrity that would soon become a regular refrain in his public comments.[27] Taking these concerns as part of the contextual motivation for *The Unconsoled*, we should note that Ryder at times functions as little more than an object who circulates as a commodified image of ostensibly disinterested artistic values in a novel that clearly internalizes and parodies the world of professionalism and prize culture that Ishiguro inhabits. The novel thus subjects the creation of a niche avant-garde, as distinct from commerce, to protracted parody. Fictitious musical titles, like Mullery's *Verticality*, sound "archly highbrow," and the avant-garde conductor Christoff speaks in musical terms like "a crushed cadence" and a "pigmented triad,"[28] invented phrases that, as Lemon notes, "remain comically opaque to the reader."[29] While these poke fun at the notion of an exclusive field of cultural values, they also fit with the novel's larger comic suggestion that the production of those values depends on their integration with shifting forms of mass cultural production in the ongoing history of the market for modernism.

Perhaps nowhere is this send-up more apparent than in the plan, hatched by Hoffmann, to use the electronic scoreboard from the local sports stadium during the climactic lecture Ryder is to give on the final evening of his visit. Staged as a series of questions concerning the current state of musical society, Hoffmann explains his idea in a way that clearly conflates sport, high culture, and commercial spectacle. The auditorium will be completely dark:

> And then a single spot will come on, revealing you standing at the centre of the stage at the lectern. At that moment, obviously, the audience will burst into excited applause. Then, once the applause has subsided … a voice will boom out across the auditorium, pronouncing the first question. The voice will be that of Horst Jannings, this city's most senior actor. He will be up in the sound box speaking through the public address system. … And as he does so—this is my little idea, sir!—the words will be spelt out simultaneously on the electronic scoreboard fixed directly above your head. (*U.* 381)

Hoffmann's plan (unfolding over the course of several pages) describes a collective investment in a scripted and spectacular ritual necessary to upholding a lofty idea of the artist. The passage amounts to a comically inflated expression of Ishiguro's publicly stated concerns about the necessity of literary self-promotion, and it clearly functions as a "burlesque of expert-celebrity culture," in Sim's words, meant "to uncover the awkward truth that art has become a business much like sport."[30] But Ishiguro also brings the implications of the plan full circle later to suggest how celebrated cultural figures like Ryder are compelled to indulge in such business as, paradoxically, the means of propping up a belief in their own contribution to high art. Feeling anxiously unprepared for the upcoming event, Ryder complains to Sophie (allegedly his wife) that she fails to understand its significance, emphasizing it by repeatedly telling her, "There are people out there depending on me. There's going to be an electronic scoreboard, everything. They want me to come to the edge of the stage after each answer. That's a lot of pressure" (*U.* 473). This kind of semi-scripted event, obviously, mocks the commercialization of cultural production, but also hints at the loss of authorial control that Ishiguro at times suggests about his own reception, the latter comically reduced to Ryder's unquestioning complicity in a fetishized spectacle of high art.

So if Ryder is a rather dull character, that is because he figures as a kind of pawn in Ishiguro's satire on a contemporary culture industry obsessed with the private lives of public figures. In this regard, Ishiguro's depiction of Ryder turns modernist impersonality, as a textual mode of producing the celebrity author, utterly inside out, often doing so through familiar clichés about narcissistic celebrities, thoroughly mediated figures that circulate as products of a postmodern system of publicity. Ryder is repeatedly praised for his accomplishments, something he internalizes according to an immaterial circuit of aesthetic judgment that constitutes cultural values and the figures who embody them. This is hilariously, and uncharacteristically, borne out in Ryder's surrealist and passive submission to the will of the unnamed journalist and photographer who convince him to leave Boris, Sophie's son, waiting in a café while they conduct a photo shoot and interview. Within Ryder's hearing, the journalist repeatedly tells the photographer to keep "feeding his ego," that as an artist he is preternaturally vain, and that someone named Schulz, perhaps his editor, "warned me what a difficult shit the guy is" (*U.* 167, 166). Playing along, without even questioning these insults, Ryder agrees to pose on the windswept hill before the enigmatic Sattler monument, a site that the journalist tellingly suggests will capture the performer's "unique charisma." The novel goes on to subject this myth of the artist's special charisma to that of a manufactured and mediated object when Ryder notices his image on the front page of the paper bearing "an expression of unbridled ferocity," fist raised and appearing to issue a "warrior-like roar." Unable to fathom how "such a pose had come about," he then notices the only text on the page—"RYDER'S RALLYING CALL"—before opening the paper to discover "six or seven smaller pictures, each a variation of the one on the front" and each reproducing the same "belligerent demeanor" (*U.* 267). Cultural celebrities are products of their own objectified images that circulate within the intersecting networks of aesthetic and economic values. The Sattler photo suggests the death of the cultural producer, absorbed as he is into images that publicly circulate to stimulate demands irrelevant to his artistic intentions. Other examples abound, but the point is that Ryder's physical presence is repeatedly eclipsed by his circulation in service to manufacturing a belief in lofty and unalloyed cultural values.

What makes this caricature of the commodified culture industries interesting, though, is its dramatization of the constitutive tension between commerce and what English calls the "collective make-belief" in disinterested aesthetic values that serve, in part, to prop up "the economy of prestige." Almost every character in the book, not least Ryder himself, expresses a belief in symbolic values as a redeeming force in a disconsolate society. Ryder repeatedly insists to his pseudo-wife Sophie, "People need me," expressing an inflated sense of the artist's role in contemporary society, a vague belief that is shared by the city's unconsoled citizens. Later in the novel Ishiguro will comically deflate this hope through a musical performance that never takes place, but over much of the book he slowly builds a fictional social fabric desperately dependent on the cultivation of cultural values through high artistic expression. Stephan Hoffmann, modestly bemoaning his own failed efforts as a pianist also boasts to Ryder of the town's history of promoting the arts, telling him of his good fortune to study under Mrs. Tilkowski, "a very revered figure in this city" who "will only take children of the city's artistic and intellectual elite" before going on to sing the praises of his own parents—"very cultured people who appreciated the importance of the arts in our society"—and their role in cultivating the artistic capital so desperately needed by the city's inhabitants (*U.* 71–2). And elsewhere we find the local citizens lamenting the unstated "crisis" they face if Ryder or some other celebrated figure of artistic authority doesn't redeem them, and many of them tenaciously cling to a belief in the power of the aesthetic, embodied by celebrated artistic figures, to alleviate their collective feelings of alienation. Karl Pedersen, an active member of the local civic council and partly responsible for bringing Ryder to the city, expresses a vague hope that Ryder's visit will somehow redeem the town in the face of its current existential "crisis": "In the trams, in the cafés, people are talking of virtually nothing else," desperately insisting that Ryder's lecture will somehow spur the community to "re-discover the happiness we once had" (*U.* 114–15). Again, Ryder echoes these sentiments and feels compelled to uphold public faith in immaterial artistic values. As he tells Boris at one point, "I have to keep going on these trips because, you see, you can never tell when it's going to come along. I mean the very special one, the very important trip, the one that's very very important, not just for me but for everyone, everyone in the whole world" (*U.* 217). The hyperbole thoroughly explodes Shelley's famous dictum about the "unacknowledged" legislative power of the poets.

Notice, though, that while the target of this parody is the conflation of high art and commercial spectacle, much of the novel also elides references to economic exchange. While it makes sense to say that Ishiguro adopts an "emphatically modernist" position in its "sneer" at a postmodernism embrace of sheer commercialism (whether ironic or not), Ishiguro also empties out any residual Romantic or modernist belief in completely disinterested aesthetic values.[31] And the novel does so, paradoxically, by foregrounding a collective belief in art as a consoling fetish, only to hollow out precisely such a promise for social consolation by aesthetic values alone. Recall that, as English argues, the noneconomic "notion of art and of artistic value requires continual acts of collective make-believe to sustain it."[32] In its elision of the commercial factors that sustain symbolic values and keep them in circulation, *The Unconsoled* effectively foregrounds this kind of collective make-believe and, most importantly, shows it to be symptomatic of a collective alienation linked to what Linda Simon describes as "the anxiety of contemporary culture about the ability of art to offer enlightenment and consolation."[33]

And yet, while the novel openly parodies those contemporary conditions of cultural publicity, it also mediates its representation with a disorienting form reminiscent of Kafka or Beckett. In its pattern of near endless digression, circling, and temporal dilation, the novel's estrangement of realism's diegetic conventions goes to work on the "real-world" content of celebrity culture that it internalizes, allowing Ishiguro to transform that content and comment on the state of literary fiction as a privileged cultural commodity in ways that exceed mere parody. Most tellingly, Ryder's performance and lecture never occur. Instead, he finds a brick wall blocking an entire street on his route to the concert hall, compelling him to repeat a pattern of circling toward his destination. When he finally enters the labyrinthine auditorium, he is first ushered to comfort the dying Gustav, then speeds off to find Sophie, and when he returns he finds himself in a curious cabinet high above the stage where he observes the ill-received performances of Stephan and the local pianist Brodksy. At the novel's close, Ryder has not given his performance or lecture, and instead finds himself repeatedly circling the city in a tram and thinking that the trip has been a success after all. The point of this admittedly reductive summary is to suggest that at the center of the novel's digressive and inconclusive form is an unyielding temporal protraction. That dilated and disconsolate form, then, goes to work on the social content the novel reflects, effectively hollowing out both the cyclical patterns of commercialized prize culture and the belief harbored by its characters that high art will redeem them from their sense of alienated crisis, implicitly refusing to offer consolation for the latter from the position of privileged literary fiction.

So call it Kafkaesque expressionism, surrealist distortion, dreamlike "oneiric realism," or what you will (and I think that each of these applies), the immediate point here is that Ishiguro revives a modernist penchant for creating irreal fictional worlds that mostly conform to our epistemological experiences of gravity or city-driving, while also subjecting that reality-effect to a form that stretches and distorts their ontological coordinates. As Sim observes more generally, Ishiguro is working "to clear new ground for aesthetic development," and he even "courts incomprehensibility to achieve this goal," something many of the novel's initial reviewers took him to task for.[34] If the novel can be said to clear a new aesthetic terrain out of the familiar stuff of celebrity culture, though, it does so by constructing a dialectic between modernist form and postmodern social content, or between its internal diegesis and the extradiegetic world it internalizes and parodies. This dialectic might be understood in terms of Eric Hayot's notion of "aesthetic worldedness." "Aesthetic worlds," he writes, "are among other things always a relation to and a theory of the lived world, whether as a largely preconscious normative construct [as in most kinds of unalloyed realism], a rearticulation, or even an active refusal of the world norms of their age." Thus, the "diegetic" content of a literary work

> refers directly to the kinds of content located *inside* the aesthetic world of the object as such ... [and] articulates a relationship with its opposed term, the *extradiegetic*: the world "outside" the aesthetic object, otherwise known as *the* world, frames and worlds it in turn, and constitutes the frame of judgment against which the diegetic content's worldedness will be evaluated.[35]

The Unconsoled engages a disorienting "rearticulation" rather than an "active refusal" of the culture industries it parodies, and it reshapes that social content according to its own formal principles. Further, if the novel can be said to frame that content in such a way that "constitutes the frame of judgment against which the diegetic content's worldedness will be evaluated," then it also throws into question both the celebrated reception of Ishiguro's work and the kinds of critical praise ascribed to literary fiction as the privileged site of a return to high modernism, a view that, as I argued in the introduction, fails to take into account how that return is part of the continuing institutionalization and marketing of the term as both a historical period and a set of aesthetic concepts. Foregrounding the "aesthetic worldedness" in such a dialectical fashion, *The Unconsoled* actually marks a radically effective reprisal of a disconsoling modernist aesthetic, emptying out the pretensions of high culture and commerce to claim, as I will show in a moment, a paradoxical and severely limited formal autonomy from within the circuit of prizes and publicity.

This dialectic of form and social content, more specifically, is what makes *The Unconsoled* most compellingly Kafkaesque. As I noted above, Robert Lemon provides a useful counterpoint to Chaudhuri's acerbic dismissal of the "unKafkaesque" in *The Unconsoled*; where the latter complained about the novel's "refusal" to engage with "the social shape of our age," Lemon finds that a comparative reading of Ishiguro with Kafka reveals "the different modes of narrative alienation and consolation offered by modernist and postmodernist fiction." As I have been arguing, this Kafkaesque revelation lies at the intersection of the novel's formal experiment and the total commodification of contemporary cultural production. We can begin to understand the stakes and limits of these modernist designs on the postmodern culture industries by comparing them to

Theodor Adorno's take on Kafka. For Adorno, literary naturalism "finds itself in agreement with the bourgeois personality type" because it "is prone to derive satisfaction from the penury and depravation [it] castigates," whereas Kafka exemplifies a productive counterpoint by expressing social content in disjunctive formal structures:

> Nowhere in his work did he address monopoly capitalism directly. Yet by zeroing in on the dregs of the administered world, he laid bare the inhumanity of a repressive social totality, and he did so more powerfully and uncompromisingly than if he had written novels about corruption in multinational corporations. That form is the key to understanding social content can be shown in Kafka's language, ... the contrast that exists in Kafka between stylistic sobriety and highly imaginary happenings.[36]

Like Adorno's Kafka, in *The Unconsoled* Ishiguro doesn't merely reflect or denounce the social conditions of commodified cultural production, but twists them to the novel's own disconsolate aesthetic form. Taking a cue from Adorno, and contra Chaudhuri, we might say that Ishiguro's formal distortions of the material conditions of celebrity are what make the novel most manifestly Kafkaesque, bringing a socially distorting aesthetic form to bear on the market's constraints on contemporary literary and artistic values. Refusing to address the larger economic determinants of literary marketing—the commercial sphere on which the novel as a commodity depends—Ishiguro instead foregrounds the fetishistic belief in cultural values, in both their purely aesthetic and spectacularly commercial forms, and stretches their intersecting logics beyond the limitations of realism or autofiction. As a Kafkaesque allegory, *The Unconsoled* not only stretches rigid period concepts, effectively revivifying modernist form for postmodern market conditions, but it also hollows out the pretentious power of a belief in the consoling symbolic value of elite artistic culture, suggesting how art as a fetish—when blinded to its economic determinants—can at best mask an unremitting alienation. Now, we've seen how the kind of reflection at work in this novel is comically distorted and temporally dilated in a way that mediates the social content of celebrity culture, subordinating it to its own formal designs, and so its "reflection" is one that self-consciously unsettles that content, as well as the equally fetishistic belief in the transformative powers of the singular artist. In the novel's refusal of the realist terms with which Ishiguro's previous work had been received, it dramatizes a process of testing—or flaunting—the limits and possibilities for literary autonomy by returning to modernism as a defining historical moment in the history of the concept. The result is a weird formal engagement with the economy of cultural prestige, an internal parody and repudiation of Ishiguro's own celebrated reception and the market constraints by which it is governed. But that repudiation remains confined to the pages of the novel.

This limit is the defining contradiction that binds celebrity authors who wish to reflect critically on the conditions of their success. Ishiguro remains a public figure for lofty literary values within the commercial sphere of literary production. Situated within this contradiction—between the novel's repudiation of the economy of prestige and its author's unalloyed reputation—we might say that the real accomplishment of *The Unconsoled* lies with its necessary failure to transform the real world of celebrity culture, a limit that is made clear by the very fact that Ishiguro continues to win prizes. Initially greeted with "consternation," *The Unconsoled* is no exception, short-listed for the prestigious Whitbread award and going on to win the Cheltenham Prize for 1995. So how might we try to reconcile the formal autonomy the novel strives for and its place within Ishiguro's oeuvre of prized and best-selling novels, and what does this teach us about the increasingly delimited possibilities for authorial independence within the constrained market for literary fiction? As Brouillette writes of the contemporary culture industries, "Art becomes ... a space where the struggle between autonomy and the market takes place—a space in which the possibility of establishing some sort of autonomous relation to capital is imagined and negotiated and in which the limits of the market are made plain."[37] Mediating and parodying his authorial platform in a novel as formally and imaginatively distorted as *The Unconsoled*, Ishiguro at this point in his career exemplifies the subtle kind of negotiation Brouillette describes, and does so more imaginatively than the works I have addressed so far in this book. And so this fictional negotiation has to be viewed as unconditionally immanent to those conditions in which Ishiguro has successfully provided what the public wants, even at the expense of his more disinterested literary intentions.

Let me turn again to Adorno who, writing in the early 1970s, presciently describes something of the state of literary production that became increasingly clear over the next couple of decades. We might qualify the performance of formal autonomy that *The Unconsoled* tries to articulate—fraught with the tension between diegetic form and a mainstream and marketable oeuvre—as mutually constitutive parts of what Adorno describes as an "absolute commodity." As Adorno insists, the work of art is unable to escape the "antagonism" between "the social forces of production" and the "commodity form"—particularly since the age of high modernism. This means that

> works of art are absolute commodities; they are social products which have discarded the illusion of being-for-society, an illusion tenaciously retained by all other commodities. An absolute commodity rids itself of the ideology inherent in the commodity form. The latter pretends it is a being-for-society whereas in truth it is only for-itself, i.e. for the ruling interests of society. ... Alas, even as an absolute commodity art has retained its commercial value, becoming a "natural monopoly." Offering art for sale on a market ... is not some perverse use of art but simply a logical consequence of art's participation in productive relations.[38]

As a marketable commodity signifying literary prestige, and as a work of fiction that refuses "the illusion of being-for-society," *The Unconsoled* imagines a kind of autonomy for itself, but does so by actively dramatizing this contradictory logic of modern aesthetics. Ishiguro's novels—successfully marketed, stylistically savvy, serially prized, and commercially viable—meet the demands of what the public wants, and thus take their place within the "ruling interests" of a competitive book market. And yet, in its internal refusal of the socially instrumental, its comic exposure and formal disorientation of the fetishistic belief in immaterial values, the novel reflects on itself as an absolute commodity. This is not to suggest that Ishiguro undermines his own enterprise, or that he utterly dismisses the social and symbolic value of contemporary literature. Rather, it is to argue that if we read *The Unconsoled* for its governing tension between a bid for formal autonomy and the material conditions that seem both to enable and constrain that aim, then we might say that the novel gestures toward a horizon of autonomy by performing and mediating its status as an absolute commodity. And the novel is fundamentally *about* this tension. Its parody of Ryder as a fully mediated, circulating commodity, for one, reflexively dramatizes the processes by which Ishiguro had been turned into an object meant to embody the unique, expressive personality of the artist. And yet, this parody is part of the novel's larger formal attempt to frustrate the prevalent logic of contemporary cultural production. What the novel's comically distorted parody of art as commercial spectacle achieves resonates with Nicholas Brown's understanding of aesthetic autonomy under neoliberal production, a limited autonomy based in "the claim that its form is self-legislating," a form that can articulate, moreover, "an internal suspension of the commodity form" as a mode of resistance to the market's totality but that remains, in itself, incapable of undoing the market's hold as the source of literature's material support.[39] As a best-selling author, Ishiguro exemplifies this productive bind. In refusing to offer consolation for the ideological contradictions of capitalism—an impulse that arguably runs throughout the history of the novel as a genre—*The Unconsoled* exploits rather than resolves the contradictory economic forces it engages, and so its claim to formal autonomy is a paradoxical one dependent on foregrounding its status as an absolute commodity. As an object, the novel participates in the productive relations of contemporary capitalism; in its internal diegesis, though, it refuses the fetish (or "illusion") of consolation that otherwise masks the material conditions that enable it. This is the striking thing about Ishiguro's formal engagement with the economy of prestige: rather than merely capitalizing on modernist clichés, his work foregrounds a disconsoling negotiation with the market as the enduring legacy of modernism under contemporary capitalism.

How to Clone a Modernist Aesthetic

If *The Remains of the Day* dramatizes the tragedy of a life spent in submission to instrumental reason masquerading as dignified duty, and *The Unconsoled* deflates a fetishistic belief in art as a disinterested source of consolation, then *Never Let Me Go* provides a disturbing synthesis of those concerns. Narrated by Kathy H. and comprising mostly linked flashbacks, the novel depicts her upbringing at Hailsham, an apparently privileged boarding school, where she and fellow students are encouraged above all to cultivate their artistic abilities. It soon emerges, though, that Hailsham harbors a darker reality: the students are clones designed expressly to provide "donations," when their vital organs will be harvested for the natural-born population within a publicly funded system. The science-fiction premise here suggests a horrifying literalization of the older Marxist model of labor power. For Marx the problem of industrial capitalism is that it relies on the ongoing reproduction of a class of workers who sell their labor power for subsistence and the perpetuation of wealth, while Kathy H. and the other clones are produced to serve an efficiently managed system that relies on the literal extraction of life-giving value from their bodies. Kathy's narrative arouses readers' sympathies, begging for the outrage over the monstrous limits to their lives that the clone characters themselves never express. Indeed, this anger, managed and mitigated within the novel and invoked in readers, is the pivot on which the most compelling political readings of the novel turn. For Bruce Robbins, the novel critically reflects "the ideology of the welfare state, which gives a grateful semblance of meaning and legitimacy to the stopgap efforts of every day."[40] Moreover, Kathy's role as a dispassionate carer figures the gross compromises and stifled anger inherent in the welfare state; her narrative in this regard is "bureaucratic, cravenly accepting of monstrously limited expectations," such that the novel "obliges us to wonder whether the freedom on which his uncloned readers pride themselves is anything more than a similarly managed ignorance."[41] Picking up on the New Labour implications of Robbins's reading, Brouillette steers away from his skepticism about the welfare state to argue, instead, that "the novel's unseen government is more akin to the neoliberal state that has eroded the relationship between the governance and public welfare" and that in questioning "how particular ideologies of individuation and creativity either directly serve or inadequately mitigate the harms that exist," the novel is ultimately concerned with "the delimitation of art's radical possibility."[42]

Taking cues from these important readings, I want to suggest that *Never Let Me Go* resonates beyond the political limits of the welfare state and the compromises that have become normalized by New Labour. From its disconsolate reflection of an ideology of the redemptive and consoling power of artistic expression to its mimetic narration suggesting a manufactured subjectivity, the novel reprises a modernist strain of inhuman aesthetics to articulate a dark allegory, taken to a horrifyingly logical limit, of the neoliberal instrumentalization of the arts and humanities—raising further implications about the institutionalized place occupied by mainstream literary fiction.

In what at first appears wholly divorced from the cold logic of instrumental reason, Hailsham encourages students to embrace, above all else, the humanist value of artistic expression. Their creative efforts are regularly rewarded, with their output of poetry, drawings, paintings, and sculpture timed to the seasonal rhythms of the quarterly "Exchanges," when they can barter their best work and individuals can add to their private "collections." While we get little description of this creative work—Kathy at one point jokes about "sculptures" made from "bashed-up cans," and Ruth later recalls "Jackie's giraffes" that "were so beautiful"—Kathy's narrative repeatedly calls attention to the immaterial expressive value of art that Hailsham teaches. Self-worth within the school community is a measure of this immaterial creative value. When Kathy thinks of the pleasure she took in adding her peers' work to her "collection," suggesting a merely decorative appreciation of art, she also muses that "how you were regarded at Hailsham, how much you were liked and respected, had to do with how good you were at 'creating'"; and "It's all part of what made Hailsham so special," she recalls Ruth saying, "The way we were encouraged to value each other's work."[43] And while the reasoning behind this excessive valuation of creativity as a measure of self-worth largely eludes the students until late in the novel, the system of artistic creation, exchange, and merit mirrors the logic of the modern symbolic economy we're familiar with. For example, Kathy recalls a time when students questioned "this whole notion that it was a great honour to have something taken by Madame" because without material compensation came "a feeling that we were losing our most marketable stuff," a contention the guardians attempt to resolve with a policy whereby students "*would* get tokens" for their valuable work, "but not many because it was a 'most distinguished honour' to have work selected by Madame" (*NLMG* 39–40). Within this selective economy, the use of tokens is meant to mirror the material exchange for art beyond the confines of the school, but it's a strikingly enclosed economy, sealed off from the larger social order it serves.

Hailsham's creative indoctrination, we learn, is a fetishization that directly serves monstrously instrumental aims. Late in the novel Tommy and Kathy seek out Madame and Miss Emily to inquire about deferrals, based on a rumor that students might be allowed to postpone their donations if they can prove they truly love each other. Having come to believe that their capacity for creative expression is an indication of their humanity, that they are not merely bodies designed for organ extraction, Madame suspiciously confirms their hopes: "Because of course ... your art will reveal your inner selves! That's it, isn't it? Because your art will display your *souls*!" (*NLMG* 254). But this affirmation is really the prelude to the novel's cruelly ironic twist. As Miss Emily goes on to tell them, their artwork was collected "to *prove you had souls at all.*" Displaying their art around the country in galleries attended by "cabinet ministers, bishops," and other influential organizations in charge of "large funds," was part of an elaborate social experiment in which the humane treatment of clones—making them "educated and cultured"—would allow beneficiaries to identify with clones and thereby justify the otherwise exploitative means and ends of the entire system. As Shameem Black argues, the novel shows how an essentially Romantic conception of creative expression operates in service to an underlying system of instrumental reason and callous exploitation. "Concealed within their Romantic logic," Black writes, "lies a far more dystopian goal that colludes with the exploitation of the students [the Hailsham authorities] claim to protect," such that even Madame's specific phrasing—art will "reveal your inner selves"—"suggests that making such art actually prefigures the process of organ donation."[44] In this vein, *Never Let Me Go* reprises disconsolation as a master theme in Ishiguro's fiction, focusing it specifically on the question of art's ameliorative function in an exploitative society. The students' art and its circulation are fully integrated within a monstrously exploitative system and the novel ultimately reveals that Hailsham's role in the system is "managerial rather than political: it will perfect the running of the existing order rather than attempt to transform it."[45]

Of course the novel prepares us—and its characters—for this revelation all along: the students at Hailsham are granted privileged access to a "cultured" life of ostensibly free expressive subjectivity while being taught at the same time to internalize the fact of their purpose. This monstrous resolution of what we normally understand to be a contradiction is radically estranging because artistic creation doesn't merely mask a grossly instrumental logic underlying it, as traditional ideology critique would have it.[46] Rather, the legacy of a Romantic model of expressive subjectivity found in the aesthetic object—complete with its assumptions of nonutilitarian authenticity—is inseparable from and in direct service to a totally utilitarian end: an efficient and morally justified economy dependent on reproducing clones for a form of exploitation that goes by the charitable name of "donations." While Black sees all this as an allegory for exploitation in the contexts of global economic imbalance and war, and Robbins just as compellingly argues that the novel models a negative critique of the failures and compromises of the welfare state, I want to ask how it comments on the social conditions by which the arts and humanities are made to serve conflicting institutional aims. The novel imagines a perversely logical limit to the contradictory position of serving instrumental economic ends under neoliberal capital, while preserving a belief that the production and reception of nonutilitarian humanist values is important in its own right.

For one, "the arts," along with notions of flexible free expression and individualist innovation, have become integrated in an unprecedented fashion with the "creative economy" favored by contemporary corporate forms of productive social organization.[47] But what is also particularly apparent, and especially pertinent to Ishiguro's novel, is the rationalization of the British and American university systems that we've witnessed since the rise of the New Right and the subsequent ideological financialization of education as both a product and a promise of economic success. In this sense, the novel registers, at a perverse extreme, something of the contradictory social forces, as well as common reactions to them, that have come to pressure the residual *raison d'etre* of literature and the arts from the time of the massive restructuring of economics and culture (or a cultural economy) since the 1980s. Consider in particular how those pressures play out in the public university and its alignment with corporate interests. It is in the university that literature and the arts function on multiple levels to subsidize and lend cultural capital to the aims of higher education, specifically its increasingly visible cultivation of corporate values. Corporate-funded business buildings might liberally display the creative work of students and faculty from around the corner; general education requirements in the humanities generate tuition streams (and this is primarily the case in the United States) to subsidize the more immediately profitable preparation that goes on in accounting, tech training, or scientific research. Moreover, faculty and students face enormous pressures from corporate managerial initiatives, administrators, and parents, to justify the aims and outcomes of humanistic inquiry and aesthetic values. Thus a well-established scholar and public intellectual like Stanley Fish can reassert what Jeffrey Nealon derides as a futile "old-school humanities" model of relative autonomy by defending their work in "contrast with the kind of thing done by members of other enterprises (history, sociology, statistics)."[48] Or, at the other end of the spectrum an equally respected figure like Cathy Davidson writes in response to the same apparent "crisis" or "decline" that "reading, writing, evaluating and organizing information have probably never been so central to everyday life," a perfectly viable defense that is also perfectly amenable to the flexible and "creative" skills and service demanded by corporate organization.[49] And neither of these positions is inherently wrong, but their opposition signals their limits as progressive promises. We read literature and look at art with undergraduate students in an effort to teach them to care about ethics and empathy, aesthetics and intellectual curiosity, while knowing that many of them will trade those values for cloney service to corporate branding and capital management. We train graduate students to theorize and historicize that kind of caring and cultivation, while it's increasingly the case that many of them will wind up teaching the humanities because of their supposedly in-built "skills in critical thinking and communication" and the like.

The shocking premise of *Never Let Me Go* is not such a far cry from this move to instrumentalize training in the arts and humanities, including, as we will see, Ishiguro's secure status in the college curriculum and beyond. By saying this I by no means want to suggest that artists, writers, or above all "students" are clones according to some reductive metaphorics and the outworn snobby position that would imply, nor do I think the novel makes exactly that point. It does, though, imagine a culture of total irrational submission to a hyperrational regime, and not merely as far-fetched science fiction, but in a way that prompts us to think about the real world of neoliberal training.[50] The Cottages seem a striking parallel to the neoliberal university, functioning both as a haven for the reproduction of creative values and in service to purely instrumental economic aims. Clearly resonant with "colleges," this is where certain Hailsham students go as part of an ostensibly liberating period—"a cosy state of suspension," Kathy calls it (*NLMG* 143)—between their time at school and their subsequent time spent as carers and donors. The Cottages tellingly occupy "the remains of a farm that had gone out of business years before" (*NLMG* 116), disused agricultural land that has been efficiently reclaimed for the cultivation of bodily organs. But it also serves a belief in the cultivation of minds, in that students are given free time to work on something like an honors thesis; Kathy recalls her own project, an essay on Victorian novels, and hours spent leisurely reading in the fields between unregimented "meandering discussions … about Kafka or Picasso" with her peers (*NLMG* 120). This life of the mind is fully integrated with preparation for the future, as the students begin to go off for training sessions, so that their creative and intellectual activity is unquestioningly understood to be mutually compatible with the instrumental ends for which they were designed.

A further parallel with the corporate training model I've outlined also takes place during their stay at the Cottages, when Ruth entertains a fantasy of working in a slick corporate office. Ruth becomes intrigued by rumors that others have found her "possible," the person whose DNA she carries, working in such an office; and the fantasy itself is directly inspired by "a glossy double-page advert" showing a "beautifully modern open-plan office" where both the workspace and the people "looked sparkling." Ruth, for whom "*that* would be a *proper* place to work," even comes to mimic the language of the ad in her spoken desire to be among such "dynamic, go-ahead types" (*NLMG* 144). The language—"modern," "sparkling," "types"—clearly suggests a cloney kind of manufactured desire, one that colors their perception of those non-cloned, or normal, types. As they peer through the polished plate-glass into the "smart" office, Kathy gives us her description of Ruth's "possible":

> Her hair was darker than Ruth's but it could have been dyed—and she had it tied back in a simple pony-tail the way Ruth usually did. She was laughing at something her friend in the red outfit was saying, and her face, especially when she was finishing her laugh with a shake of her head, had more than a hint of Ruth about it. (*NLMG* 159)

The scene ultimately culminates in Ruth's bitter disillusionment (again, prepared for by their time at Hailsham). But it also signals, more radically, a manufactured-mimetic affectivity within the being of the non-cloned, such that the figure of what they believe to be more authentically human is herself cloney. The anonymous woman's gestures, seen through clear plate-glass, figure a simulated affect, itself something like a copy of the advertised image Ruth had seen, and neatly fitted to the recognizable social organization of office management rather than determined—as the students assume—by genetic coding.

All of this makes for a pretty grim picture, no doubt, especially if we consider that the novel imagines an extreme manifestation of the corporate-driven synthesis of flexible aesthetic self-expression and an instrumental devotion to the bottom line. But Tommy's mature art provides a critical counter to the pacifying function of the instrumentalized economy of the aesthetic, and his art recalls some of the radical avant-garde work of the modernist period. At Hailsham, recall, we get a sense that the students' artwork is of a fairly conventional, representational type (cute giraffes and such). Tommy's drawings, on the other hand, adopt an "inhuman aesthetic" (in Black's accurate phrase) that earlier avant-gardes had developed to critique a modern mass culture that they perceived as either excessively Romantic or geared toward automated dumb desire.[51] Having failed at Hailsham to produce anything that might reveal his soul, or human authenticity, Tommy produces a series of minute drawings that cross the organic-mechanical divide and that would have been familiar to the radical practitioners of Dada and Surrealism. Here's Kathy's description:

> I was taken aback at how densely detailed each one was. In fact, it took a moment to see they were animals at all. The first impression was like one you'd get if you took the back off a radio set: tiny canals, weaving tendons, miniature screws and wheels were all drawn with obsessive precision, and only when you held the page away could you see it was some kind of armadillo, say, or a bird. (*NLMG* 187)

In Tommy's drawings, Ishiguro reprises a modernist avant-garde that alternately sought to question, critique, or cultivate the transformations to subjectivity being wrought by technology, mass commodification, and industrialized military production. These mechanical representations of the living appear very much like the work of surrealists who were drawn to automatons, mannequins, and machines, producing strangely familiar visual objects that, as Hal Foster argues, "could insist on the uncanny effects of mechanization and commodification; more, they could exploit these perverse effects to critical ends" meant to challenge "the very order [of industrial capitalism] that produced them."[52] Tommy's drawings also give an analogous expression to the instrumental lives of the clones rather than the innocuous, decorative art held to reveal their "inner selves." Their vulnerability, despite "all their busy, metallic features" (*NLMG* 188), also parallel Ishiguro's characters: perceived by the rest of the fictional society as other than fully human, the students are also the subjects of our sympathy as readers. In this sense Black is right to argue that Tommy's modernist "inhuman aesthetic"—albeit one that overturns an earlier revulsion at an automated mass culture—marks the novel's appeal to the simulated, cyborgian subjectivity in all of us, a critical move away from the Romantic conception of a unique expressive subject.

But we should note, too, that Tommy's art remains incomprehensible to Kathy: "I didn't know how to judge it," she says (*NLMG* 187). The drawings remain outside the kind of aesthetic frame of judgment cultivated by the Hailsham system. Within the novel's diegesis, then, Tommy's drawings not only bear a figural relationship to the lives of the clones, but that aesthetic also remains conceptually and ontologically autonomous from what Kathy allows herself to understand. As an uncanny expression of the instrumental logic of Ishiguro's imagined regime, the artwork also resists incorporation into its deployment of supposedly authentic or humanist values. Tommy's inhuman aesthetic experiments retrieve a modernist deadness, or mechanization of organic life, but rather than using it as a proclamation on the automated masses of modernity it features as both a direct expression of the devious designs on the clones and as a synecdoche for Ishiguro's novel more generally. Typical of Ishiguro's work, this novel refuses consolation for readers or the clones with whom we sympathize.[53] Tommy's inhuman art critically reflects on the novel's evacuation of a scripted humanism that in fact serves instrumental reason and the economic rationalization of culture and aesthetic expression. Tommy's failure to produce consoling, soul-revealing pictures, combined with his experimental designs on inhuman existence, gestures to a form of resistance to neoliberal capitalism by pushing it to its logical limit in a radical alternative to art's false consolation in a world of corporate efficiency and a creative economy in which an appreciation of aesthetic and ethical ambiguity are valued as slick, marketable skills badly needed in our increasingly "flexible" market society.

Of course Tommy's art and the novel in which it features refuse to offer any direct opposition to the instrumental values that creativity is made to serve. Instead, Ishiguro's allegory fully inhabits and twists that instrumental logic to its own dispiriting ends. Taking issue (or asking us to do so) with a widespread imperative to behave like clones serving a totalizing market, while transforming that logic with a sympathetic cloney style, *Never Let Me Go* raises the question of aesthetic autonomy, a central problem for claims about "the contemporaneity of modernism" within a hyperrationalized contemporary society. The novel straddles the "unstable distinction" between art and society that Adorno identifies in late modernism and which prompts him to insist that "all aesthetic categories must be defined both in terms of their relation to the world and in terms of art's repudiation of that world."[54] In their recent reply to Adorno, Michael D'Arcy and Mathias Nilges reflect on this instability and its implications for contemporary claims for a modernist autonomy: "To dissolve altogether the distinction between art and the rationalizing processes of late capitalist society runs the risk of collapsing the distance between art and the empirical world, thus foreclosing the possibility of aesthetic autonomy."[55] If *Never Let Me Go* articulates any kind of autonomy from late-capitalist society, it does so by fully inhabiting the grossest logic of its rationalizing totality and denying the false promises of a consoling humanism.

In giving the lie to an idealized humanism as a holdout against more transparent forms of training in marketable skills and selves, *Never Let Me Go* indirectly engages with the instrumentalized economic conditions for cultural value in which Ishiguro's work is necessarily implicated. Just as Ishiguro's work is regularly read in the university classroom—where literature and the humanities bear a conflicted identity of a source for free expression and an imperative to quantify the production value of the self for neoliberal capital—and slotted into marketable academic categories, whether it's called a belated modernism or the new world literature, *Never Let Me Go* brings those former poles into monstrous alignment in such a way that refuses the pathos of easy consolation. If *The Remains of the Day* is fundamentally concerned with the tragic consequences of a life devoted to serving power, and *The Unconsoled* mocks its dependence on the prestigious economy of cultural celebrity, then this novel extends and synthesizes those previous projects by imagining the totalizing instrumentalization of aesthetic expression and value. The novel thus acknowledges that process while refusing to accept its paltry promises. It is a powerfully moving imaginative work and an absolute commodity which, again, refuses to offer false consolation to an alienated society. Ishiguro has managed consistently to provide what the public wants, as a gesture of negative capability, and here he offers a bleak warning, albeit from the compromised position of a celebrity author, to those of us who face an uneasy and indeterminate future of service to instrumental corporate values.

5

Zadie Smith, Inauthenticity, and Multicultural Modernism

Since the appearance of her ultra-hyped debut novel, Zadie Smith's name and authorial persona have been securely established as a metabrand for multicultural British fiction. *White Teeth* stormed the literary scene in the wake of a codified popular postcolonial genre—most visibly associated with Rushdie and Hanif Kureishi—and the novel knowingly invokes and appeals to the familiar tropes of migration, hybridity, and the historical contingencies of multicultural belonging. Indeed, the novel clearly situates itself at a moment of arrival, largely unburdened by the defensive posturing with regard to racial or religious difference that fueled the work of a previous generation of postcolonial, Asian, and Black British writers.[1] In *White Teeth* and subsequent novels, Smith portrays a taken-for-granted multicultural British society, or what Laura Moss neatly terms "everyday hybridity," that is at once mundane and comically inflated, bringing a long tradition of the English comic novel right up through a celebrated postcolonial hybridity and appealing to a perception of a diversifying field of minority literary expression.[2] Positioned within a market bent on celebrating Black and multicultural British fiction—and this is a problem I discuss in detail below—Smith was quickly singled out as a new and authentic expressive embodiment of minority voices of all tones.

The story is well known: in a two-book deal with Hamish Hamilton that included an advance rumored to be around £250,000 while Smith was still a Cambridge undergraduate, *White Teeth* was ushered into print amid a frenzy of hype in the literary press. Focusing on the novel's sassy style, multicultural optimism, and capaciously mongrel depiction of contemporary London, the marketing campaign and early reviews of the book launched its young, attractive, biracial writer as the first literary celebrity of the twenty-first century and "the multicultural voice of England."[3] Even before its publication, *White Teeth* and its formerly unknown author were heavily showcased by the literary media, exemplified by a prominently placed interview on the cover of *Bookseller* accompanied by the publisher's promotional tagline, "Hamish Hamilton are proud to launch a dazzling new literary talent," itself followed on the inside cover with a photograph and bio of Smith.[4] That same publication included the brief yet glowing prepublication remark by Rushdie, which then also appeared on the cover of the hardback edition of the novel, a move that was further inflated after its appearance when Robert McCrum wrote in the *Observer*, "It's perhaps too early to say exactly how good this novel is, but there's no doubt that it marks an important literary watershed in much the same way as the publication of *Midnight's Children* or *The Buddha of Suburbia*."[5] As we've seen, this is the clever yet typical marketing scheme that invokes originality and familiarity simultaneously, slotting the novel into line with the proven formula established by Rushdie and Kureishi, seminal figures in the market for postcolonial and multicultural fiction.[6] And that, of course, anticipated the chorus of journalistic praise that would follow, much of which stuck to the formula, hailing the book as "a restless hybrid of voices, tones, and textures" that gives literary expression to a multicultural London at the dawn of a new millennium.[7] The celebratory terms of postcolonial hybridity and mongrel identities making up a multicultural millennial London dominated the initial marketing and reception of the work and, more importantly, the author herself as its new expressive embodiment. As Claire Squires neatly summarizes the picture, with *White Teeth* and subsequent novels, Smith's "work came to be seen as an example of the *zeitgeist*, a new, multicultural, multicoloured Britain," supposedly emblematic of New Labour's "Cool Britannia" and its cultural embrace of multiculturalism.[8]

As hype, all of this of course reflects the reductive logic of manufacturing a multicultural fiction, and it quickly generated some critical pushback. Camilla Palmer notes that the rising popularity of African, Caribbean, and South Asian forms of cultural expression during the 1990s "directly precipitated Smith's success and laid the groundwork for the enthusiastic reception of *White Teeth*." That reception was a form of "simulated optimism," in Katarzyna Jakubiak's terms, a case of "international book-marketing" at the turn of the century that worked "to turn Smith's multidimensional novel into a 'safe' and easily consumable product."[9] In a particularly biting criticism that sums up a range of arguments on Smith's status as product and participant in the literary industry for multiculturalism, Tobias Wachinger writes that

> a look at the way Smith has been publicised and mediatised as "young, black, British" writer sensation (*The Observer*) indicates the machinery of the market

recuperation of a certain type of "in-between" fiction is well lubricated. This fashioning by the metropolitan cultural industries that have turned *White Teeth* into the latest "hot" commodity from multicultural London (complete with Rushdie's appraisal on the cover blurb), however, would not have been possible without Smith's novel's own stressing of its undeniably multicultural sweep.[10]

Wachinger risks overstating Smith's authorial agency and the centrality of *White Teeth* to a commodified multiculturalism, but his somewhat reductive account usefully points to the deeper political, social, and economic conditions that immediately came to shape the ways in which Smith's work and persona were received, conditions that have necessarily enabled and restricted her writing since.

My point here is not to dispute either of these conflicting accounts of Smith's early work and the question of its complicity in the mass market for clever multicultural commodities. Rather, I take the hype as seriously as the materialist criticism leveled at the undeniably commercial fashioning of Zadie Smith; each of these participates in a network of publicity, one that includes a countering skepticism, that constitutes the visibility and viability of the field of multicultural and minority fiction and its prominent place in contemporary economies of prestige (to paraphrase James English again). Taken together, the celebratory and skeptical accounts of Smith's multicultural celebrity hint at the tensions—even contradictions—inherent to the political, economic, and cultural discourses of diversity at the turn of the twenty-first century, the constitutive contradictions that Smith's fiction often explicitly engages. Smith's instant celebrification in the field of new multicultural fiction is itself indicative of the contradictions that guide my reading of her work.

Reading her work within and against market trends and the university institutionalization of her authorial position, I show how Smith's major novels reproduce familiar forms of multiculturalism and hybridity while they self-consciously subject a market demand for "authenticity" to an ironic exposure of the role that celebrated cultural commodities play in mediating identity. When we read *White Teeth* together with its mainstream reception, we see how the novel knowingly plays up the familiar tropes and themes of popular postcolonial fiction while, at the same time, it pits its vision of a "multicultural millennium" as an organic process ostensibly distinct from a commodified hybridity; the novel thus reflects the contradictory demands of a multicultural market caught between what Timothy Brennan calls the "celebratory claims and despairing recognitions" of liberal cosmopolitanism.[11] *On Beauty* and *NW* register a clear shift away from these preoccupations with a fashionable multiculturalism, and they do so by way of two different kinds of engagement with the legacies of modernism. *On Beauty* is a formally conservative homage to Forster's *Howards End*, thus affirming the institutionalized cultural capital of her modernist predecessor while, at the same time, it brings Forster's problematic reflection on class and exclusion into a critical reflection on the failures of contemporary liberal diversity discourse and implicitly contests the hyped claims for a multicultural authenticity. *NW*, on the other hand, moves beyond modernism as a heritage industry, and instead reanimates its experiments with different stylistic registers and an impersonal narrative aesthetic, bringing their unresolved implications to bear on the alienating conditions of neoliberal society in the age of austerity. That move toward a modernism after multiculturalism, however, depends on the author's privileged position in the corporate field of production, such that Smith's effort to imagine new horizons beyond a fashionable multiculturalism offers a striking example of how such a bid for authorial autonomy is necessarily negotiated within a market in which modernism serves as an elite form of cultural capital that underwrites a corporate and highly selective model of diversity.

Playing the Market for Multicultural Fiction

Writing about the staggered emergence of multicultural British fiction in the wake of the racially charged and politically volatile 1980s, James Proctor notes that *White Teeth* often "flirts with" the exotic and hybrid models of multiculturalism from which it also satirically distances itself.[12] A model for an "everyday hybridity" or a "mundane" kind of multicultural London largely unburdened by the anxiously defensive postures of Smith's immediate postcolonial predecessors, her first novel can be said to "deliver Rushdie's future in [a] realistic view of present-day multicultural identity."[13] Here I want to extend and complicate these observations to show how Smith's first novel imagines into fictional existence a "multicultural millennium" by consciously positioning itself as the culmination of a popular postcolonialism, one that is equally subject to ironic reflection on Smith's self-authorizing complicity with the market for optimistic multicultural fictions.

Smith openly appropriates and satirizes the dominant themes and tropes of postcolonialism as a self-authorizing gesture, a move that is particularly borne out in the novel's comic dramatization of the riotous and divisive British reception of *The Satanic Verses*. The date is January 14, 1989, and the scene features Millat

Iqbal and his teen gang buying return tickets to Bradford to participate in the infamous burning of Rushdie's novel, the spark that ignited the Rushdie Affair. Smith's slyly acknowledged debt to Rushdie and the event that prompted his global notoriety is telling.[14] As the jumpy Millat shouts to his loyal peers on the question of Rushdie's guilt, "We've taken it too long in this country. And now we're getting it from our own man. … He's a fucking bādor, white man's puppet," later telling them, "You don't need to read shit to know that it's blasphemous," a point about not reading that his father echoes at home when he says to his cool-headed wife Alsana, "I don't *need* to read it. The relevant passages have been photocopied for me."[15] Millat's and Samad's reactions and their shared refusal to read the text in question directly echo the claims by Islamic fundamentalists that were castigated in the Western liberal press. In a novel published shortly after the unofficial lifting of the *fatwa*, and one that is also brimming with interracial tensions based in the long history of colonial migration, the dominant tone of the passage is one of irony that knowingly establishes (or assumes) the sympathy of readers and contributes to Smith's mockery of tautological fundamentalist discourse. This intertextual return acknowledges a literary debt while capitalizing on Rushdie's notoriety, thereby aligning Smith with what one critic calls a "post-Rushdie orthodoxy."[16] Indeed, through the novel's recurrent themes of East-West migration, multiracial families, numerous returns to the colonial "roots" of the present, not to mention jokes at the expense of the Chalfens, white middle-class liberals who first appear dressed in "pseudo-Indian garb" (*WT* 110), Smith's narrator openly "employs the tropes and archetypes with which any student of postcolonialism would be well aware," as Benjamin Bergholtz observes.[17]

What's more, neither Rushdie nor his inflammatory novel is named, which serves to flatter readers already familiar with the Rushdie Affair, and this too plays into the larger paratextual properties of the novel that go to make up an economy of literary exchange and publicity. Rushdie's name is prominently tagged in the promotional blurb on the cover of the first edition of *White Teeth*, and his praise for the young writer's "assured" sense of individual authenticity—"the voice has real writerly idiosyncrasy"; the novel has "bite"—fulfills the absence within the novel that readers have most likely already identified. If the passage itself acts as a kind of ironic acknowledgment of influence, a symbolic debt, then when we zoom out to the celebrity author's name that circulates with the novel we see a perfect example of how the intertextual and paratextual constitute a network of promotion, based in the interchangeability of literary acclaim and economic capital, and in which Smith's debut can be fitted into the market for an established genre. Rushdie, as a signifier of postcolonial fame, circulates within and outside the pages of *White Teeth*, enacting a literary economy that not only promotes the young author but, more importantly, also affirms the cultural authority of the industry for elite postcolonial and multicultural fiction.

But if this intertextual return within the novel acknowledges a literary debt to capitalize on Rushdie's notoriety, the passage also strains to distance Smith's writing from its influence. The echoes of the reactionary fundamentalist rhetoric that greeted *The Satanic Verses*—which isn't Millat's own but the heavily mediatized language that speaks through him—and the comic irony that permeates it suggest how the Rushdie Affair had itself become a historical event, a settled feature of literary publicity and promotion. Moreover, and from that vantage of historical hindsight, Smith's narrator can ironically reflect on how a postcolonial celebration of hybridity had gained mainstream recognition not only as a mark of authenticity but also as a trope that had already been appropriated by the logic of global capitalism. The intertextual drama of the Bradford book burning frames the narrator's intrusion, itself featuring as a comic send-up of a "hybridity" that implicitly conflates Rushdie's fiction and celebrity persona with an expanding market for manufactured multiculturalism. Millat's "hybrid" crew, Smith's third-person narrator jokes, can be summed up by their performance as "Raggastanis [who] spoke a strange mix of Jamaican patois, Bengali, Gujarati, and English. Their ethos, their manifesto, if it could be called that, was equally a hybrid thing: Allah *featured*, but more as a collective big brother than a supreme being, a hard-as-fuck *geezer* who would fight in their corner if necessary" (*WT* 192).

Clearly a parody of the terms of Rushdie's fame, the "hybrid thing" of their unwritten manifesto finds its expression and approval in the logic of 1980s corporate multiculturalism. The kids' bandanas, baggy jeans, and big sneakers look "like trouble," a subversive performance of the badass gang culminating in the fact that "everything, everything, everything was *Nike*™; wherever the five of them went the impression they left behind was of one gigantic swoosh, one huge mark of corporate approval" (*WT* 192–3).

The joke here is aimed not only at Millat's naïve accusations that the infamous author is a "white man's puppet"—ironically applicable to Bengali-British teens craving the corporate approval of a multinational company notorious for its exploitation of third-world labor—it also takes a satirical "bite" (to extend Rushdie's term of praise) at the dominant trope of a heavily commodified form of postcolonial fiction. In this instance, the comically overdetermined hybridity points to the convergence of postcolonial fiction's radical claims and a corporate multiculturalism that capitalizes on mixed and manufactured differences to reflect how identities are produced by "the dynamics of market exchange-value" in which "the consumer becomes the model hybrid subject."[18] Smith thus knowingly appeals to the familiar tropes of postcolonial fiction, simultaneously capitalizing on them and subjecting them to comic irony, a double move that, we'll see, reveals how even her first novel reflects on its own complicity in meeting market demand for celebratory multicultural fictions. The novel's metafictional mode reflects on this bind and twists its commodified status into an enabling factor by foregrounding its comic inauthenticity.

This satirical position on capitalist hybridity also acts as a foil against which Smith constructs an alternative "everyday hybridity" others have found refreshing, specifically in its portrayal of organic social change that unfolds within a narrative arc of postcolonial arrival.[19] The school, always a prominent site for the formation and testing of identities in the coming-of-age novel, features as a synecdoche for this pattern. Glenard Oak Comprehensive is a liberal lab for the promotion of diversity, and Smith mocks those institutional initiatives even as she appeals to and affirms their ideal effects within the larger narrative of social change structuring the novel as a whole. As a microcosm for late-twentieth-century multicultural London, the school figures as a site of an evolving hybridity, despite its institutional trappings, and as a distinct alternative to readily marketable representations of difference. Consider the following oft-quoted passage:

> This has been the century of strangers, brown, yellow, and white. This has been the century of the great immigrant experiment. It is only this late in the day that you can walk into a playground and find Isaac Leung by the fish pond, Danny Rahman in the football cage, Quang O'Rourke bouncing a basketball, and Irie Jones humming a tune. ... It is only this late in the day, and possibly only in Willesden, that you can find best friends Sita and Sharon, constantly mistaken for each other because Sita is white (her mother liked the name) and Sharon is Pakistani (her mother thought it best—less trouble). (*WT* 271)

Exemplifying the kind of taken-for-granted multiculturalism that pervades the novel and that readers celebrate, the passage is often read in isolation as evidence that Smith and her generation are freed from the burden of historical "roots" so anxiously present in an earlier and more contentious postcolonial fiction, or as a naïve fictional optimism that merely anticipates and affirms the hype that in many ways shaped the ensuing reception of *White Teeth*.[20] Outside the novel, Smith herself seems to have adopted a similar position. Initially, and perhaps basking in the glow of newfound celebrity status, Smith suggests a genuine optimism about the kind of social diversity depicted in *White Teeth*, telling one interviewer that "it's optimistic, I think," and another that a heterogeneous North London school, one like Glenard Oak, "is amazing," and imagines taking an outside observer and saying, "Look at this, look at how well it can work."[21] Again, I don't aim here to debunk the hype, nor merely to confirm it with yet another reading of this novel, but to suggest, instead, the rather simple premise that Smith here knowingly plays up to the ready-made tropes of postcolonial fiction as part of a self-authorizing gesture. Smith lays claim, not without the tempering force of irony, to a moment in literary and social history that the novel imaginatively wills into being; "It is only this late in the day" that a genuinely hybrid London society can be envisioned.

That vision is not isolated from history, however, and the novel's projections into the colonial past on which Glenard Oak's diversity program is structured further establishes Smith's self-conscious appeal to postcolonial tropes that aim to move beyond them and into a new fiction for multiculturalism. That utopian image of the playground has been prepared for, in other words, and Smith locates the origins of a present and future pluralism from within the dark and exploitative history of Victorian colonialism. Importantly, we get this history, again, in a narratorial aside. The school evolved out of the establishment of an experiment that the PTA promotional booklet describes as "a 'shelter, workplace, and educational institute'" founded by its namesake, Sir Edmund Flecker Glenard (*WT* 252). In what reads like a knowingly familiar introduction to Victorian colonial philanthropy, Glenard invested surplus funds from his Jamaican tobacco estate in the institute devoted to joining Jamaican religious devotion and an English work ethic, and had three hundred Jamaicans shipped to London to work side by side with English employees in "packaging Sir Edmund's cigarettes and taking general instruction from the Englishmen in the evening" (*WT* 254). After Glenard died in the 1907 Kingston earthquake, dwindling funds left the Jamaicans stranded, many of them dying of hunger or drifting into the English working class until some of those remaining were reduced to acting out their Jamaicanness as spectacle in the 1924 English Empire Exhibition (*WT* 255). One point of this historical aside is to stress that its story of colonial philanthropy gone wrong repeats itself in the form of late-twentieth-century institutional diversity initiatives. Caught smoking pot on school grounds, Irie, Millat, and Joshua Chalfen (privileged English-Jewish son of the geneticist Marcus) are summoned to the headmaster's office and introduced to a new program of "bringing children of disadvantaged or minority backgrounds into contact" with their more socially privileged peers under an institutional diversity initiative that, he hopes, will receive public funding (*WT* 256). Irie and Millat, second-generation children of immigrants, are the unwitting case studies in what amounts to a repetition of the old colonial model of bringing them "to work side by side" with those more socially and economically privileged.

Smith of course mocks this reinscription of colonial philanthropy in the dehistoricized form of institutional diversity, but the kind of organic multiculturalism she imagines comes about, in part, by way of this return to a colonial history of contingent migration and encounter. The novel tempers its irony, that is, with a narrative structure that posits a multicultural moment of arrival in the wake of its more internally fraught postcolonial predecessors. I will qualify this in a moment, but here we might argue that *White Teeth* participates, from within the commercial field of literary fiction, in bringing to the mainstream a model of postcolonial pluralism also advanced by cultural critics like Paul Gilroy. Just as Smith satirizes postcolonial fictions that came to appear amenable to consumerism in service to global capital, her depictions of "everyday hybridity" work to articulate a space for contemporary identities that are not reducible to either their market or institutional dimensions, promoting "forms of conviviality and intermixture," in Gilroy's words, "that appear to have evolved spontaneously and organically from the interventions of anti-racists and the ordinary multiculture of the postcolonial metropolis." And if this optimistic ordinariness pervades the novel's present, then Smith, like Gilroy, also looks to the past, to the "untapped heterological and imperial histories"—like the role of Jamaican migrants in shaping a diasporic London—"in the urgent service of contemporary multiculture and future pluralism."[22] Smith's first novel is something of a postmodern creole fiction in which "the past is prologue" and the future is plural.

This utopian pluralism as it's imagined in the novel is not, however, to be understood as somehow autonomous from or in opposition to the marketing of multicultural fiction written by celebrity authors. As a heavily mediatized and marketed literary commodity, one promoted on the logics of multicultural authenticity and the author as its representative, *White Teeth* cannot avoid complicity with the commercial conditions of hybridity it so stunningly satirizes. What's interesting about this, though, is that the novel demonstrates Smith's awareness of this bind, particularly insofar as it internalizes that commercial contradiction as a constitutive part of its own self-conscious play with form. The novel ends by self-reflexively synthesizing this twinned irony and complicity, at once commenting on and satirizing its own commodified status. The event is the televised millennial presentation of Marcus Chalfen's FutureMouse project and it assembles the novel's sprawling cast of characters across a vast social swath of generations, national origins, political persuasions, religions, and ethnicities, and the mediatized event itself, the narrator jokes, has been carefully prepared for by market research on preselected "focus groups." Smith both foregrounds the postmodern commonplace that all experience is pre-mediated while, at the same time, playing up to consumer demands and niche marketing on which the production and promotion of celebrity fiction depends. After describing the use of "focus groups" in aligning the spectacular presentation with the right "demographic pattern," and to bring the novel to its close, the narrator speculatively asks, "Is it young professional women aged eighteen to thirty-two who would like a snapshot seven years hence of Irie, Joshua, and Hortense sitting by a Caribbean sea …?" Having offered this happy projection into the future, though, the narrator immediately undercuts it as fantasy, saying, "But surely to tell these tall tales and others like them would be to speed the myth, the wicked lie, that the past is always tense and the future, perfect" (*WT* 448). Coming at the tail end of a novel structured on a "myth" of socially organic postcolonial arrival, here Smith both grants a happy ending tailored to targeted marketing groups while admitting her self-conscious concession to the same kind of market demands. Benjamin Bergholtz draws a similar conclusion, suggesting that "it is difficult to decenter *and* placate the preferences of focal groups at the same time, and Smith seems to openly admit that she is subordinating the former to the latter at novel's end" but, rather than signaling a hopeless nihilism, "the narrator's acknowledgment of her market-driven 'snapshot' is analogous to a 'wicked lie'—demonstrates" that the "rootless" postcolonial fantasies the novel sometimes indulges in are impossible.[23] Considering, as I have done here, that *White Teeth* is a commercial product appealing to a demand for multicultural optimism, its author does anything but disguise that fact. Smith knowingly appeals to a demand for more diverse representation within the field while cleverly reminding readers that the kind of multicultural representation the novel indulges in is, itself, a marketable fiction.

All of this makes Smith's first novel a stunning reflection on the intersections of commercial and aesthetic considerations in the market for multicultural fiction, and the novel thus anticipates the hype that helped usher it onto the best-seller and prize lists. Presenting a hopeful multicultural fiction that self-consciously concedes to a market demand for diversity is no bad thing. But reading *White Teeth* and its ironic embrace of multicultural marketing together with the promotion of its author provides a different picture of the field as a whole.

In other words, if we position this hybrid novel of postcolonial arrival at the intersection of the market promotion of Smith as a "master" of "mongrel" styles and hybrid identities, then the knowing irony that permeates *White Teeth* appears inseparable from a monopoly logic that seeks to capitalize on a manufactured diversity. Smith's stardom and her status as a distinctively representative figure for the new multiculturalism reflects, in part, what Mark Stein calls an issue of "containment" in the big book trade. "By concentrating disproportionately on a small number of recognizable voices, post-colonial polyphony is in danger of being muffled," and the potential "heterogeneity of [B]lack British cultural production" becomes reduced to a few select writers who can be marketed according to an institutionalized or "'official' multiculturalism."[24] This process of marketing the novel is most reductively reproduced in the author images accompanying the initial publications of *White Teeth*; as Dominic Head observes, the photo on the first hardback edition has Smith appearing "bespectacled and studious" under her "Afro hairstyle," while that on the subsequent paperback, with Smith in straight hair, suggests an identity that is at once "Asian" and "indeterminate."[25] Promoting Smith and her first novel according to this kind of essentialist logic of representative hybridity both affirms and contains that novel's ironic reflections on its market appeal, so that its hopeful depiction of an organically evolving multicultural Britain serves, in the mainstream literary establishment, "to articulate an ostensibly whole and organic community" that, as Sarah Brouillette argues, is based in questionable "assumptions about authenticity and representation." In this context, the twinned promotion of *White Teeth* and its author reproduces a logic of representation based on the exclusion of potential polyphony in the literary field, and exemplifies the problem that is already implied in *White Teeth*, in which "the language of cultural diversity entrenches the inequality it seems to want to erase."[26]

In the few years following the stellar success and optimistic reception of *White Teeth*, and in acknowledgment of the economic and institutional discourses of multiculturalism into which that novel was incorporated, Smith came to deplore the position of a "poster child for multiculturalism," and shifted to a defensive mode of critical reflection on the marketing of her novel and public persona.[27] In a statement directly contradicting her earlier musing on the successful functioning of a young migrant community, she says, "I didn't want the community in *White Teeth* to be representative of immigrants in England, that's not my job really, I'm not a politician."[28] Even more tellingly, on another occasion she openly rejects the labels ascribed to her work and public image, telling *Kansas City Star* interviewer Mark Eberhardt: "Before we begin, there are certain words that make the author very tired. These words are: multicultural, post-colonial, archetype, stereotype, post-millennial, literally, identity, zucchini." Smith's preemptive statement reveals an "author" who is perhaps genuinely exhausted by the popular "buzzwords," to use Lexi Stuckey's term, that conditioned her success.[29] In her drily comic conflation of "multicultural," "stereotype," and "zucchini," she clearly rejects the demands for a mainstream and marketable fiction of multicultural identities, a branding that Smith plays up to and precociously ironizes in her first novel. In the next section I want to couple this particular authorial intention with Smith's turn to a more established literary tradition, seeing her homage to Forster's *Howards End* as an exploration of the possibilities of a canonical, if marginalized, modernist writing for critically reflecting on the limits of institutionalized and market-mandated diversity initiatives playing out within the commercial literary field.

Institutions of Modernism and Multiculturalism

On Beauty (2005) extends Smith's signature mode of ironic detachment—in part exemplified by a modernist deployment of narrators who are "in total control of their narratives"—and the novel marks her first explicit engagement with the legacies of modernism.[30] The novel's open homage to Forster's *Howards End* is, on the one hand, a conservative reprisal of the earlier novel's structure and perspectival preoccupations. In this regard, *On Beauty* exhibits what Neil Levi calls a "fidelity to the institution of modernism" in contemporary literature that serves as a "conservative affirmation of what is."[31] In this case, the "what is" points to the settled and canonical status of Forster's liberal and marginal modernism, an inheritance that, in turn, affirms Smith's secure possession of established literary capital and her shared space on the university syllabus. There is something to be gained here, though, in that this transhistorical literary dialogue raises questions about the limits of institutionalized liberalism and how they are reproduced in elite literary fiction. Adapting Forster's own reflection on those limits—figured by him in the lower-middle-class Leonard Bast—to contemporary diversity initiatives that often reproduce structures of economic inequality, *On Beauty* extends Smith's critical negotiations with the conditions of her singular success while implicitly pointing to the inadequacy of this kind of modernist inheritance for transforming the social relations of literary production and reception.

Smith's homage is not merely a boilerplate imitation of Forster, so I won't belabor a comparative structural analysis here, as others have done.[32] Indeed, the correlations of character especially, but even of plot, are loosely worked out, and strike me not merely as an act of subtle "subversion," but also as something of a red herring.[33] It is worth noting, however, that the adaptation work that *On Beauty* conducts is importantly on the level of class difference and clashing ideologies among the major characters, and in this Smith extends Forster's reflection on a crisis of liberalism that can only acknowledge its exclusion of the working class without offering a resolution, social or aesthetic. The novel's homage turns the crisis of liberalism as it plays out in Forster's novel into a critical reflection on the blind spots and contradictions structuring contemporary liberal diversity initiatives in the academic setting, where they can obscure underlying economic inequality or, worse, reinscribe the social and material conditions of that disparity. Multiple plotlines bear this out. One of them concerns the contrast between Howard Belsey and Monty Kipps, both professors of art history and experts on Rembrandt. Howard, an out-of-date and underpublished critic of the economic conditions structuring artistic genius, and married to African American Kiki, half-heartedly believes in liberal diversity programs like Affirmative Action; Monty, a well-traveled Caribbean who enjoys an enviable international scholarly reputation, vehemently opposes such measures and, in light of his obvious privilege, is shown to be a rather vile hypocrite. As in Forster, Smith's novel is not interested in taking sides, but rather with probing the ethical implications of perspectival narrative. Smith allows each character's contradictions to play out and expose their flaws, ultimately suggesting that, as Dorothy Hale observes, "the perspectivalism that grounds the aesthetics of alterity also causes problems for its perfect realization."[34]

This is the updated Forsterian reading the novel invites, but those main plotlines also form the social and institutional ground on which the novel engages with class and diversity. Like Forster's Leonard Bast, Smith's Carl exhibits artistic aspirations, but as working-class subjects they are both denied entry to a social order that would provide material support for those endeavors. Focusing on Carl, as a marginal figure for Smith's metamodernist engagement with *Howards End*, stresses the role he inadvertently plays in exposing the contradictory dictates of contemporary liberalism, and it provides a sense of how Smith's novel pressures us to place more emphasis on the minor and socially marginalized figures in the literary tradition she occupies, providing as it does a mode of reading that is critical of the contradictory social conditions it reflects. Sharing Forster's liberal and aesthetic values, Smith also reprises the failed reconciliation at the heart of

Howards End in a way that registers the contradictory privilege and exclusion structuring institutional liberalism and its favored genre, the lyrical realist novel.

Carl's appearance in the novel comes rather late and is almost fortuitous, but his marginal status to the main plot is key to how the conservative Forsterian form of *On Beauty* dramatizes the conditions by which liberal privilege is structured on institutionalized exploitation. A Black spoken-word artist whose aesthetic sensibilities range from Mozart to hip-hop, Carl lacks the outward signs of formal education that define the private and public lives of the Wellington College community. Carl's presence exposes the unacknowledged privilege enjoyed by those comfortably occupying the academic sphere, particularly Claire Malcom, a white, quirky cosmopolitan and professor of poetry. Claire regularly meets with select students from her poetry class at The Bus Stop, "a Wellington institution" that draws a big crowd to its "bi-monthly Spoken Word nights."[35] Fully in her element and basking in the glow of student worship, it is at The Bus Stop that Claire and her groupies "discover" Carl. After two other performances, one in which a Black girl "rhymed brashly" about white patriarchy, and Levi, Howard Belsey's teenage son, raps out a critique of American imperialism in Haiti, Carl finally appears, "like Keats with a knapsack" (*OB* 220, 228, 230). The theme of his rap is an unwanted pregnancy and abortion, in which the male has no say, and his performance wins the night. The chapter ends with Claire presumptuously asking Carl, "Are you interested in refining what you have?" a question that elicits from Carl a rather nonchalant agreement to join Claire's poetry class at the white and well-to-do Wellington campus.

Thus begins Carl's narrative arc, but in the story of his brief passage through Wellington, Smith makes clear that his agency is an illusion governed by Claire's representative liberal voice and position. She recruits Zora, fittingly biracial and the daughter of Howard, to argue at an upcoming faculty meeting that Carl be admitted to her creative writing class without the usual protocols of applying. Claire cues Zora's participation, telling her "there are people in the college who don't approve of our class," especially the inclusion of "people like *Carl*," and that a student like Zora, who "has benefited from the experience of learning alongside these people," would make the most effective appeal. Her argument, in terms of cultural inclusion as institutional management, prompts the right response: "I mean, what are we *doing*,' asked Zora loudly, 'if we can't extend the *enormous* resources of this institution to people who need it? It's so *disgusting*" (*OB* 263). Zora's words in turn prompt Claire's own self-satisfied rhetorical rejoinder, itself a twisted blend of self-awareness and pandering. She would prefer to send Carl to make his own case, but depressing as it is, the truth is these people won't respond to an appeal to their consciences in any language other than Wellington language. ... And I don't mean to get overly dramatic here, but when I think of Carl, I'm thinking of someone who doesn't have a voice and who needs someone like you, who has a very powerful voice, to speak for him. I actually think it's that important. I also think it's a beautiful thing to do for a dispossessed person in this climate. Don't you feel that? (*OB* 263)

Of course we do. Ostensibly feeling for Carl's position among the "dispossessed," while possessed of a desire to help him "refine" his talents, Claire's rhetoric is at once genuine, typical, and laden with irony in Smith's handling. His talent clearly resides with his voice and confident ability to engage an audience, but over the course of Carl's part in the novel it's clear that his voice and fate are subject to Claire's direction and Wellington's discretion. Carl moves quickly from the role of guest student to a new position as musical archivist for the Black Studies Department—a dream job for him, a checked box for the college. The full brunt of the irony, though, comes from Zora, who conveniently occupies a position that straddles Wellington and Carl's outsider status. When she jealously accosts him while drunk at a party, and he points out the painful truth of liberal self-deception, she unknowingly expresses the material hypocrisy structuring any allowance of his presence on campus. "'You go to Wellington for a few months,'" she shouts, "'You hear a little gossip and you think you know what's going on? You think you're a Wellingtonian because they let you file a few records? You don't know a thing about what it takes to belong here'" (*OB* 417). Revising the miscommunication that leads to Leonard Bast's ousting from *Howards End*, Carl is instantly made a suspect in the case of a painting stolen from Carlene Kipps and, seemingly taking his own initiative, he quickly and quietly disappears from the novel. In his temporary presence and disappearance, Carl figures as a token in the school's diversity program; the cultural clout and veneer of inclusion that he was made to serve ultimately reinscribes his "dispossessed" position, while the economically and racially marginalized community he ostensibly represents remains unaltered and even beyond the representational scope of the novel.

If this narrative arc suggests a continued capacity for the novel to reflect on the limits of its own middle-class liberal tradition, it leaves open the question as to why Smith writes an homage to Forster to engage with the contradictions of contemporary multiculturalism. In his astute exploration of class evasion in contemporary British fiction, Lawrence Driscoll takes up this question, arguing that Smith's emphasis on a postmodern multiculturalism fails to resolve or move beyond the "liberal guilt" in Forster.[36] As Driscoll notes, Smith clearly assumes, with her readers, that affirmative action is "vital." But "Zora's voice works to undermine the stated desire of the novel," he argues, "which is to somehow include Carl in the middle-class world, but sadly no amount of multiculturalism will change the problems of inequality that are due to class."[37] Citing the examples of Belsey and Kipps, and seeing them as analogous to Smith's position, Driscoll rightly suggests that "multiculturalism is not a personal threat to" their jobs and that, "[in] fact, multiculturalism operates with, not against, the desires of their jobs and the market."[38] As I have shown in the cases of Amis, McEwan, and Rushdie, the evasion of real working-class issues is a central limitation to literary fiction, whether or not it is concerned with multiculturalism. And while I generally sympathize with the kind of readings Driscoll carries out, I think this one misses the point. For one, it implicitly assumes that Smith's job is to imagine a radical solution to inequality. Further, *On Beauty* is equally bent on exposing the contradictory idealisms and class-based privilege operating in the liberal academy, a crucial site for the value-making of her novels. It seems fair, in fact, to read the novel, with all its limitations, as critical of precisely the "fairytale" version of multiculturalism that Driscoll ascribes to it.[39] Smith exposes the way diversity initiatives fail to address underlying economic structures. And in doing so, we might say that she writes a counter-narrative to her own elevation as a selective representative of multiethnic and minority communities.

And yet, while Smith effectively shows the limits of an institutionalized multiculturalism as they operate in a privileged academic setting, *On Beauty* remains bound to the marketable version of the same problem. Reading the novel as an expression of "the anxiety of authorship" in light of Smith's own position as celebrated writer, public intellectual, and creative writing professor, Patrick Herald argues that her fictional "probing of the boundaries between campus cultures, and between the university and the world outside it, frees her from its grasp even as it ensnares the characters she writes."[40] But that position-taking (to adopt a term from Bourdieu) is articulated on a privileged fiction of autonomy, one afforded by both the tradition Smith engages and her position at the intersections of the market and the academy. Written by an author who is at least as prominent on the university syllabus as Forster, her dialogue with *Howards End* might be understood as an extension and consolidation of the canon. On the one hand, it participates in a "conservative affirmation of what is," in Neil Levi's observations on modernism as an institutional inheritance. At the same time, Smith's style even reproduces a Forsterian (and Jamesian) perspectival realism—a conventional literary aesthetic that has an established commodity value as "literary fiction," that nebulous market genre in which the cultural capital of the canon is sustained and consolidated as a mark of prestige.[41] While *On Beauty* exposes the failures of institutional liberalism, its formally conservative aesthetic also registers a failure to contest the social contradictions within the novelistic tradition on which Smith draws, in Forster's time and our own.

Modernism after Multiculturalism

By the time we get to *NW*, her most pronounced engagement with the legacies of modernism, we get a sense that, as David James notes, Smith "has been changing her mind about the kind of novel she wants to write."[42] The novel's cast of characters, primary and minor, carries forward Smith's celebrated capacity for creating a heavily stylized and densely localized multicultural fiction; and it presents the Northwest London of its title as a kaleidoscopic center of global capitalism and the diasporic dynamics of twenty-first-century cosmopolitanism and class anxiety. But it also reads as a deliberate alternative to a fashionably ironic multicultural fiction, subsuming its vivid cross-section of identities inflected by race, class, and gender to the shifting stylistic registers that the novel foregrounds. In its restless shuttling across stylistic modes, all loosely cohering under a decidedly detached narrative aesthetic, Smith seems to be struggling, within the pages of a single novel, to elude the fashionable demands of the literary market that have so conditioned her reception.

Smith's widely read essay "Two Directions for the Novel" signals something of this motivation. There, she pits lyrical realism's continued embrace of the "consoling myth" of the self's "beautiful plenitude"—a mark of "our ailing literary culture"—against Tom McCarthy's *Remainder*, an avant-garde novel that "empties out interiority entirely," insists on the "inauthenticity" of being, and poses a mode of resistance to the mainstream market for literary fiction.[43] While not necessarily a "drawing board" for her own novel, as one reviewer has suggested, Smith's bifurcated anatomy of the state of the novel nonetheless hints at her ambitions for *NW*, where alternations across a detached visual poetics and free indirect style mark a clear return to a detached strain of modernism by the privileging of style over the consoling plenitude of self, and show her struggling to wrestle free from the mainstream demands for lyrical realism and marketable multicultural themes.

Indeed, its fairly long first section, "Visitation," focuses on Leah Hanwell and her paralyzing ambivalence about work, marriage, and pregnancy, but foregrounds a stylistic fragmentation shored against the realist ruins of the post–welfare state and the subjective plenitude of "our ailing literary culture." The novel's opening lines abruptly announce this modernist ambition toward a detached and self-legislating style:

> The fat sun stalls by the phone masts. Anti-climb paint turns sulphurous on school gates and lampposts. In Willesden people go barefoot, the streets turn European, there is a mania for eating outside. She keeps to the shade. Redheaded. On the radio: I am the sole author of the dictionary that defines me. A good line—write it out on the back of a magazine.[44]

Alliterative visual poetics and an imagistic detachment subordinate psychological perspective to the novel's apparently self-legislating will to style. This nod to Joyce's impersonal narrator-artificer then seamlessly swoops into Leah Hanwell's minimalist stream-of-consciousness, which in turn quickly shifts to the fragmented aural intrusions into Leah's "Fenced in" solitude, rendered in a free indirect style where "a grim girl on the third floor screams Anglo-Saxon at nobody. … It ain't like that. Nah it ain't like that. Don't you start" (*NW* 3). Point of view is refined into a kind of narrative autogenesis, while Leah's near mechanical mental reproduction of the mass media appeal to being the "sole author" of one's definition underscores a "fenced in" consciousness that is tenuous, subject to the controlled free indirect style that takes in the intrusive and anonymous voice of urban cacophony. From its beginning, then, *NW* echoes a familiar modernist style, its narrator situated above or beyond or behind its handiwork and distilling, in this case, a self-referential aesthetic effect out of the mundane material stuff of an alienating contemporary London.

But if *NW* marks an explicit return to modernism as an alternative to fashionable multiculturalism and lyrical realism, it also prompts us to reflect on the value of an institutionalized modernism and to question its historically latent designs on transforming our expectations of commercial fiction. The novel's reception, we should note, has been divided along similar lines; and upon its 2012 publication, reviewers and critics were quick to reflect on the Joycean legacy it clearly bears out. David James highlights the novel's "accretive presentation" of shifting stylistic registers that subordinates "the connective sinew between diegetic events" to "the punctilious yet oblique manner of their description," to argue that Smith engages a metamodernist alternative to her previous successes with lyrical realism.[45] Joyce Carol Oates similarly praises the novel for its "boldly Joycean appropriation," suggesting that its alternating stream-of-consciousness, free indirect style, and directly reported speech reprise those defamiliarizing techniques for their relevance in depicting the epistemological flux of global capitalism as it impinges on the localized contemporary setting.[46] David Marcus usefully qualifies these generic accounts of Smith's metamodernism, noting that "instead of Joyce's roving and associative stream of consciousness, Smith's is empirical, cartographic," attenuated by the depleted public planning of the post–welfare state and the constraints that neoliberal capitalism exercises over subjective plenitude.[47] Other reviewers have questioned the relevance of the novel's late or metamodernist appropriations. Christian Lorentzen reads it as a "dip into the modernist toolkit," an emulation of Joycean fragmentation that at time borders on pastiche, while Adam Mars-Jones sees the novel as caught between confidence and uncertainty, its first section in particular "defined by its resistance to genre, by what it doesn't want to be," but he adds that "the touches of dilute Joycean play are less like new ways of looking at the world than mildly adventurous ways of organising a narrative."[48] Despite differences of opinion, these conflicting accounts agree that *NW* boldly engages in an act of metamodernist appropriation, but without asking how such a strategy is conditioned by a contemporary market for modernism where its institutional legacies and its historical potential for aesthetic innovation continue to be negotiated.

In other words, *NW* presses us to address evaluative questions concerning contemporary literary production and the value or prestige that modernism affords, not only to celebrity writers but to everyone invested in sustaining its cultural capital, from editors and publishers to academic critics and mainstream reviewers. If her emulation of modernist aesthetics amounts to a self-legislating drive to explore new horizons of possibility from within the commercial sphere of its production, then that remains a powerful mark of class privilege, one that depends on and extends modernism's own vexed strategies for articulating an autonomous aesthetic in the face of the social and material conditions that enable or constrain them. If the novel makes a bid for stylistic autonomy from lyrical multicultural fiction, it also depends on the accumulated cultural capital of modernism's legacy. At the same time, though, *NW* implicates that privileged claim to autonomy in the pressing material and social conditions of inequality, asking us to question our own abiding investment in modernism's legacy as a formerly autonomous bearer of cultural and economic capital.

If the first page of the novel announces Smith's "boldly Joycean appropriation," a kind of mimicry of the modernist master of mimesis, then this opening bid alerts us to the cumulative play with different stylistic registers that are nevertheless organized by Smith's detached and impersonal narrative aesthetic. And while it may be that "every page of *NW* exudes a will-to-experiment," as

David James writes, that will is most pronounced in its longish and fragmentary first section.[49] For example, as a fatally bored Leah zones in and out of her boss's bureaucratic monologue on the neoliberal necessity of "efficiency" in managing public services, Smith disrupts the alternating flow of direct speech and free indirect style to mediate Leah's visual apprehension of the speaker's mouth, rendering it into a concrete imagistic poem set off on the page:

> Tooth gold tooth tooth gap tooth tooth tooth
> TONGUE
> Tooth tooth tooth tooth chipped tooth filling (*NW* 35)

If Smith alludes to the malleable toothy trope of her first novel, here she reduces it to a visual echo of Joycean hyperrealism. Leah's perception focalizes the narrative, but rather than featuring as a mark of a distinct subjectivity, it becomes distilled down to a detached and free-floating concrete image that preemptively disrupts a demand for lyrical progression or plenitude.

Elsewhere Smith stretches her detached and impersonal styling beyond focalization altogether, where jarring shifts in style can generate, for example, conflicting epistemologies of the city as a localized nexus of global capitalism and late modernity. Turning from Leah as a central subject produced out of a disjointed style, chapter 9 of the same section reproduces what appears to be the objective walking routes "From A to B"—Yates Lane to Bartlett Avenue in NW— from Google Maps, with the directions set off in columns and followed by the qualifier that unforeseen events "may cause conditions to differ from map results" (*NW* 41). In its emphasis on the materiality of the text, devoid of a human user, the odd appearance may be designed to hint at the distinction between virtual and lived realities, but as Wendy Knepper points out, the directions themselves are also false, including parallel streets that would lead nowhere so that, by extension, the chapter refers to itself, to the deceptive fictionality that trumps the demands of realistic representation.[50] The text interrupts and implicitly parodies a reading practice trained in realism. This affectless materiality is immediately followed by a shift to an immersive stream-of-consciousness prose poem whose sense of moving through the same space takes in the cacophonous sensory vitality of the city as center of global capital and commodity circulation. Multisensory experience is aestheticized into a feverish play with prose possibilities as it moves through the "sweet smell of the hookah, couscous, kebab, exhaust fumes of a bus deadlock," its flowing and fragmented style momentarily alighting on a catalog of international newspapers, black market phone deals, global banking and brand name fashion icons (*NW* 42–3). Echoing the defocalized cinematic techniques we find in *Ulysses*, but subjected to a radically accelerated narrative pace, Smith forges a prose poetry of frantic sensory rhythms, underscoring the decentered and depersonalized flow of international capital and multiethnic local identities. Instances like these mark a clear break from lyrical realism and its consolations of authentic selfhood, reprising a Joycean technique that creates its own plenitude in and of style, itself a stream-of-consciousness without a singular focalizing subject. The highly localized sensory impressions of the city are rendered in an impersonal aesthetic, and the accelerated narrative pace and disorienting focus alert us to the latent potential of modernist style to capture and compress something of the anonymous experience of the global flows of capital.

The will to style that Smith adopts here points to a paradox that reaches back to a modernist impersonality while, at the same time, it raises questions about the function of a formerly defamiliarizing literary technique in the contemporary commercial field. Consider two conflicting takes on the stream-of-consciousness treatment of Leah. Oates suggests that "perhaps it's because we come to know Leah through her meandering stream-of-consciousness thoughts that she remains indistinct and improbable, and not sharp-edged."[51] Christian Lorentzen takes a more critical tack. After cataloguing in detail the narrative contours through which Smith presents Leah's inner life, he concludes that it amounts to "thin stuff, and it's hard to tell whether Smith has kept Leah's story simple, even clichéd, as a delivery device for her modernist repertoire, or if the repertoire has gotten the better of the characters."[52] Stream-of-consciousness always revels in fragmented indistinction, and yet I think we do well to take Lorentzen's criticism seriously, not to grade Smith's literary talent but to ask how this particular Joycean legacy squares with a mainstream market for a selectively received model of modernist aesthetics. Maybe, that is, Smith's point is to foreground that modernist repertoire, so that the pared-down and fractured sense of interiority reminds us that, at least since modernism, characters are always fashioned out of textual designs assembled by the author or narrator. Interiority in the novel has always been the privileged reserve of bourgeois consciousness, and the shifting stylistic registers that *NW* plays with serve to expose that conventionality and to question the "consoling myth of our beautiful plenitude" by way of a mimetic return to an impersonal modernist aesthetic.[53]

This flattening of subjectivity under an impersonal style is oddly apparent in the novel's longest section, "Host," which provides something of the backstory of Leah and Keisha/Natalie's lifelong friendship, the connective sinew between main characters, and features as a mini-*Bildungsroman* of Natalie's transition from the child of a working-class Caribbean family through her university days and culminating in her status as a successful corporate lawyer and perfect host. In this more traditionally realist section, Smith trades those earlier Joycean flourishes for alternating third-person and free indirect style, all organized by titled and thematized subsections apparently modeled on the "Aeolus" chapter of *Ulysses*. But if "Host" seems openly "modeled" on Joyce's newspaper scene, with titles that similarly "joke, pun, allude, or explain" (as Lorentzen suggests), it also flattens that appropriation into an ironic reflection on neoliberal subjectivity as conditioned by economic rationalization and the dubious promises of meritocracy. As a child, Keisha's young consciousness is thoroughly interpellated to the ubiquity of brand names—supposedly significant moments in her individuation are comically riffed by titles such as "Evian" and "Sony Walkman"—and yet, in a neat reprisal of Joyce, Smith pushes commodity fetishism to its limits by aestheticizing it: "That obscure object of desire" introduces the semidetached description of "the red and white air technology of the Greek goddess of victory," effectively obscuring the object itself (Nike shoes) under a mock iconicity (*NW* 211). "The sole author," an echo of Leah's earlier stream-of-consciousness, introduces Natalie's "self-invention," her coming-of-age efforts to break with the nets of class and religion coupled with a newfound "faith" in "politics and literature, music, cinema"; but that thin promise of self-authorization becomes fitted to the demand to "*Claim your future*," the promotional tag on an energy drink provided at a job fair for aspiring bankers and lawyers (*NW* 247, 253).

Comprising fragments of varying lengths and narrative pacing, the entire section is organized around impressionable "events" within a cumulative and prosaic style in which the "plenitude" of a self amounts to an unfulfilled and alienated Natalie, her neoliberal "self-invention" leading to social subjectivity as "an ensemble of entrepreneurial and investment capital," in Wendy Brown's terms.[54] So while the novel has elicited a number of comparisons to Joyce, the passages devoted to Natalie's story seem more indebted to Woolf's use of free indirect style aimed at a critical reflection on self-satisfied liberal privilege. As Natalie and her husband Frank brunch with a group of like-minded professionals whose lives reflect the gentrification going on around them, fragments of direct speech and narrative commentary flow into and out of each other, so the question of how much to tip is followed by the narrator's clipped comment: "Global consciousness. Local consciousness. Consciousness." The private domain of modernist consciousness bleeds into an ironic reflection on the power of property values: a £1 million house on the park, the narrator slyly interjects, doesn't signify the "brick and mortar" of "these poky terraced houses," but rather "the distance the house puts between you and Caldwell" (*NW* 299–300). Plenitude equals economic acquisition and attention to property values, which Smith presents as a false autonomy based on social exclusion and smug complicity.

All of this makes for a cleverly detached reflection on concerns with neoliberal austerity, liberal guilt, and the polarizations of wealth following the 2008 global economic crash. But it also registers and negotiates some of the authorial anxieties about commercial complicity and the question of literary autonomy I have been tracing throughout this book. While the cumulative events narrated in Natalie's section ultimately reveal "a terrifying emptiness at the heart of her story," she also shares a number of telling character traits with her author.[55] Superficially, Keisha/Natalie shares Smith's socioeconomic background, Caribbean parentage, and the merits and privileges of a university education. But Smith is also consistently detached from her creation, especially when the character most resembles something of the author. Burdened by a self-conscious sense of her own "inauthenticity," at one point Natalie features as a would-be author of a familiar lyrical multicultural fiction:

> Walking down Kilburn High Road Natalie Blake had a strong desire to slip into the lives of other people. It was hard to see how this desire could be practicably satisfied or what, if anything, it really meant. "Slip into" is an imprecise thought. Follow the Somali kid home? Sit with the old Russian lady at the bus-stop outside Poundland? Join the Ukrainian gangster at his table in the cake shop? A local tip: the bus-stop outside Kilburn's Poundland is the site of many of the more engaging conversations to be heard in the city of London. You're welcome. (*NW* 334)

Oates calls this "a convincing account of the fiction writer's predilection," and it certainly suggests Smith's celebrated ability to "slip into" a range of experiences, while also hinting at an all-but-suppressed anxiety about authorial authenticity. Any hint of autobiographical anxiety, though, is dispensed with by Smith's unrelenting narratorial detachment from her character. She is almost always referred to as "Natalie Blake," a distancing formality that reminds us of the author's act of fabrication, an effect that is here underscored by the narrator's knowing intrusion, her tip on locating authenticity followed by the self-satisfied "You're welcome." Smith does not indulge in the overt kinds of authorial self-fashioning that Amis, McEwan, and Rushdie are variously prone to; rather, the detached presentation of Natalie participates in a long history of free indirect style as a novelistic convention. As Elaine Freedgood argues in her revisionary study of Victorian realism, in free indirect style "the narrator splits away from [her] creation, giving us the characters we think of as people—even though they are made up of textual bits and pieces that the narrator knits into sentences" to produce that narrator as "a superhuman being" asserting her control.[56] If realism works by obscuring this conventional effect, then *NW*, appropriating its modernist ramifications, lays it bear so that stylistic detachment seems designed both to assert narrative control and, more importantly, to distance Smith's authorship from the kind of economic rationalism that her characters are subject to.

The fact that so many reviewers and critics (myself included) feel compelled to comment on this novel's metamodernist aspirations is enough to suggest, I think, that *NW*'s stylistic strategies rely on and appeal to our own modernist credentials. Smith's impersonal aesthetic offers a refreshing and challenging alternative to lyrical multicultural perspectival fiction, but in so overtly dipping "into the modernist toolkit" to support that move, *NW* also participates, along with its critics, in sustaining the institutional reception of modernism as a brand name and mark of literary capital and social privilege. Alys Moody, for example, has recently argued that a contemporary return to a detached modernist style constitutes, for novelists and critics, a "selective memory" clustered around a narrow canon that reflects an academic consolidation and contraction of modernism's aesthetic legacy. "In this sense," Moody writes, "the aestheticized indifference of contemporary writing is … a retrospective one, filtered through the legacy of modernism's reception in the university." And that selective reception plays out in the redefinitions of modernism that take place in its contemporary market formations; as Claire Barber-Stetson suggests, "this is how it consolidates an audience and thus sustains itself. … The concept constitutes and is constituted by the people and texts that participate in the industry; the more participate, the more activity takes place off which certain parties can profit."[57] This profitability is, of course, something I have stressed throughout this book. If impressionism once reshaped the writing of perception and consciousness but has since been filtered through institutionalization and consolidated into mainstream fiction by prestigious publishing firms, as Jesse Matz argues, then it might be that a style of studied and aesthetic detachment reflects a similar market trend. As a product of the consolidated publishing industry, *NW* clearly appeals to a modernist prestige that is also sustained by our critical and institutional investments in its legacy at the intersection of cultural and economic capital.

And yet, and while I think *NW* revels in its "boldly Joycean appropriation" in a way that reflects and appeals to that modernist inheritance as a mark of consolidated cultural capital in the market for literary fiction, I want to argue that it is on the level of form that the novel enacts a more compelling and critical kind of metamodernist writing, one that prompts us to reflect on the privilege that our investments in modernism's legacy uphold. Formally embedded between the detached Joycean poetics of the first section and the ironic distancing of the third, "Guest" narrates the last day in the life of the working-class recovering addict, Felix Cooper. The section deviates from the experiments in stylistic detachment that the rest of the novel foregrounds, settling instead for a "conventional realist narration" in which "the representation of the external world is accompanied by a portrayal of the subjective world of the focalizer."[58] And if Smith's detached aesthetic elsewhere subordinates a demand for consoling plenitude to impersonal style, this is the only section that seems concerned with eliciting sympathy for her character, the novel's thematic and formal "guest."

As a minor character and a socially marginalized figure, Felix is doubly dispossessed. Each of these effects comes together, for example, in depictions of his disoriented relation to the networks of public transport that otherwise provide a spatial and thematic link among the city's diverse and disparate populace. Consider the matter-of-fact depiction of Felix's entry into the Underground: "Mind the gap. Felix stepped in the second carriage from the end and looked at a tube map like a tourist, taking a moment to convince himself of details no life-long Londoner should need to check" (*NW* 135). The same experience is repeated later, shortly before the pointless altercation that will lead to his death: "Felix inched deeper into the carriage. He gripped the safety rail. He considered the tube map. It did not express his reality. The center was not 'Oxford Circus' but the bright lights of Kilburn High Road" (*NW* 190). Felix's affective detachment or unbelonging in these moments is, of course, a result of the narrative's focalization, inverting the novel's detached aesthetic through its proximity to his lived experience. It marks a stark contrast to the earlier use of a collective stream-of-consciousness and its heavily stylized immersion in the city's affective sensorium. If this section otherwise disrupts the novel's more modernist ambitions, its return to a more conventional realism underscores Felix's dispossessed status, so that his death is at once presented as statistically normal and a source for readers' sympathetic response.

Felix's story is rendered in a lyrical social realism that sets it off from the rest of the novel, and it might be tempting to argue that Smith brackets its focus on social inequality in such a way that highlights the stylistic panache her metamodernism aspires to. On such a reading "Guest" and the utterly contingent death it concludes with would fit a containment strategy, its sociological realism subordinated to the dominance of modernist aesthetics. But I think it also helps to throw into question the self-legislating aesthetics elsewhere in the novel and hint that our literary and critical investments in modernism's cultural and economic capital are fully the reserve of class privilege. Rather than merely containing this narrative of systemic social inequality, Smith reprises a vexed modernist preoccupation with autonomy which, in Andrew Goldstone's words, is "sensitive to the ways autonomous form carries troubling social entanglements along with it."[59]

News of Felix's death repeatedly punctuates the novel and contributes to its recursive form, itself a modernist technique that mediates social inequality and a questionable claim to aesthetic autonomy. Warping throughout the novel's chronology, news of Felix's death twice interrupts the strained intimacy between Leah and Michel. On their way to Natalie's dinner party, wine bottle in hand, Michel is randomly threatened near a public phone box, and a stereotypical Felix figure intrudes into Leah's anxious consciousness: "From where Leah stands anyway it is still all dumb show, hand gestures and primal frowns, and of course some awful potential news story that explains everything except the misery and the particulars: one youth knifed another youth, on Kilburn High Road" (*NW* 91). The general reference foreshadows Felix's death, while the free indirect style casually reminds us that "the misery and the particulars" of violence stemming from austerity and inequality are elided by the mass media and are all but incomprehensible to a middle-class consciousness. The next day, as Leah and Michel attend a Carnival pre-party at a friend's flat, Smith's strangely iterative and detached style—"Michel goes to help in the kitchen. Leah accepts a rum and Coke and sits in a corner chair"—is suddenly disrupted by the television announcement that the festivities have been "marred by reports of a fatal stabbing" along with the bare "particulars": Felix Cooper, "32 years old" who moved from "the notorious Garvey House project" to Kilburn "in search of a better life" (*NW* 104). Later, in the protracted stream-of-consciousness narrative that tracks a disoriented Natalie wandering the streets after her split with Frank, she first observes a 98 bus, one of the final images Felix saw before dying, before her route is blocked by police cars at the entry to Albert Road (*NW* 359–60). Finally, and as the novel winds down to its grim anti-epiphany, Natalie sees a photograph of Felix and his family in the local newspaper, and faintly recognizes "a depth of misery" in their faces that compels her gaze to keep "returning to the same block of text, trying to squeeze a little more meaning from it." While she vaguely recognizes him "as a local," she also finds she is unable "to say anything else definitive about him" (*NW* 392–4).

Smith uses a recursive pattern centered on a local figure whose appearance and death feature as little more than a mildly disturbing statistic or a source of uncanny recognition, thereby implicating the novel's main characters in the social inequality that is otherwise set off from their sections. Their affective detachment underscores their relative insularity from local poverty and violence. And this recursive structure is perhaps the most convincing adaptation of the latent social implications of an impersonal modernist form. Think, for example, of the recurring reports of Septimus Smith's suicide in Woolf's *Mrs. Dalloway*, the contrasting reactions among characters producing an eerie sense of ethical connection across a spectrum of social class. As a governing formal device in *NW*, the recurring presence of Felix's murder "makes apparent," to borrow from Goldstone again, "a relationship between aestheticist form and social inequality," or that between "a 'dominant' aesthetic form and social domination."[60] Just as the novel helps make this relation apparent through characters' affective detachment, it also implicates the novel's detached modernist aesthetic—as a residual mark of an older claim to formal autonomy—in the inequality that the corporate publishing industry and a culture of celebrity perpetuate and disavow.

Embedding its metamodernist appropriations of a self-legislating style in a recursive form attentive to unequal social relations, *NW* also prompts us to reflect on our own abiding critical investments in modernism's contemporary legacy as one that is fraught with institutional privilege. Since her first novel, Smith's major fiction has creatively and critically reflected on its necessary complicity in its own commodification. And *NW*, her most overtly metamodernist work, at once flaunts and questions its own reanimation of an institutionalized modernism that continues to circulate as a resource of cultural prestige and economic capital. This raises additional implications about our own critical investments in a contemporary market for modernism and celebrity fiction. On the one hand, *NW* contributes to a recurring interest in "the ethics of form," implicitly positing its performance of stylistic "singularity" on the "alterity" of the economically excluded, thereby answering to Derek Attridge's call for "the demand of the literary work as the demand of the other."[61] As such, *NW* exemplifies a brand of metamodernism concerned with exploring the latent social and ethical implications of its historical antecedents. At the same time, though, this ethical gesture comes from a self-conscious position of literary privilege, asking us, too, to acknowledge and question our investment in sustaining modernism's experimental legacies as conditioned by corporate branding and the increasingly polarized social relations structuring contemporary capitalist society. In other words, the metamodernist dialogue that Smith engages in the novel's diegesis should also prompt us to engage in a metacritical reflection on the rebranding of an institutionalized modernism in the market for best-selling books and celebrity authors. If the novel registers a continuity with historical modernism, it does so primarily on the level of style and form, as a source of inspiration for experiment. That renewal, though, is one that requires attention to a historical dissonance marked by the structural transformations to the literary industry and its corollary culture of celebrity. As both an experimental metamodernist text and a privileged cultural commodity, *NW* forces us to rethink aesthetic autonomy as a fetishistic form of privilege in the commercial field, and to attend to the troubling social and ethical implications of its production.

6

Marginal Literary Values, or, How Eimear McBride and Anna Burns Reframe Irish Modernism

In this book I have shown how some of the most critically acclaimed and commercially successful authors of contemporary fiction align their work with the legacies of modernism—whether to affirm, repudiate, or extend its influence—while capitalizing on its institutionalized value as a sign of literary prestige. As we've seen, modernism's formal and institutional legacies afford contemporary authors with a wide range of strategies for negotiating market constraints and literary celebrity, expanding the horizons of formal possibility, and distinguishing their work from mass market genre fiction. These contemporary engagements with modernism as both a source for authorial self-fashioning and an inspiration for critical reflection on the social and material conditions of literary production repeatedly return us to the vexed question of aesthetic autonomy, perhaps the most pronounced and problematic inheritance of modernism's accumulated cultural capital when seen in the context of the twinned commercialization of literature and celebrity culture. If modernism historically sought to create a market for literary experiment within a "shadow economy" of publicity and promotion that could be seen to operate alongside the instant commodification of mass cultural production, then by the time of the conglomerate era its established canonicity has come to circulate within a large-scale field of commercial production, its symbolic value sustained by celebrity authorship and the economy of prestige in which a claim to authorial and aesthetic autonomy now functions according to the logic of the brand name.

This chapter diverges from my forgoing case studies, and focuses on the work of Eimear McBride and Anna Burns, experimental writers who extend and contest a modernist Irish tradition and who have only recently emerged from the margins of commercial literary production into mainstream visibility. It may seem odd, I should note right away, to place McBride and Burns together when considering the geopolitical differences that mark their respective backgrounds and fictional settings: while both currently reside in England, Burns grew up in Belfast during the tumultuous peak of the Troubles, while McBride was born in Liverpool, raised in the rural west of the Republic, and later moved to London to study drama. If we wholly deny ongoing consequences of Irish partition, we risk making an uncritical assumption about ethnocentric identity that belies the stark political and cultural differences between the two Irelands. McBride and Burns, however, reflect broadly shared literary and cultural traditions of Irish modernism and, as Paige Reynolds observes, "modern Irish cultural production has always moved across national and ethnic boundaries," giving its vitality an "international character" that "was long typified by European exile."[1]

That said, while the prize-winning novels I analyze here have enjoyed an international reception and circulation—based in part on their stylistic affiliations with modernist experiment—their settings, themes, and cultural concerns are decidedly local. McBride's *A Girl Is a Half-Formed Thing* is set in the rural Republic during the 1980s and 1990s, and Burns's *Milkman* during the nightmarishly protracted violence of 1970s Belfast. McBride and Burns also bear out a different set of relations to modernism, both as a historical formation and a contemporary legacy for new experimental styles and forms that alert us to the varying "contingencies of historical reception."[2] McBride's debut novel, as many reviewers were quick to note, channels the broken syntax of Beckett in its stream-of-consciousness style, overtly writes back to Joyce's quintessentially modernist *Bildungsroman*, *A Portrait of the Artist as a Young Man*, and specifically reframes the latter's heroic masculine aesthetics around the voice of the female embodiment that it suppresses. Burns's *Milkman* seems unburdened by such an anxiety of influence, and deploys a digressive stream-of-consciousness that destabilizes the constrictions of patriarchal structures, both in its fictional past and its present. As David James asks in a related context, "In what terms can such distinct novelists be brought together so that their incongruities are as edifying as their complementarity. And how might they then help us to recognize that the modernist 'inheritance a writer receives,' in Sarah McKibben's phrase, is 'not fixed but subject to challenge' because 'the possibilities to be extracted are not finite but unbound'?"[3] James here usefully embeds an answer within his question, and we'll see that for Burns and McBride the formal legacies emanating out from the history of Irish modernism are neither a template nor an iconic model, but constitute instead a tradition of remaking the marginal value of literature whose contemporaneity requires an ongoing dialogic challenge to and within that tradition itself.

One of my aims here is to tease out the productive "incongruities" and "complementarity" of these two authors, and to situate their distinctive styles and geopolitical positions within the larger sphere of an evolving and hybrid canon of modern Irish literature. For one, the work of reframing modernism and its will to aesthetic autonomy in the novels of Burns and McBride is gendered, and the diegesis of the fiction and its marginal relation to the conglomerate field of production signal the possibilities for extending and radically contesting a predominately male Irish canon. *A Girl* and *Milkman* are fundamentally antidevelopmental, resisting the heroics of masculine literary authority, and they each reflect a vision of the "backwardness" that David Lloyd and Paige Reynolds align with the modernist potentialities of postcolonialism as it's understood in the vexed historical and political context of Ireland, north and south. For Lloyd, a major political aim of postcolonial thought is to "represent the possibility of as yet unexhausted alternatives to the unidirectional progress of modernity," giving a futural aspect to Irish modernism and its complex and evolving relationship to the history of colonialism.[4] And a recapitulation of an incomplete Irish modernism "testifies to the enduring potentiality of modernist forms, themes, and practices," as Reynolds writes, for a gendered literary politics in which "old modernist form provides women writers with a valuable new tool for the critique of abusive patriarchal structures and practices."[5] In this sense, reading McBride and Burns together reveals a rich terrain for an emerging body of experimental writing by Irish women who creatively and critically reframe the gendered restrictions of the political and literary traditions they inherit.

Finally, McBride and Burns take up distinctively gendered engagements with modernism's experimental legacies from the margins of mainstream literary fiction and thus provide a compelling rationale for placing their work at the conclusion of this book. As I elaborate in more detail at the end of this chapter, both novels were first picked up by independent publishers based in the UK and, following their respective reception of prestigious prizes, were bought and repackaged in the United States (again, by independents) with the financial support of public and corporate sponsorship. Acknowledging these sources of financing in the front and back matter of these novels, when read as part of the text, amounts to what Paul Crosthwaite calls "highlighting its own commodity status."[6] But in the cases I take up here, that status is not merely a sign of the market's complete co-opting of the potential value of experimental writing, but rather a post facto material supplement to a claim to literary autonomy that precedes its absolute commodification. In reframing and destabilizing a masculine Irish tradition, McBride and Burns create self-legislating fictions of formal autonomy that precede the corporate support that their novels came to acquire. Whereas the commercially consecrated authors I address in previous chapters take up a modernist legacy in ways that make clear the convertibility of its cultural capital into prestige and financial rewards, we turn here to an emerging engagement from the literary and economic margins, in which "low financial returns" and "relative autonomy," to paraphrase Alys Moody, mark a deliberate expansion of the potential, latent within historical modernism, to momentarily elude the constraints of commercial publishing.[7]

These unique material conditions of publication shed light on an additional commensurability between the novels, signaling a space for a genuinely resurgent modernism outside the conglomerate commercial operations that have dominated contemporary literary culture. These novels create experimental aesthetic forms to advance a relative autonomy both from the canon they rework and the commercialized forms of a received modernist legacy circulating within mainstream cultural production. Both authors, again, revive the potentialities of Irish modernism in ways that elude, if only momentarily, a predictable market branding of modernism's institutionalized status. The geopolitical, generational, and formal incongruities of their work will yield a rich sense of the untapped literary-historical potential of a modern Irish tradition that remains stubbornly marginal even as it reflects its canonical position within "the world republic of letters."[8] Writing a gendered politics of literary autonomy from the margins of mainstream literary publishing, McBride and Burns point to a new horizon in the market for modernism.

McBride's Metamodernism

A Girl comes ready-made with its own widely disseminated myth of modernist commitment and autonomy. McBride refused to capitulate to market demand for autobiographical "misery memoirs," and struggled for nine years to find a publisher until the independent Galley Beggar Press picked it up.[9] This twinned struggle and commitment plays in nicely to the heroic story of Joyce's difficulty in getting *Dubliners* published (although his problems concerned threats of censorship and liability rather than the market constraints for "difficult" form that McBride faced). More to the point, the novel explicitly channels the trinity of Yeats, Joyce, and Beckett, especially its middle figure, in a strong example of "metamodernist writing [that] incorporates, adapts, reactivates and complicates the aesthetic prerogatives of an earlier cultural moment."[10] This appeal to an established Irish modernism was quickly picked up in the literary press. For example, Alice O'Keefe writes that McBride "set out to pick up the experimental modernist baton from James Joyce and Samuel Beckett, and she has done just that."[11] Such reviews, while usefully revealing a renewed general interest in the afterlives of Irish modernism, are less concerned with close analysis to support those findings than they are with promoting and sanctioning the value of new work, and one result is a kind of pigeonholing of McBride's novel into a restrictive recapitulation of an established historical canon, one that is tied "firmly" to its historical male predecessors.

Academic criticism, which moves at a comparatively glacial pace, has extended and complicated this reception, giving rise to a mini-debate that raises further questions about the viability of modernism's legacies for contemporary writing, particularly with regard to the politics of gender. In an insightful early essay, Paige Reynolds brings close attention to the modernist form of the novel, specifically its response to Joyce's *Portrait*, to bear on its sexually traumatic content and its effects on readers. McBride's novel, she argues, "uses modernist form to remind us of our alienation and distance from her protagonist's experiences. ... The armature of modernist intertextuality provides readers protection from identifying too closely with the protagonist's abnegation."[12] This identification of form with containment prompted a rigorous counterresponse from Ruth Gilligan. Following James and Seshagiri's model of a metamodernism that balances "attention to the textures of narrative form and an alertness to the contingencies of historical reception," Gilligan criticizes Reynolds's praise for *A Girl*'s formal dialogue with modernism, which she sees as upholding "a fixed, finalised construct that exists and can be added and removed at will."[13] This complaint applies, as well, to Reynolds's otherwise hopeful argument that "old modernist form provides women writers with a valuable new tool for the critique of abusive patriarchal structures and practices."[14] In what seems to be an implicit response to these jabs, Reynolds later refines the terms and methods of her first reading, and argues that *A Girl* "retools Joyce's modernist epiphany to launch a feminist critique" of contemporary sexual abuse, a move that exceeds mere formal parroting.[15] Reynolds identifies in McBride's novel a pressing example of contemporary writing that "can move us beyond the satisfactions of our own virtuosity" as readers and "expose the social and political implications of using modernism after modernism," specifically a use that "cannily resurrects the legacy of modernism to enable a uniquely potent critique of childhood sexual abuse."[16] Beyond her argument with Reynolds, Gilligan is critical of the marketing and reception of McBride's first novel, arguing that its alignment with a male modernist tradition adds to the ongoing marginalization of experimental women writers.[17]

I want to expand on the key terms of this debate and to ask how *A Girl* both begs and complicates its reception as model of the so-called "Joycean legacies." In a wide-ranging essay collection of that title, contributors explore the myriad ways in which writers have felt compelled to address the inescapable shadow of Joyce and the Joyce industry, especially among Irish writers. As Derek Attridge argues elsewhere, "we are indirectly reading Joyce … in many of our engagements with the past half century's serious fiction," a point that Martha Carpentier extends in her introduction to the volume: Joyce's "cultural pervasiveness," she writes, "results in a challenging inheritance for the creative writer, one that is oppressive as well as inspirational."[18] And writers frequently negotiate the binary terms of this inheritance, as Attridge argues, by appealing to one or more distinct modes: "the *assertion*, the *nod*, the *echo*, and the *counter-signature*."[19] The stronger of these modes, the echo and the counter-signature, shed some light on McBride's revisionary approach to Joyce's legacy. An echo "establishes a link" through thematic or formal similarity," while the counter-signature affirms the originality of an existing work and the singularity of its counter through the "exploitation of existing shared codes."[20] In *A Girl*, McBride echoes Joyce in order to authorize her own counter-signature, specifically in her radical reframing of the centrality of the epiphany to the aesthetics of *Portrait* and her creative channeling of Molly Bloom's unregulated stream-of-consciousness. In doing so, McBride engages in a radical intertextual dialogue with Joyce—as a dominant model of male Irish modernism—that at once acknowledges and destabilizes his centrality to the canon. More than merely "using old forms" derived from modernism, or capitulating to institutional and market demands to follow in step with an established patriarchal canon, McBride's novel adds a new chapter to an evolving history of women writing back to a sprawling Joycean legacy. In its strategically stylistic echoes of Joyce, *A Girl* forges its own claim to aesthetic autonomy, one that reflects and critically contests the marginalization of experimental Irish women's writing from canonical consecration.

Across its taut narrative, *A Girl* channels juxtaposing echoes of Molly Bloom's flowing monologue and a minimalist and broken syntax reminiscent of Beckett's late prose, embedding each within an overarching form that cites and subverts that of *Portrait*, perhaps the most influential modernist *Bildungsroman*. Joyce's novel famously opens with the young Stephen at the threshold of language and consciousness and ends with his plan to flee Ireland and its "nets" of "language, nationality and religion" and "to forge in the smithy of my soul the uncreated conscience of my race."[21] McBride's novel denies this developmental pattern altogether. Its first chapter, for instance, begins with the unnamed narrator still in utero and waiting to be named and concludes with a strangely preemptive erasure of her story after birth: "Something's coming. Wiping off my begans," her own uncreated conscience already "Going dim. Going blank. Going white."[22] And the novel ends with a circular return to this metaphor of erasure: as she drowns herself, her name, writ in water, vanishes before it can materialize. I will unpack the significance of this erasure below, but for now let me simply suggest that this grimly subversive reframing of Stephen's story contains the crucial themes and motifs of a long Irish literary tradition—the mother's oppressive Catholicism, abusive or absent fathers, guilt-ridden sexual desire—all violently punctuated by the narrator's sexual abuse by her uncle which, in turn, is thematically linked to a series of questionably consensual sexual encounters. All of this serves the novel's larger formal counterpoint to a Joycean heroic-aesthetic of development, dramatizing the traumatizing constraints on the narrator's self-consciousness—there's no reproductive development and the girl remains "half-formed," her subjectivity always a condition of the bonds of familial love, unruly sexual desire, and religious authority. But as a grim counterpoint to the liberating effects of Joyce's male modernist epiphany, McBride uncovers and occupies what its aesthetic suppresses, translating that marginalized otherness into the productively enabling conditions of her own radical metamodernist critique, one that plays out in patterns of appropriated and reworked motifs.

Most tellingly in this vein, McBride radically reworks the famous "bird girl" epiphany of *Portrait*, adopting the perspective of the silenced female body in a way that subverts the controlling gaze of the aspiring modernist male aesthete. In Joyce's canonical *Künstlerroman*, Stephen Dedalus's epiphany marks a climactic point in his turn from the call of the church to become instead a "priest of the eternal imagination" and to "create proudly out of the freedom and power of his soul ... a living thing, new and soaring and beautiful, impalpable, imperishable." Stephen's conscious metamorphosis finds its object in the silent and unnamed girl wading along the beach, "like one whom magic had changed into the likeness of a strange and beautiful seabird."[23] Replaying the traditional Irish figure of the "colleen," the beautiful girl "who typically serves as a metaphor for Irish kinship and sovereignty," Joyce's bird girl features as a silent and symbolic figure that inspires Stephen to become a solitary artist free to "fly by" the "nets" of a repressive Ireland and to create a new national consciousness.[24] As the silent subject of his adolescent gaze,

> she was alone and still, gazing out to sea; and when she felt his presence and the worship in his eyes her eyes turned to him in quiet sufferance of his gaze, without shame or wantonness. Long, long she suffered his gaze and then quietly withdrew her eyes from his and bent them towards the stream, gently stirring the water with her foot hither and thither. (*Portrait* 186)

Joyce's repetitive and alliterative poetics flow from the girl as the subject of Stephen's will to artistic autonomy into his very being: "Her image had passed into his soul for ever" in the moment of "ecstasy" that will spurn him on "to recreate life out of life!" (*Portrait* 186). Imaginatively translating her silent "suffering" image to his aspirations to artistic flight, the bird girl in *Portrait* "remains troublingly silent as she is reduced to a mere symbol for the male artist who grants her no space or possibility for an identity of her own."[25]

McBride's nameless narrator, in contrast, occupies something like the bird girl's position, inverting Stephen's male epiphany so that we experience the narrative from her first-person perspective rather than Joyce's omniscient one. In the section of the novel aptly titled "A Girl Is a Half-Formed Thing," McBride stretches avian and watery tropes across the narrator's extended and life-altering experience of sexual abuse, and in doing so she radically reframes Joyce's epiphany and its central place in the canon of the modernist novel of the artist's free development. At thirteen, and having been subjected to her uncle's lurid gazes when he and his wife visit, the narrator is wracked with guilt and unruly desire, made to feel "not me" as she's on the threshold of a sexual awakening that is fraught with violence. Unlike Stephen's Dedalus-inspired desire for creation, she imagines herself "turning to the sun" like Icarus, "Me who is just new. Fallen out of the sky" and "Going to the bad. To the somewhere new" (*Girl* 55). Reeling from conflicted desire after her uncle first kisses her, the next morning she wanders to the nearby lake in what becomes McBride's explicit reframing of Joycean epiphany as the province of the singular and self-authorizing male artist. Imagining her own form of self-creation, she says, "I will gush myself out between my legs," and then performs an inverted baptism that begins as an act of purification and ends in an embrace of dirty desire. Thinking "The thing I want I should not get. I'll put my head in for discreet baptize," her silent prayer to be cleansed of "this bloody itch" of desire is followed by a drowning reverie and a consummation with the murky filth of lake water (*Girl* 60). This key passage is one "in which she transports herself," as Paige Reynolds writes, "from clean to dirty, from youth to adulthood," and at its heart McBride situates the narrator within the bird girl tradition in an overt reprisal to Stephen's epiphany.[26] Signaled by the host of curlews, swans, ducks, and heron, and getting out of the cold, grimy water, she sees on its surface "my cold body reflected back up to my face as I stand there. Look down. I see my sorry self. That girl. My wicked" (*Girl* 61). The narrator's strangely disembodied identification with her "wicked" reflection is at once a decentering of her self and a reframing of Stephen's aesthetic epiphany, taking on the silenced perspective of the bird girl as symbolic figure for the equally subjugated and marginalized position of women in the tradition that McBride cannily appropriates.[27]

After this realization of her split-subjectivity, contra Stephen's sense of his own creative coherence, she concludes, "I don't think I will be clean now," and returns home to the gaze of the lascivious older man (*Girl* 61). This in turn points to another split. On an intra-diegetic level, the narrator's willing abjectification here is an initiation into her partly willed embrace of her uncle's sexual abuse that immediately follows, itself prompting a series of transgressive sexual encounters that make up her attempt to forge an identity freed from the dictates of Catholicism and constrictive family bonds, all of which radically revise Joyce's portrait of artistic development as a transubstantiation of desire and guilt, religion and national identity. As the unnamed subject of repeated violent abuse, and for whom agency and identity will remain "half-formed" until her death, McBride's narrator clearly figures as the obverse of Stephen's epiphany, presented here as the silent, suffering image of feminine sexuality long obscured by a male literary tradition. As that suggests, McBride's novel engages in a radical extradiegetic dialogue, one that self-reflexively dramatizes Joyce's legacy as simultaneously oppressive and as a source for experimental and transgressive revision.

Admirably situating McBride's transformation of the bird girl trope within an extensive genealogy of Irish women writers who have adapted Joyce's epiphanic mode to represent "interior revelations" from the perspective of the girl, Reynolds argues that this revisionary strategy is one in which "McBride cannily resurrects the legacy of modernism to enable a uniquely potent critique of childhood sexual abuse."[28] This is a compelling argument and an important intervention, but I would add that McBride's debut, clearly attuned to the long shadow that Joyce and fellow Irish modernists cast over contemporary writers, takes up a radical intertextual dialogue to forge her own work's aesthetic autonomy, and in a way that both contests masculine literary authority and resists the constrictions on formal experiment imposed on literary fiction in the large-scale field of commercial publishing. McBride signals this ambition, for example, in her dialogue with Joyce's monologue, the famous and flowy final chapter of *Ulysses* ending the novel in Molly's affirmative "yes I said yes I will Yes."²⁹ In *A Girl* we find McBride echoing Molly's lusty language in an almost playful parody, implicitly taking aim less at Joyce's construction than at his very audacity in doing it. In an accelerated passage of narrative montage that ironically sums up a series of abject sexual encounters during her time at university, the narrator echoes Molly's erotic excess but in a style of mock-romance. "I met a man. I met a man," the passage begins, and runs the quick litany of lovers and what they had to offer, winding up to say, "I met a man who was a priest I didn't I did. Just as well as many another one would. I met a man. I met a man" (*Girl* 105–6). The joke about the priest and the "well as many another" echo and parody Molly Bloom's sexually wandering stream-of-consciousness; and yet McBride goes a step further. In the same passage, the language itself losing control under the pressures of returning home, the narrative erupts with: "If Jesus was here he'd have gone. Running. Screaming with his sandals all flapping through the cow shit. O God get me out of this" (*Girl* 107). Yearning to be freed from the burden of homecoming, McBride's narrator indulges in a bit of comic blasphemy, and this also echoes and alters Molly's voice at one point in the "Penelope" section of *Ulysses* when she interjects her interior monologue to plead with her authorial creator: "O Jamesy let me up out of this pooh sweets of sin."³⁰ Substituting a desacralized God for the self-authorizing Jamesy by thus mediating Molly's voice, McBride subjects Joyce's influence to productive parody and a critical appropriation of his claim to authorial autonomy. McBride's acts of reframing Joyce forge a creative counter-signature that, as Attridge argues, "will require new interpretive strategies, just as Joyce's works did. It will have its own singularity, created out of the inventive manipulation of existing cultural materials"—just as, we might add, Joyce famously got up to himself.³¹ Like her reframing of the Joycean epiphany, these echoes clearly exceed simple imitation and generate instead a radical metamodernist reframing of a male-centric canon of modernist aesthetic autonomy.

One way in which McBride's novel articulates "its own singularity" in relation to the Joycean tropes it reworks is in its creation of a "distinctive" style, most notably through its radical disruptions of syntax.³² In this vein, McBride has said that in her first novel she aimed to write in a style that captures "the moment just before language becomes formatted thought."³³ Contrary to Molly's monologue and its freely flowing, unpunctuated affirmations of desire, McBride writes a halting prose, her narrator's desire often on the verge of choking in its own visceral stream-of-consciousness. This stylistic singularity is most keenly legible in moments of acute anxiety brought on by those forces of repression—religion, family, sexual abuse—that go to make up the thematic content of a familiar Irish literary tradition, alongside the narrator's attachment to her dying brother. If the novel as a whole invokes Joycean stream-of-consciousness—whether that of Molly's first-person monologue or the poetic and self-generative style of *Portrait*—it does so in ways that go about fracturing the very conventions it uses, frustrating their developmental desire in order to contest its influence.[34] This style of a "broken bildungsroman" comes to a fevered pitch in the series of sexual abuses that occur between the disorienting death of her brother and her final watery oblivion at the novel's end. Having fled the house of hypocritical mourners and feeling utterly bereft, she is assaulted by a young man she had previously rejected, and the violence aptly works at the level of language, even breaking up individual words to register the visceral destruction of the self: "Crushing I hear boines on done he up me fuck me. ... Stucks the fck the thing in. Me. In. Jesus. I nme" (*Girl* 215). Returning home, bruised, dirtied, and distraught, she encounters her uncle, and what begins as an attempt to soothe her becomes yet another scene of abuse that culminates in a complete loss of self under the violence of possession:

> Give it to him if he wanted it. I don't. I think he did. Fuck the. I'm the girl. Did that is that love to me. I'm. Spite and spit and sick. That's me that was. Is now. What me? ... Where do I live? Where am. Someone he can see and cut into. ... What he takes is the what there is of me. Now you've. I thought there was nothing left. (*Girl* 220–1)

The direct treatment of violence—registered in the equally violent distortion of the boundaries of pronoun and time—in a scene like this one make for some genuinely disturbing reading on the level of content, and that is appropriately matched by McBride's difficult and distinctive style, the unflinching violence done to language and convention. The echoes of Joyce that the novel carries out at once extend a longer tradition of modern Irish women's writing, and amount to a larger counter-signature at the stylistic level of the sentence, comparable to Beckett's minimalist and broken syntax and yet performing its own commitment to an anti-lyrical literary aesthetic. That anti-lyrical style does not so much denigrate or subvert Joyce or even his privileged place in a mostly male canon, but rather extends and destabilizes the institutionalization of that canon.

It is these intertextual acts of destabilizing the pervasive presence of a "Joycean legacy" that I identify as key to McBride's early (and ongoing) "aesthetic agenda," one that aspires to no less than a politics of literary autonomy with the potential to play a role in reshaping the gender of a resurgent modernism, particularly when writers like McBride refuse to conform to the constrictions on formal experiment in the larger commercial literary field.[35] If the novel advances its own productive counter-signature, as I have been arguing, as a means of extending and contesting a modernist legacy, the full brunt of that comes full circle, paradoxically, at the novel's final point of erasure. Returning to the lake near the end, the narrator repeats the earlier baptismal rite, only this time it's an attempt to become "all the purity I can"—to be cleansed not only of the unbearable grief she feels at the loss of her brother, but also the serialized abuse she's experienced and, indeed, the whole history of repressive Irish literary motifs and themes that subjugate her. The scene is also a self-reflexive return to that earlier bird girl moment and its engagement with Joyce's epiphany-driven aesthetic as the narrator first thinks to herself, "Not a new girl here," and then, focusing on her reflection on the water's surface, she thinks, "Deepest mirror of the past and in it I am. Drowned no fine" (*Girl* 225). The distorted syntax here is suggestive: it anticipates the drowning that she imagines as a reunion with her brother in a present-past she sees herself in, while, at the same time, the past is a mirror that precedes and reflects the narrator's whole being as a literary creation, suggesting an overwhelming pervasiveness of an Irish literary tradition that one cannot fully escape. And just as the narrator's name never materializes in the text, it is here, at the moment of her death, that we witness its full dissolution, as she thinks, "My name is. Water." As her name and consciousness become one with the deathly stream, McBride concludes with a powerful counterpoint to Joyce's lyrical epiphany; the echo of Stephen's self-authoring proclamation—"Welcome, O life!" (*Portrait* 275)—dissolves as her own creation thinks, "That was just life" before we read the novel's last line: "My name is gone" (*Girl* 226–7).

Diegetically, this dissolution and the forces of repression and abuse that lead to it make for a bitter reflection on a history that remains all too real. The novel channels all the familiar themes that make up Ireland's chief literary export, but within an experimental form that appropriates signature tropes of an Irish literary tradition, doing so from the perspective of what the institutionalized canon historically suppresses. Fully inhabiting this repressed position in the tradition, and subjecting its protagonist to the demands of McBride's self-legislating style, *A Girl* marks a return, from outside the commercial literary field, to a late-modernist mode of autonomy constituted in "unfreedom." As Alys Moody writes, the trope of hunger within a minority modernism after modernism "imagines the aesthetic as a realm of unfreedom and physical suffering, marked by a refusal to bow to necessity that nonetheless fails to end in liberation."[36] McBride's aesthetic, too, engages in an autonomous will to style that is steeped in the female suffering that its counter-text, *Portrait*, overlooks, and it's an aesthetic that refuses to indulge in the consoling demands of mainstream fiction. Committed to a nameless difficulty and a self-legislating style that subversively occupies the margins of modernism and the market for its legacies, *A Girl* teaches us not only that there is space for experimental women's writing that builds on the tradition it contests, but also for one that lays claim to its own autonomous capacity to alter, if ever so slightly, the social expectations of contemporary fiction.

Milkman as Modernist Suspense

Unlike McBride's first novel, Anna Burns's *Milkman* seems unburdened by a specific modernist precedent, a point perhaps underscored by its setting in the late 1970s as a moment of protracted suspense in the Northern Irish Troubles. Whereas McBride's novel takes up a position in the suppressed margins of Joyce's epiphanic aesthetics so as to claim a place for her own radical experiments with style and form, Burns deploys a tightly constricted yet digressive style in the spirit of late modernism to present an arrested history of political violence from a marginalized woman's perspective. The different geopolitical and cultural backgrounds of these writers, then, also point to distinct literary traditions. More specifically, *Milkman* extends the work of earlier writers from the province—such as Seamus Deane, Deirdre Madden, and Robert McLiam Wilson—that tend to depict the Troubles and its afterlives in a state of violent "suspension," as John Brannigan writes, caught "between the 'bad,' dark notoriety of the past, and the precarious and tentative visions of an infinitely abortive future."[37] Burns's novel brings that focus into the twenty-first century, but by way of a belated modernist return to a digressive stream-of-consciousness that both dramatizes and resists the repressive ideological forces of Irish history. From the perspective of its 2018 publication, *Milkman* also registers the Janus-faced backwardness and futurity of a postcolonial Irish vision, reflecting the renewed relevance of Northern Ireland's dark history during the stalled Brexit debates and their implications for the region's political future, while it also aspires to the universal in its critique of the "totalitarian" tendencies of modern nationalist and imperial states from within its narrowly local setting in an unnamed Belfast.[38]

Despite these differences in style and geopolitical setting, Burns, like McBride, contributes to a resurgent Irish engagement with modernist form from the gendered margins of the canon to articulate a politics of literary autonomy.

Before taking up the ways that these authors signal a new development in the market for marginal modernist experiment, with which I will conclude this study, let me note that McBride and Burns forge their autonomous fictions from within the violently circumscribed conditions of possibility for women within their respective literary contexts. In the case of *Milkman* we might take a cue from Eoin McNamee, who suggests that the novel "invents its own context, becomes its own universe,"[39] one that certainly reflects the violently splintered politics of modern totalitarianism within its undisclosed yet closely local setting, but also translates the constrictive force of ideology into a formally digressive surrealist fiction.[40] Claustrophobically focalized, nightmarishly surreal, and funny as hell, *Milkman* invents a literary context in a form that recalls the work of earlier belated modernisms by "dramatizing," to adopt Moody again, "an unfree and embodied mode of aesthetic autonomy." In its acute reflection of ideological repression coupled with its circular and digressive narrative form, *Milkman* implicitly stakes a belated modernist claim to a literary politics of autonomy from the oppressive patriarchal structures of contemporary history, literary tradition, and even a reified institutional legacy of modernism itself.

It is within the unfree and ideologically circumscribed society of 1970s Belfast, the "context" that the novel "invents," that Burns forges a detached and darkly comic "conscience" of a fractured Irish identity arrested in historical time. Always voiced from the communal perspective of "our side," Catholic and loosely affiliated with various levels of "state renouncers" that sometimes evokes the IRA without naming it, middle sister is fully cognizant of a local identity defined against anything that might be associated with the site of political power "over the water." Proper names, newspapers and TV programs, and trivial everyday objects are policed, marked out as symbols of political loyalty or disloyalty: "As regards this psycho-political atmosphere, with its rules of allegiance, of tribal identification, of what was allowed and not allowed, matters didn't stop at 'their names' and at 'our names', at 'us' and 'them,' at 'our community' and 'their community,' at 'over the road,' 'over the water' and 'over the border.' "[41] In this deeply divided totalitarian socius, where objects of everyday consumption such as butter or tea are automatically inscribed with "allegiance" or "betrayal," it's perhaps of little surprise that when middle sister's "maybe-boyfriend," a mechanic, acquires a discarded bit of a Bentley supercharger—still bearing the flag of British manufacture—it sparks one of the most tense and absurd disputes in the early pages of the novel. As friends and neighbors gather at his ostensibly neutral home to admire the bit of engine, one of them "homed in on that flag issue, the flags-and-emblems issue, instinctive and emotional because flags were invented to be instinctive and emotional—often pathologically, narcissistically emotional" (*Milkman* 25). As the excessive quotation followed by her sense of a collective pathology suggests, middle sister cultivates a stubborn detachment from within the very "psycho-political atmosphere" that constricts and contains the possibilities of language, narrative, and identity.

More generally, the novel is organized around a formal tension between those repressive ideological forces that mark social identity on the one hand, and its circular and digressive stream-of-consciousness on the other, both of which are dramatically punctuated by the repeated and increasingly threatening encounters the narrator has with the anti-state terrorist milkman. Within that larger structure, *Milkman* comprises a series of smaller digressive patterns that critically reflect on the violence of unwavering political affiliation and hypersexualized fantasies of patriarchal power.

Take, for example, middle sister's excessively protracted third encounter with her nemesis, which serves as something of a synecdoche for the novel's larger formal tension between a policed and circumscribed socius and Burns's use of a digressive stream-of-consciousness. The entire passage is claustrophobically framed by the milkman's unexpected appearance in the dead of night, but also gives rise to an internal stream of finite digressions, making the scene a dissociative yet tightly contained surrealist nightmare. After previous encounters with the enigmatic figure, the narrator alters her route home one night, choosing to walk through the notoriously deteriorated "ten-minute" area to avoid him, so his sudden appearance affirms his omnipresent stalker-status. And omniscient as well: the milkman lets on that he not only knows of her job and her evening French classes, but menacingly mentions maybe-boyfriend's possession of the Bentley supercharger, which then sparks a series of thinly veiled threats and the narrator's own spiral of "fearful fantasies and catastrophic thinking" that lead her to suspect maybe-boyfriend's impending "death by carbomb" (*Milkman* 109–15). She also realizes that this stalking doesn't even conform to the normalized categories of binary political violence, but is instead the expression of misogynistic masculine possessiveness: "maybe-boyfriend was going to be killed under the catch-all of the political problems," she thinks, but "in reality, the milkman was going to kill him out of disguised sexual jealousy over me" (*Milkman* 115). What's more, this internalized paranoia triggers her recollection of her previous stalker, Somebody McSomebody (whose own possessive fantasies will later lead him to threaten the narrator at gunpoint). His aggressive pursuit of her included posing as a committed "renouncer of the state," aligning his fantasized image with the so-called "legendary warriors" with "superhuman endurance" willing to sacrifice their lives at any moment fighting for the district, which the narrator identifies as the cocky masculine pose that it is, remarking that "they don't see you as a person but instead as some cipher, some valueless nobody whose sole objective is to reflect back onto them the glory of themselves" (*Milkman* 118, 131, 133).[42] Like the passage in question, I could go on, but the point is the formal tension unfolding here: middle sister's stream-of-consciousness is associative and digressive, but confined to a serial pattern governed by a paralyzing political paranoia embodied by predatory masculine figures. If one effect of this is the suspense it generates, along the lines of the classic psychological thriller (one of the genres the novel exploits), then that in turn depends on the foreclosure of personal autonomy reflected in the circular constriction of the narrative itself.

Faced with the omnipresent threat of the milkman and the socially repressive force of rumor, the narrator tries, impossibly, to detach from it all, to set up and "maintain a border to keep my mind separate" (*Milkman* 54). In other words, her only means of survival is to occupy a place of individual political neutrality and affective detachment from the ideological borders and predatory masculinity that so violently police her social world. By the age of eighteen middle sister had "dropped all interaction surplus to requirement which meant they got no public content, no symbolic content, no full-bodiedness, no bloodedness, no passion of the moment, no turn of plot, no sad shade, no panicked shade, no location of anything. Just me, downplayed. Just me, devoid" (*Milkman* 174–5). This affective and imaginative withdrawal from the symbols and plots of the political problem is figured throughout the novel by an immersive, antisocial, and ostensibly "deviant" habit of "reading-while-walking," a response to hypervigilant social surveillance manifested in local rumors as they congeal into oppressive and collectively presumed fact. Her awareness "of rumour and actuality," she observes, fails to offer even the illusion of control over her social existence, so that "reading-while-walking" is a defiant act of not-knowing, of "a vigilance not to be vigilant" in the face of the coercive and self-generating power of "fabrication" (*Milkman* 65). That effort at withdrawal from personal threats and the larger "political problem," however, contributes further to the dangerous proliferation of rumors that increasingly circumscribe her narrative and foreclose personal autonomy. As her "longest friend" tells her, "reading-while-walking" is "disturbing" and "deviant" and "not public-spirited," whereas "'Semtex isn't unusual'" in the normalized world of the Troubles and its symptomatic male violence. The narrator's blanket refusal to answer "social questions" about her movements and affiliations only serve to place her "into the difficult zone" of suspected informers (*Milkman* 201, 200, 204). And rumors multiply beyond questions of state- or anti-state affiliation. When the local serial poisoner "tablets girl" turns up dead before the "renouncers" could get to her, everyone in the district assumes the milkman did it to take revenge on her attempt to kill middle sister, and she becomes totally alienated from local society, greeted in public with an eerie collective silence (*Milkman* 231–42). Subjected to the nets of rumored fabrication that her antisocial withdrawal fails to resist, she is reduced to an object to be interpreted, possessed, or cast beyond the pale. Social and personal autonomy, in the novel's dark diegesis, is impossible, always subject to unwanted and paranoid political interpretation.

And yet it is within this sphere of social constraint that *Milkman* forges a paradoxical form of literary autonomy, so that even as the narrator's agency is progressively stripped away, her narrative in its digressive circularity stretches the ontological binds of, say, the generic conventions of social or historical realism the novel draws from (and which tends to be favored by the Man Booker prize committees, more on which below). In other words, if the novel's constrictive content acts as a kind of centripetal force of social constraint, its unruly and digressive stream-of-consciousness provides a centrifugal counterpressure, in a protracted experimental form of imaginative excess articulated from within the gendered and finite fields of history, religion, and literary realism. Whereas middle sister's mental border fails to secure any effective resistance to the violent banalities of politics and masculine power, *Milkman* just keeps "going on," to paraphrase Beckett's *Unnameable*, and its deviant and digressive style suggests an anti-political claim for aesthetic autonomy that might be forged from within a collective memory of Northern Ireland that is suspended between a deadly past and "an infinitely abortive future."[43]

Milkman achieves its autonomy from both the deadlock of history and the conventions of social realism when it erupts into the serialized styling of slapstick comedy, a mode that recalls the dark laughter and formal minimalism of a late modernist like Beckett. An exemplary moment concerns two lovers' unexpected reunion, in which the narrative temporarily breaks free from the violently reductive power of patriarchal politics. Still recovering from the poisoning at the hands of tablets girl and ostracized by everyone in her district, middle sister finds herself at the center of a reunion between tablets girl's sister, temporarily blinded by poisoning, and her own exiled brother, and the scene erupts into an extended moment of choreographed physical comedy. Physically shaking while carrying out a litany of verbal self-laceration for having left the girl behind—shouting, "Buck idjit! ... Dammit! ... Fuckit! ... Immature!"—the narrator's brother finally notices that his lover can't see him shaking, and Burns translates her tragic condition into the comic limitations of the suffering body: "'Cannot you see me shaking?' he said. Then he said, "*Fuck! You can't see me shaking! You can't see!*" (*Milkman* 270). And this gives rise to middle sister's detached observation of a wayward moment of slapstick spectacle, trading the forces of social repression for the comic finitude of embodied repetition. She watches as the characters perform a comic ballet of serialized action and reaction: pushing away and drawing toward each other, fully embracing only to withdraw again until, finally wrapping arms, the little routine draws to an exhausted conclusion:

> And now, permitting him to bring his arms around her, while she herself held on to him while managing at the same time to push away at him, she admonished, saying, "I think I hate you," which meant she didn't because "I *think* I hate you" is the same as "probably I hate you," which is the same as "I don't know if I hate you," which is the same as "I don't hate you, oh God, my love, I love you, still love you, always, always have I loved you and never have I stopped loving you."
> … There was a second of nothing, a blip of suspension, then they fell—no more talk, no more dramatics—with relief into each other's arms. (*Milkman* 272)

This scene is in turn framed by another slapstick skirmish: prior to this reunion, middle sister had noticed an utterly odd and seemingly orchestrated fight silently taking place between two men: "They were at it in silence, absolute quietness—fists up, lunging, jab-punch, jab-jab-hook, undercut, evading, leaping around, grabbing hold of each other" (*Milkman* 260). She turns again to the two men after witnessing the lovers' squabble, noting the "disconcerting" silence of the fight, "one which worked largely perhaps by association of ideas, some modern, stylistic *art nouveau* encounter" that makes no sense to those observing it, accustomed as they are to the "realism" of the normalized violence of the Troubles.

Such scenes (and there are a number of others) break free of the novel's otherwise enclosed serial violence and social repression, taking the narrator's sstream-of-consciousness outside itself to focus on an exteriorized and wayward comic moment. Oddly framed by that silent and mechanical fight scene that just keeps going on for no apparent reason, the lovers' tousle bears comparison with the various forms of comic modernism, from slapstick film to the avant-garde work of writers like Beckett. As Michael North writes, so much of the comedy from the modernist period worked by "extract[ing] novelty from repetition"; and in "the common practices of doubling, repetition, and seriality" in Beckett's work, we see "how an apparently repetitious insistence on a limited set of possibilities enables the works to break out of closure into comedy."[44] In Burns, slapstick encounters use repetition within a finite field to generate comic effect and affect, breaking out of the closure of the novel and the profoundly troubled historical moment it fictionalizes and turning the claustrophobic violence and reduced agency of its narrator to a disruptive comic style.

We should note that Burns hadn't read Beckett until after she wrote *Milkman*, but the novel's flights into detached comic style, and its larger patterns of digressive permutations within a finite realm of formal possibility, justify reading her as a belated modernist within a longer tradition of experimental Irish writing.[45] Strikingly different as these writers' styles and circumstances are, the comparison to Beckett's late modernism yields additional implications about Burns's insistence on a literary form that claims autonomy from the restrictive politics it reflects. Alys Moody eloquently argues that Beckett's closed-system narrative form "refuses the conventional link between aesthetic autonomy and freedom, reimagining autonomy not as an expression of the artist's freedom, but as subjugation to the limitations of the aesthetic or artistic condition," a reimagining of aesthetic autonomy that requires, in part, a "radical divorce from … the exterior world in which politics unfolds."[46] In its effort to divorce its aesthetic from the "real" restrictions of narrow ideological positions, *Milkman* makes constraint a condition of its relative aesthetic autonomy, and does so in stark contrast to celebrity modes of authorial self-fashioning attuned to the logics of branding and literary prestige. Burns's aesthetic project, coming into the field from the margins of the mainstream, counters the ideological appeal inherent to the commercial production of contemporary literature that Brouillette calls "freedom from constraint of any kind" and "expressive of individual genius," once the mantra of Romanticism and then modernism but now fully conducive "to neoliberal capital" and its demand for constant (but often predictable) "innovation."[47] *Milkman* draws on the conventions of the suspense thriller and the historical novel and subjects them to a disorienting and belated modernist form. In this light the novel isn't concerned to assert authorial singularity but to articulate an autonomy for literary form that takes the violently gendered constraints of its specific historical context as its condition for an experimental critique of patriarchy. In rejecting the mere politicization of violence (or vice versa), *Milkman* performs a politics of literary form that exceeds the historical constraints that bring it into being.

As always, this kind of self-legislating formal claim to literary autonomy is necessarily relative, especially when we address it within the context of the politics and prestige of the Man Booker Prize that helped bring mainstream attention to the book. Here we might note that Burns is the first author from Northern Ireland to have received the prize, reminding us that together with the province's vexed political history, fractured cultural identity, and distinct literary traditions, it remains peripheral to the Anglo-Irish and US literary establishment. On the institutional level, we should recall that like other widely publicized cultural prizes, the Man Booker works to affirm its own authority "to produce cultural value" and to assert "control over the cultural economy."[48] As a curious hybrid that adopts some of the familiar conventions of, say, the thriller, noirish memoir, and historical fiction, Burns's writing blends the genres that have been favored in the recent history of the prize, especially that of the historical novel.[49] But if *Milkman* evokes the conventions of historical fiction, it also stretches them beyond formal recognition. Not only does it withhold specific names, places, or historical figures but, more importantly, it engages an immersive and digressive stream-of-consciousness in a belated modernist mode of disorienting the ontological coordinates of history or historical fiction, subordinating them to its own formal and stylistic principles. The novel's setting and style render it out of joint, foregrounding its self-legislating form to stake a position from which to critically reflect on universally repressive patriarchal structures.

Milkman's distortion of time and memory are intrinsic to its fictive historical setting, and in this it both reanimates modernism's challenge to a traditional historiography organized around causal events and obliquely meditates on its present.[50] If Northern Irish novelists writing during the Troubles sometimes turned to earlier periods of history to reflect on and order their own chaotic present, then Burns's fictional return to the period resonates with real-world concerns of its moment of composition. The novel's concern with real and imagined borders and their violent, reactionary policing (strongly gendered in this case) bears an urgent resemblance to the political climate that includes recurring questions about the status of Northern Ireland in international affairs, a problem that has become especially pronounced during the stalled Brexit debates. Burns had been working on *Milkman* well before the 2016 referendum, and while there would be little point in arguing for the novel's prescience, we might say that its sensitivity to questions of borders and violence brings to the literary establishment the reverberations of a colonial past that Brexit debates made audible again. More tellingly, Burns seems to anticipate the rise of the MeToo Movement. The novel's contemporaneity with regard to our current climate of gender politics, then, speaks well of the committee for a prize that is equally "revered and reviled."[51] For in this singular instance the prize provides institutional and cultural affirmation of the value of experimental work by women from the geopolitical margins of the literary market, in effect bringing it into the mainstream, boosting sales, and renewing international attention to the region. And this brings me to one further implication: the prize and ensuing sales of the novel merely provide the material and social support for its larger claim to a literary autonomy as a modernist inheritance, particularly in its modernist mode of "disrupting ordinary perceptions of time" with the formal effects of a wayward stream-of-consciousness.[52] Inventive of its own belated modernist techniques and contexts, *Milkman* illustrates, together with McBride's work, that emerging women writers taking up an experimental modernist style can do so in ways that draw from and contest the gendered and classed constraints within the industry for literary fiction, especially at a time when big commercial publishers have shied away from such non-lucrative ventures in the recent economic contractions.[53] Again, the time of *Milkman* is out of joint—registering a resurgent modernist impulse to experiment that is also powerfully of its time. Staking out their own subversive gender politics through a claim to formal autonomy from within the constraints of history and on the margins of the mainstream literary industry, McBride and Burns renew a modernist commitment to experimental, autonomous form and point to the emerging market conditions for the production and reception of imaginative writing.

Marketing Modernism from the Margins

From "the conglomerate era" to "the age of Amazon," corporate production has dramatically shaped and constricted the possibilities for literary fiction since the 1980s, legible in part in the promotion of select number of celebrity authors. These conditions have also prompted aspiring and successful writers to negotiate their position within the commercial field by aligning their work with a modernist tradition and its legacy of relative autonomy, one that has become increasingly indistinguishable from market branding. In many cases, this has meant learning from the historical modernists, for whom the complex interactions between aesthetic autonomy and the market became defining concerns in any attempts to assert a distinctive value for literature in the face of capitalism's encroachments into cultural production. In contrast to the celebrity authors I addressed in previous chapters, McBride and Burns expand and contest a modernist legacy, in an Irish context, and demonstrate a commitment to autonomous forms of writing from the margins of mainstream literary production. In this regard, the incongruities of their respective geopolitical backgrounds and fictional settings yield a comparative, and admittedly partial, picture of a renewed commitment to experimental writing by contemporary Irish authors, from both sides of the still-provisional border. And while the texts I have discussed demonstrate a will to self-legislating formal autonomy, I want to close by considering how the emergent market conditions of their production and reception provide the material support for that autonomous aesthetic, thus pointing both to a recent shift in literary production and a new historical chapter in the market for modernism.

This shared investment in a modernist legacy of formal autonomy can be understood, in part, as an authorial positioning at an angle to the mainstream corporate production of contemporary fiction, their work only coming slowly to wide visibility and indicative of a new interest in the marginal literary value of an experimental writing that reanimates and destabilizes modernism's complex aesthetic legacies. Like some of the modernists before them, McBride and Burns have moved from a marginalized and restrictive field to positions of relative prominence afforded by, in this case, a decentered field of corporate support, and their careers illustrate this recent transformation. *A Girl* was first published by Galley Beggar Press, a small independent publisher based in the UK; after receiving a number of prestigious prizes, it was picked up by the American nonprofit, Coffee House Press. *Milkman* was originally published by the independent but historically established Faber before it, too, was brought out under the imprint of another small American press, Greywolf. Both Coffee House and Greywolf operate as nonprofits through various grants, gifts, and, most tellingly, corporate sponsorship, so that the US editions in my hand not only acknowledge those sources of financial support, but come with the visible logos of major multinational corporations, including the Amazon Literary Partnership, Wells Fargo, and Target. As John Thompson points out, the public and private grants provided to and enabling nonprofit publishers and their writers help "cushion them to some extent from the harsh realities of the marketplace."[54] This development is not ideologically neutral, however; as Lee Konstantinou argues, the corporate support for ostensibly disinterested nonprofit literary production can "institutionalize ... problems of the neoliberal nonprofit sphere" and, rather than signaling some new kind of cultural commons, it "privatizes" support through "tax-exempt gifts" that then bypass any "political or democratic accountability," bringing, I would add, a bounty of symbolic capital to a corporation's public image.[55] Finally, acknowledging corporate support in the front and back matter of these novels, when read as part of the work itself, amounts to what Paul Crosthwaite calls "highlighting its own commodity status."[56]

These specific and emerging conditions for publishing experimental fiction are neither merely good nor bad. On the one hand, we need to be wary of forms of corporate support for cultural production that mask economic self-interest with the logic of the gift, and it points to a specific manifestation of a wide-ranging privatization of the literary field. Think: "Literary autonomy brought to you by Amazon, preserving the former by incorporating it to the totality of the latter." At the same time, the commodity status that is made explicit in these novels is not merely another sign of the market's absorption of the potentials of literary experiment, but rather a post facto form of material supplement. In the cases of Burns and McBride, formal experiment in the spirit of modernism precedes its corporate sponsorship, and radically destabilizes an institutionalized and largely male tradition of Irish modernism. Coming into recognition from the literary and economic margins, these writers expand on the aesthetic possibilities latent within modernism's history, and do so in an emerging market organized around complex intersections between independent presses, public support, and corporate sponsorship, one in which "low financial returns" and "relative autonomy," to paraphrase Alys Moody, are mutually constitutive in sustaining our ongoing investment in modernism as a valued legacy. The specific conditions by which their work has been produced and distributed—published by small, independent presses committed to experimental writing with the material support of public funding and multinational corporations—mark a new transformation in the industry, an alternative response to conglomerate-driven production that, since the 2008 recession, has beat a conservative retreat from risky investments in fiction that radically deviates from familiar and market-proven forms.

Finally, this emerging cooperation between experimental style as a claim to autonomy—which draws on the latent aesthetic possibilities of historical modernism—and its belated support from the corporate sector might be understood as a weird logical outcome in the market for modernism, split as it is between a conservative legacy of cultural capital and an inspiration to resist the status quo. The logos of multinational corporations make the commodification of these novels transparent, reminding us that any fiction of autonomy depends on the market. But this new literary economy also constitutes a curious return to the older market formation of historical modernism. As materialist critics of the period have taught us, modernism instituted a form of cultural capital that could accumulate through the cultivation of an elite field and small-scale production, and did so within a system that often engaged in a fetishistic disavowal of the material support of promoters and producers whose labor could be absorbed into the cult value of the authorial name. Now we're witnessing a return to small-scale production of experimental writing, but one whereby the proposed autonomy of the work makes clear its dependence on nonliterary sources of capital. "Modernism" is a brand, and its intersecting cultural and economic capital requires continued investment by authors, publishers, readers, and critics; when that value is reproduced by a system of large-scale corporate production geared toward celebrity authorship, it also tends to reproduce an institutionalized and static fiction of modernist autonomy. In the cases of Burns and McBride, we are witnessing what might be called a metamodernism of the market in the creation of marginal literary values. Their coming into prominence, even celebrity, signals a process that still depends on the support of exploitative corporate capitalism even as they imagine new horizons for contemporary writing and a renewal of that old modernist impulse to alter the social conditions of literary production.

Notes

Introduction: Contemporary Fiction, Celebrity Culture, and the Market for Modernism

1 David James and Urmila Seshagiri, "Metamodernism: Narratives of Continuity and Revolution," 88, 89.
2 Ibid., 89.
3 Sarah Brouillette, *Literature and the Creative Economy*, 18.
4 David James, *Modernist Futures: Innovation and Inheritance in the Contemporary Novel*, 10. In addition, see James's edited collection, *The Legacies of Modernism: Historicising Postwar and Contemporary Fiction*; Madelyn Detloff, *The Persistence of Modernism: Loss and Mourning in the Twentieth Century*; and Rebecca Walkowitz, *Cosmopolitan Style: Modernism beyond the Nation*. In their different ways, each of these is concerned with showing how contemporary writers adapt modernist modes of literary representation and form to pressing ethical and political conditions in the late twentieth and early twenty-first century.
5 James, *Modernist Futures*, 30, 29.
6 Tim Woods, "A Complex Legacy: Modernity's Uneasy Discourse of Ethics and Responsibility," in *The Legacies of Modernism: Historicising Postwar and Contemporary Fiction*, ed. David James, 154.
7 David Attridge, *The Singularity of Literature*, 131.
8 See David Attridge, *J. M. Coetzee and the Ethics of Reading: Literature in the Event*, 5. My gloss on the demand to reassemble and transform inherited tradition, both within the modernist period and among contemporary authors, echoes David James's assertion that "fiction today partakes of an interaction between innovation and inheritance that is entirely consonant with what modernists themselves were doing over a century ago, an interaction that enables writers to work *with* their lineage in the process of attempting new experiments with form" (*Modernist Futures*, 2). These critical reflections on contemporary reworkings of a modernist tradition inhabit, of course, a line that goes back to T. S. Eliot's famous essay, "Tradition and the Individual Talent," which I address elsewhere in this book.
9 Alys Moody, "Indifferent and Detached: Modernism and the Aesthetic Affect," *Modernism/modernity* Print Plus 3.4 (December 2018), https://

modernismmodernity.org/forums/posts/indifferent-and-detached (accessed August 1, 2020).

10 Neil Levi, "How to Do Things with Modernism," *Modernism/modernity* Print Plus 3.4 (December 2018), https://modernismmodernity.org/forums/posts/how-do-things-modernism (accessed August 1, 2020).

11 Jeremy Rosen, *Minor Characters Have Their Day: Genre and the Contemporary Literary Marketplace*, 30.

12 Levi, "How to Do Things."

13 James and Seshagiri, "Metamodernism," 93.

14 Literary impressionism is one specific example of a modernist aesthetic that has become fully normalized in literary fiction, its once radical questioning of perception and consciousness now assumed normal by editors at elite presses. See Jesse Matz, *Lasting Impressions: The Legacies of Impressionism in Contemporary Culture*, especially chapters 2 and 7.

15 Here I channel Jennifer Wicke's provocative essay, "Appreciation, Depreciation: Modernism's Speculative Bubble," *Modernism/modernity* 8.3 (September 2001): 389–403; Claire Barber-Stetson, "Modern Insecurities, or, Living on the Edge"; and James English, *The Economy of Prestige: Prizes, Awards, and the Circulation of Cultural Value*. I return to and elaborate on these works elsewhere in this book.

16 Max Horkheimer and Theodor Adorno, *Dialectic of Enlightenment: Philosophical Fragments*, trans. Edmund Jephcott, 105, 113, 127–8.

17 Fredric Jameson, *Postmodernism, or, The Cultural Logic of Late Capitalism*, 48.

18 Ibid., 4–5.

19 Michael D'Arcy and Mathias Nilges, "Introduction," *The Contemporaneity of Modernism*, 4–5.

20 Ibid., 9.

21 Ibid., 5.

22 Ibid., 6.

23 Ibid.

24 For more on Eliot's essayistic "management of his reputation" based in a "language of elitism and exclusion to reform the expectations of and attract readers most useful to the success of his poetry," see Leonard Diepeveen, "'I Can Have More Than Enough Power to Satisfy Me': T. S. Eliot's Construction of His Audience," in *Marketing Modernisms: Self-Promotion, Canonization, Rereading*, ed. Kevin J. H. Dettmar and Stephen Watt, 37–60, 40. Mark Morrisson charts the complex historical intersections between modernist circulation in little magazines and the larger commercial culture as they emerged in the early twentieth century, showing how their apparently conflicting aims and methods of distribution were mutually transformative; see *The Public Face of Modernism: Little Magazines, Audiences,*

and Reception, 1905–1920. Regarding the founding and expansion of the Woolfs' Hogarth Press, Laura Marcus argues, "Hogarth Press represented work that cut out the middleman and escaped literary commodification. It gave Woolf a way of negotiating the terms of literary publicity and a space somewhere between the private, the coterie, and the public sphere" (Laura Marcus, "Virginia Woolf and the Hogarth Press," in *Modernist Writers and the Marketplace*, ed. Ian Willison, Warwick Gould, and Warren Chernaik, 144).

25 Pierre Bourdieu, *The Field of Cultural Production: Essays on Art and Literature*, 115.
26 Ibid., 117.
27 This is an admittedly simplified summary of Andreas Huyssen's more complicated thesis about modernists' fears of "contamination" by mass markets. See *After the Great Divide: Modernism, Mass Culture, Postmodernism*. Reference to Huyssen's study has become obligatory in materialist and sociological accounts of modernism since its appearance, despite significant critical qualifications of the divide at work in his thesis.
28 See Aaron Jaffe, *Modernism and the Culture of Celebrity*, 20.
29 Lawrence Rainey, *Institutions of Modernism*, 100, 3.
30 Jaffe, *Modernism and the Culture of Celebrity*, 74.
31 Ibid., 18–57, 20.
32 Loren Glass, *Authors Inc.: Literary Celebrity in the Modern United States, 1880–1980*, 5–6.
33 Jonathan Goldman, *Modernism Is the Literature of Celebrity*, 7.
34 Pierre Bourdieu, *The Rules of Art: Genesis and Structure of the Literary Field*, 227, 228.
35 Ibid., 229.
36 Ibid.
37 Ibid., 104.
38 Sean Latham, *Am I a Snob: Modernism and the Novel*, 2.
39 Ibid., 3; see also the chapters on Woolf and Joyce, 59–168. See also Loren Glass, *Authors Inc.*, which shows how celebrity modernist authors could resolve a tension between outright self-promotion and claims to disinterestedness by way of impersonal style (5–6).
40 Latham, *Am I a Snob*, 4.
41 Bourdieu, *The Rules of Art*, 76.
42 Andrew Goldstone, *Fictions of Autonomy: Modernism from Wilde to de Man*, 5, 23.
43 Ibid., 23, 22.
44 Ibid., 4.
45 Mark McGurl has shown at length how modernism, especially its conflicting "minimalist" and "maximalist" impulses, and its authors' textual performance of

"autogenesis," became thoroughly normalized and institutionalized in the postwar American university and with the rise of creative writing programs. While the latter only emerged much later in Britain, his study does have some relevance to the institutionalization of modernism in literary fiction in its now global production and distribution. See *The Program Era: Postwar Fiction and the Rise of Creative Writing*, especially chapters 1 and 5.

46 Morrison, *The Public Face of Modernism*, 6.
47 See, e.g., Michael Murphy, "'One Hundred Percent Bohemia': Pop Decadence and the Aestheticization of Commodity in the Rise of the Slicks," in *Marketing Modernisms: Self-Promotion, Canonization, Rereading*, ed. Kevin J. H. Dettmar and Stephen Watt, 61–89; Jennifer Wicke, "Coterie Consumption: Bloomsbury, Keynes, and Modernism as Marketing," in Dettmar and Watt, 109–32; and Donal Harris, *On Company Time: American Modernism in the Big Magazines*.
48 Catherine Turner, *Marketing Modernism between the Two World Wars*, 194, 195.
49 See Lise Jaillant, *Cheap Modernism: Expanding Markets, Publishers' Series and the Avant-Garde*. For a richly rewarding case study of the role of the Grove Press in bringing modernist and avant-garde literature into an expanding postwar American market, see Loren Glass, *Counterculture Colophon: Grove Press, the* Evergreen Review, *and the Incorporation of the Avant-Garde*.
50 Sean Latham and Gayle Rogers, *Modernism: Evolution of an Idea*, 67, 65.
51 Ibid., 52.
52 See Rod Rosenquist, *Modernism, the Market, and the Institution of the New*.
53 Claire Squires, *Marketing Literature: The Making of Contemporary Writing in Britain*, 21
54 Squires, *Marketing Literature*, 20; and Paul Delany, *Literature, Money and the Market: From Trollope to Amis*, 180.
55 Richard Todd, "Literary Fiction and the Book Trade," in *A Concise Companion to Contemporary British Fiction*, ed. James F. English, 20.
56 Delany, *Literature, Money and the Market*, 182; and Todd, "Literary Fiction and the Book Trade," 26. As Sarah Brouillette has shown, these structural changes had a major impact on the marketing of specifically postcolonial fiction, which I address in Chapters 3 and 5. See Brouillette, *Postcolonial Writers and the Global Literary Marketplace*, 44–75.
57 Claire Squires, "Novelistic Production and the Publishing Industry in Britain and Ireland," in *A Companion to the British and Irish Novel, 1945–2000*, ed. Brian W. Shaffer , 184. Channeling the work of John Thompson and others, Paul Crosthwaite has more recently contributed to this sociological history, showing how a rising emphasis on brand-name recognition since the 1980s has helped to marginalize seriously dissenting or experimental fiction and compelled the production of novels that show only a marginal difference from commercially successful forms. See *The Market Logics of Contemporary Fiction*, 18–23.

58 See Squires, *Marketing Literature*, 41. I take the phrase "journalistic capital" from James English, "Winning the Culture Game: Prizes, Awards, and the Rules of Art," *New Literary History* 33.1 (2002): 109–35.
59 Squires, *Marketing Literature*, 5.
60 Crosthwaite, *The Market Logics of Contemporary Fiction*, 24–5.
61 James F. English and John Frow, "Literary Authorship and Celebrity Culture," in *A Concise Companion to Contemporary British Fiction*, ed. James F. English, 48.
62 Ibid., 52.
63 John B. Thompson, *Merchants of Culture: The Publishing Business in the Twenty-First Century*, 141. Thompson's is perhaps the most thorough study of trade book publishing today. Chapters 1–3 provide an in-depth look at the way the players—retail, agents (and authors), and big publishing corporations—interact in the business of producing and marketing trade books, including literary fiction.
64 See Dan Sinykin, "The Conglomerate Era: Publishing, Authorship, and Literary Form, 1965–2007," *Contemporary Literature* 58.4 (Winter 2017): 462–91.
65 English, *The Economy of Prestige*, 1.
66 As English writes, "Every form of 'capital' everywhere exists not only in relation to one particular field"—such as marketing and sales or less measurable forms of prestige—"but in varying relations to all other fields and all other types of capital" (*The Economy of Prestige*, 10).
67 Richard Todd, *Consuming Fictions: The Booker Prize and Fiction in Britain Today*, 7, 59.
68 Ibid., 61, 12. For a more recent data-driven study that extends and complicates the ways the Booker affects sales, see Alexander Manshel, Laura B. McGrath, and J. D. Porter, "Who Cares about Literary Prizes?" *Public Books* September 3, 2019, https://www.publicbooks.org/who-cares-about-literary-prizes/ (accessed December 10, 2019). Graham Huggan has shown how the Booker is deeply implicated in imperial history and global capital, in *The Postcolonial Exotic: Marketing the Margins*. I engage with Huggan's arguments in Chapter 3.
69 English, *The Economy of Prestige*, 54, 52.
70 Ibid., 51.
71 Ibid., 212. As English elaborates, "The prize [depends] on this collective belief, since its own currency, however tainted or debased, is understood to derive from this other and purer form, which stands in relation to the economy of cultural prestige as gold did to the cash economy in the days of the gold standard—perfectly magical guarantor of an imperfectly magical system."
72 Nicholas Brown, *Autonomy: The Social Ontology of Art under Capitalism*, 33, 182, 34.
73 Crosthwaite, *The Market Logics of Contemporary Fiction*, 12–15, 7.
74 Brouillette, *Literature and the Creative Economy*, 50.

75 Latham, *Am I a Snob*, 8.
76 James, "Introduction," *The Legacies of Modernism*, 1.
77 See Rosen, *Minor Characters Have Their Day*, 29–30.
78 Sarah Brouillette and others have addressed the marketing of "diversity" in the literary field, from postcolonialism to multiculturalism, and how it obscures or distorts the privileges of access; I engage with this relevant work in Chapters 3 and 5. For a recent and very revealing data-based study of racial inequality in postwar publishing, see Richard Jean So, *Redlining Culture: A Data History of Racial Inequality and Postwar Fiction*.
79 Theodor Adorno, *Aesthetic Theory*, 336.

1 Signature to Brand: Martin Amis's Negotiations with Literary Celebrity

1 Martin Amis, *Experience: A Memoir*, 247.
2 Sarah Lyall, writing for the London special edition of the *New York Times*, summarized the outlook of the British literary establishment:

"Part of what took everyone aback," said Peter Straus, the editor of Picador, a division of Macmillan, "is that Mr. Amis is a literary novelist, not a commercial writer like the high-earning authors Jeffrey Archer, John Grisham and Barbara Taylor Bradford." "Commerce and literature are still meant to be separate in England,' Mr. Straus said. "If you're writing mass-market fiction, it doesn't matter your price: you can be as vulgar as you want in terms of money. But somehow that isn't the same for literary fiction." (August 14, 2013, http://www.nytimes.com/books/98/02/01/home/amis-bigdeal.html, accessed September 3, 2013)

3 Keep in mind that this was 1995, when it was still possible for some in the business, like editor Peter Straus, to see literary fiction as operating in a field distinct from its more commercial cousins, even though it's part of the same larger field of corporate-based trade publishing. Indeed, Andrew Wylie, the agent who "poached" Amis from Pat Kavanagh, played a significant role at this time in shifting the terms that star authors could expect from major publishers in the UK and the United States. Widely referred to as "the jackal," Wylie began in 1980 as an outsider with an interest in promoting the authors of serious "backlist oriented" work with lower initial sales but who would generate more revenue in the long run. To do so, he and other agents essentially challenged the existing close ties between big agencies and publishers and focused on attracting a large number of authors whose work would sell steadily over time. Wylie insists that poaching authors like Amis is par for the course: "I think it's lazy or quaint or both to assume that one doesn't poach. It is pretending that publishing is a business peopled by members of a social elite who

have a sort of gentlemanly game going, and the gentlemanly game was played to the disadvantage of the writer" (qtd. in John B. Thompson, *Merchants of Culture: The Publishing Business in the Twenty-First Century*, 66–8, 68).
4 See Paul Delany, *Literature, Money and the Market: From Trollope to Amis*, 180. Delany perhaps overstates the case that authors lost much of their control over the fate of their writing. As Richard Todd argues, publishers promote lead authors' books and brand names at the expense of lesser ones, "maintaining good relationships between author (and agent) and publisher is seen by both parties as a matter of great importance, since it may develop into a career-long cooperation" ("Literary Fiction and the Book Trade," in *A Concise Companion to Contemporary British Fiction*, ed. James F. English, 31).
5 Todd, "Literary Fiction and the Book Trade," 20. Perhaps the most thorough study of trade book publishing today is John B. Thompson, *Merchants of Culture*.
6 Delany, *Literature, Money and the Market*, 182; Todd, "Literary Fiction and the Book Trade," 26.
7 Or, as James Diedrick says of the media affair involving Amis and his publishing switch, "it became clear that for a writer who attains celebrity status, public reception of his work often has little to do with genuine questions of literary value" (*Understanding Martin Amis*, 145). While I generally agree with this statement, I also think that Amis's representative celebrity status and his place in publishing today indicates that "genuine questions of literary value," implying autonomy from market considerations, has become passé, to say the least. As I argued in the introduction, critics since Bourdieu have reassessed the notion of separate spheres in the construction of literary and commercial values.
8 I take the phrase "shithead factfile," and the general tone here, from Amis's *Experience*, 248.
9 Delany, *Literature, Money, and the Market*, 184.
10 On Lewis's capitulation to self-marketing as a necessary move in critiquing commodification, especially evident in *The Apes of God*, his scathing send-up of fellow modernists of all stripes, see Rod Rosenquist, *Modernism, the Market, and the Institution of the New*, 69–74. For a discussion of how Waugh's satirical depiction of hollow publicity in *Vile Bodies* helped secure his own celebrity, see Aaron Jaffe, *Modernism and the Culture of Celebrity*, 47–50.
11 Ian Gregson also refers to "the self-conscious cartoon flatness" of Amis's characters, seeing it as a "posthuman" device that responds to a loss of Romantic values: "Amis's caricatural vision is most accurately seen as satirizing a contemporary state of affairs in which Romantic values have been thoroughly trashed" (see *Character and Satire in Postwar Fiction*, 132).
12 While he isn't focused on Amis and modernism, my observations here align with Paul Crosthwaite's recent arguments in *The Market Logics of Contemporary Fiction*.

Concerned with how postmodern fiction internalizes the market forces that help produce it, Crosthwaite rightly asserts that that narrative act consciously mediates the process, holding out space for critical reflection that is in excess of marketing. As I go on to show, Amis also brings a self-fashioning modernist mode of satire to bear on that mediating process.

13 See Jonathan Goldman, *Modernism Is the Literature of Celebrity*, 11–12.
14 James F. English and John Frow, "Literary Authorship and Celebrity Culture," in *A Concise Companion to Contemporary British Fiction*, ed. James F. English, 48.
15 Delany, *Literature, Money, and the Market*, 182.
16 See Laura Doan, "'Sexy Greedy *Is* the Late Eighties': Power Systems in Amis's *Money* and Churchill's *Serious Money*," *Minnesota Review* 34.35 (1990): 69–80; Amy Elias, "Meta-Mimesis? The Problem of British Postmodern Realism," *Restant* 21.9 (1993): 10–31; Kiernan Ryan, "Sex, Violence, and Complicity: Martin Amis and Ian McEwan," in *An Introduction to Contemporary Fiction*, ed. Rod Mengham, 203–18; Elie Edmondson, "Martin Amis Writes Postmodern Man," *Critique* 42.2 (2001): 145–54; Jon Begley, "Satirizing the Carnival of Postmodern Capitalism: The Transatlantic and Dialogic Structure of Martin Amis's *Money*," *Contemporary Literature* 45.1 (2004): 79–105; and Nicky Marsh, "Taking the Maggie: Money, Sovereignty, and Masculinity in British Fiction of the Eighties," *Modern Fiction Studies* 53.4 (2007): 845–66.
17 For an extended analysis of Amis's doubles, see Richard Todd, "Looking-Glass Worlds in Martin Amis's Early Fiction: Reflectiveness, Mirror Narcissism, and Doubles," in *Martin Amis: Postmodernism and Beyond*, ed. Gavin Keulks, 22–35.
18 Martin Amis, *Success*, 11, 33. Hereafter abbreviated *S*. and cited parenthetically in the text.
19 Delany, *Literature, Money, and the Market*, 175.
20 For a useful summary of these economic crises and shifts leading into the Thatcher years, see Patrick Brantlinger, *Fictions of State: Culture and Credit in Britain, 1694–1994*, 253–4.
21 T. S. Eliot, *The Wasteland*, in *The Complete Poems and Plays, 1909–1950*, 37, 50 (lines 1, 431).
22 Delany calls attention to the novel's satirical representation of excessive, even "mad" consumerism in the United States (the setting alternates between New York and London), but complains that because of its totalizing focus on a money-driven society, "the novel is enfeebled by the disappearance of any rival moral system" (see *Literature, Money and the Market*, 177–8). Laura Doan argues that the novel's protagonist John Self acts as a failed metonym for Thatcherite ideology ("'Sexy Greedy Is the Late Eighties,'" 79). Begley situates the novel between a postimperial Britain in decline and an ascendant US consumerism ("Satirizing the Carnival of Postmodern Capitalism"). Nicky Marsh shows the novel's response to financial deregulation in the period, but argues that its satirical indictment of global capital

and unbridled consumerist greed fails because it ultimately equates a loss of male sovereignty with castrating women ("Taking the Maggie").
23 Tamás Bényei also points out John Self's role as an allegorical figure for a reified excessive consumption, arguing that "he is, as it were a meta-fetishist: his enjoyment is displaced onto 'money' as the *possibility of pleasure*. He craves desire itself, the endless metonymic postponement of enjoyment," and "the ultimate allegorical figure of consumer society, a figure of waste" (see "The Passion of John Self: Allegory, Economy, and Expenditure in Martin Amis's *Money*," in *Martin Amis*, ed. Keulks, 41, 48).
24 Brantlinger, *Fictions of State*, 259.
25 See Bényei, "The Passion of John Self," 36–54.
26 Begley, "Satirizing the Carnival of Postmodern Capitalism," 84.
27 Martin Amis, *Money: A Suicide Note*, 24. Hereafter abbreviated *M*. and cited parenthetically in the text.
28 Nicky Marsh provides an in-depth, if meandering, summary of this state of affairs as it pertains to the novel (see "Taking the Maggie" [cited above], 855). Building on Marsh's reading, Roberto del Valle Alcalá shows how *Money* is steeped in the crisis of post-Fordist economics, arguing that the problem of representation in the novel reflects the breakdown in referentiality brought on by decoupling money from gold. See "Martin Amis's *Money* and the Crisis of Fordism," *Critique: Studies in Contemporary Fiction* 60.1 (2019): 1–10.
29 Begley, "Satirizing the Carnival of Postmodern Capitalism," 99.
30 Diedrick, *Understanding Martin Amis*, 98.
31 See Tew, "Martin Amis and Late-Twentieth Century Working-Class Masculinity: *Money* and *London Fields*," in *Martin Amis*, ed. Keulks, 78.
32 Lawrence Driscoll, *Evading Class in Contemporary British Literature*, 100.
33 This replaying of the swindle on the part of the metafictional Amis points, again, to the recurring problem of class in his work. As Lawrence Driscoll argues (citing Gavin Keulks) about the Self-Amis relation, "while these working-class characters are at the center of these novels, they are also relegated to the margins by 'the superior, ironizing voice' of the author" (*Evading Class*, 107).
34 In a similar vein, Begley suggests that the novel's dialogical pairing works to "undermine the status of the authorial presence and his narrative designs, thereby reaffirming the premise of his cultural critique by implicating both figures within an economic system that resists the imposition of any encompassing 'Answers'" ("Satirizing the Carnival of Postmodern Capitalism," 98).
35 Amis, *Experience*, 275. For the story on Wilde's celebrity self-promotion, see Goldman's *Modernism Is the Literature of Celebrity*, 19–54.
36 This is from Amis's more recent reflections in *The Rub of Time: Bellow, Nabokov, Hitchens, Travolta, Trump: Essays and Reportage, 1994–2017*, 112. Clearly, Amis

continues to be preoccupied with the mediated conditions of his own public image and their impact on his work and reception.

37 *The Information*, 52. Hereafter abbreviated *I.* and cited parenthetically in the text.

38 We might note here another ironic allusion to Beckett. Amis writes that Richard's current manuscript, *Untitled*, uses a "rotating crew of sixteen unreliable narrators," which sounds like Molloy's scheme of rotating sixteen sucking stones in his pockets, a scheme that itself winds up being unreliable. See *Three Novels: Molloy, Malone Dies, The Unnamable*, 69–74.

39 See Niall Gildea and David Wylot, "The And of Modernism: On New Periodizations," *Modernist Cultures* 14.4 (2019): 446–68.

40 Sarah Brouillette, *Postcolonial Writers and the Global Literary Marketplace*, 65. I cite Brouillette here because she stresses the significance of marketing an author's image as part of celebrity production. For a fuller discussion of the specific and increasingly powerful role played by literary agents, from the 1970s to the present, see Thompson, *Merchants of Culture*, 59–100. Most importantly, Thompson points out how the process of rapid consolidation among publishing houses made editors more mobile, either because they were pushed out, sought out by new corporations, or moved on for better salaries. This weakened relations between authors and editors, making agents more necessary to "deal with a world that was becoming less personal and more corporate, more complex and businesslike, by the day" (73).

41 Brouillette, *Postcolonial Writers*, 66.

42 Richard Menke, "Mimesis and Informatics in *The Information*," in *Martin Amis*, ed. Keulks, 149. Menke mentions the novel's insider mockery of literary celebrity, but focuses on the more general concerns about the information age and the media environment that it reflects.

43 Brouillette, *Postcolonial Writers*, 67.

44 This synergy between the global corporate mass production of literature and appeals to its distinctly cultural value operates like "the culture of prestige" surrounding cultural prizes as analyzed by James F. English. As English shows, the apparently binary relationship between the commercial and the high cultural is better seen as part of a larger system of circulating cultural values, so that the commercial operations both prop up an allegedly antithetical desire for pure art and gain immense symbolic and cultural value—added to the commercial value—from that antithesis. So cultural prizes—like other markers of cultural prestige—"have traditionally been useful in providing regular occasions for … critics to rehearse Enlightenment pieties about 'pure' art and 'authentic' forms of greatness or genius, and thereby to align themselves with 'higher' values, or more symbolically potent forms of capital," but "such rehearsals do nothing to discredit the cultural prize, and in fact serve as a crucial support for it inasmuch as they help to keep aloft the collective belief or make-belief in artistic value as such." Thus, "without

disappearing, the modern discourse of autonomy has become a tactical fiction, or at least an imperfectly sincere one" (see *The Economy of Prestige: Prizes, Awards, and the Circulation of Cultural Value*, 212, 236).

45 This is of course a comically overblown joke about the real practice of creating an author's platform, as it's called in the business. As Thompson puts it in *Merchants of Culture*, "platform is the position from which an author speaks—a combination of their credentials, visibility and promotability, especially through the media. It is those traits and accomplishments of the author that establish a pre-existing audience for their work, and that a publisher can leverage in the attempt to find a market for their book" (87).

46 Catherine Bernard, "Under the Dark Sun of Melancholia: Writing and Loss in *The Information*," in *Martin Amis*, ed. Keulks, 132.

47 Graham Fuller, "The Prose and Cons of Martin Amis," interview with Martin Amis, *Interview* May 1995, 124.

48 I quote Daragh O'Reilly, "Martin Amis on Marketing," in *Consuming Books: The Marketing and Consumption of Literature*, ed. Stephen Brown , 77. I take the description of the London marketing campaign for the novel from Claire Squires, *Marketing Literature*, 117.

49 "Hype" in creating "big books" that *might* become bestsellers—with no way of knowing or guaranteeing that outcome—is common and explains the marketing of *The Information*. See Thompson, *Merchants of Culture*, 193–5.

50 In fact, according to Delany, the marketing for the paperback of *The Information* emphasized Amis's huge advance on the novel to arouse readers' curiosity, "encouraging people to buy the book to decide for themselves whether it was worth what was paid for it" (183).

51 Will Norman, "Killing the Crime Novel: Martin Amis's *Night Train*, Genre and Literary Fiction," *Journal of Modern Literature* 35.1 (Fall 2011): 38.

2 "To Invent a Literature": Ian McEwan's Commercial Modernism

1 Aida Edemariam, Interview with Ian McEwan, *Guardian*, August 18, 2007.
2 See Kiernan Ryan, *Ian McEwan*, 2.
3 Ibid., 5, 4. In his monograph on McEwan, Dominic Head elaborates on this assessment of the strange ethical impulse that is especially evident in his earlier fiction, noting in particular the tensions between "an ongoing search for systematic ways of knowing the world" and "a keen anxiety in McEwan about the absence of foundational beliefs" (see *Ian McEwan*, 15).

4 Daniel Zalewski, "The Background Hum: Ian McEwan's Art of Unease," *New Yorker*, February 23, 2009, qtd. in David James, *Modernist Futures: Innovation and Inheritance in the Contemporary Novel*, 136.
5 Zadie Smith, Interview with Ian McEwan, *The Believer* 26 (August 2005): 53.
6 Ambivalence is central to David James's assessment of McEwan's use of impressionist formal strategies. I address that argument in what follows.
7 See Jonah Siegel, "Looking at the Limits of Autonomy: Response," *Victorian Studies* 51.3 (Spring 2009): 497; Sebastian Groes, "Ian McEwan and the Modernist Consciousness of the City in *Saturday*," in *Ian McEwan: Contemporary Critical Perspectives*, ed. Sebastian Groes, 104; and Laura Marcus, "Ian McEwan's Modernist Time: *Atonement* and *Saturday*," in *Ian McEwan*, ed. Groes, 83–98.
8 See Derek Attridge, *J. M. Coetzee and the Ethics of Reading: Literature in the Event*, 5; and David James's edited volume, *The Legacies of Modernism: Historicising Postwar and Contemporary Fiction*.
9 See Marcus, "Ian McEwan's Modernist Time," in *Ian McEwan*, ed. Groes, 85.
10 James, *Modernist Futures*, 136, 138.
11 Ibid., 137.
12 Pierre Bourdieu, *The Field of Cultural Production: Essays on Art and Literature*, 115, 169.
13 Sean Latham, *Am I a Snob: Modernism and the Novel*, 2.
14 Andrew Goldstone, *Fictions of Autonomy: Modernism from Wilde to de Man*, 4.
15 I draw here on Brouillette's useful generalization that "the figure of the author becomes an increasingly important marker of differentiation, a way of concealing mass production in individuation" (*Postcolonial Writers and the Global Literary Marketplace*, 66).
16 As Jeremy Rosen suggests in his reading of the immensely popular genre of "minor character elaboration," or the rewriting of canonical works from the perspectives of marginalized figures, authors who deploy this strategy are "in possession of significant quantities of cultural capital" that they can "leverage … to gain strategic advantages in a highly competitive literary marketplace" (see *Minor Characters Have Their Day: Genre and the Contemporary Literary Marketplace*, 29–30).
17 Jesse Matz, *Lasting Impressions: The Legacies of Impressionism in Contemporary Culture*, 229.
18 See Dominic Head, *Ian McEwan*, 144.
19 Frank Kermode, "Point of View" (Review of *Atonement*), *London Review of Books* 23.19 (October 4, 2001): 8. In her review of the novella Juliet Waters also places its satire firmly within the literary establishment it inhabits, noting "a satisfying irony in knowing that this is exactly the kind of book that the society McEwan satirizes would pick as the best book of the year" ("The Little Chill: Has the Booker Prize Chosen the Noveau Beaujolais of Fiction?" cited in Head, *Ian McEwan*, 144–5).

20 Head, *Ian McEwan*, 145, 154.
21 As Richard Todd notes, "controversy has in many respects been the making of the Booker Prize," and "it is surely by 'getting it wrong' that the Booker survives," a point James English elaborates on in arguing that "modern cultural prizes cannot fulfill their social functions unless authoritative people—people whose cultural authority is secured in part through these prizes—are thundering against them" (Richard Todd, *Consuming Fictions: The Booker Prize and Fiction in Britain Today*, 64; James English, *The Economy of Prestige: Prizes, Awards, and the Circulation of Cultural Value*, 25).
22 English, *The Economy of Prestige*, 212.
23 Adam Begley, "The Art of Fiction CLXXIII," interview with Ian McEwan, *The Paris Review* 44.162 (Summer 2002): 30–60; rpt. in *Conversations with Ian McEwan*, ed. Ryan Roberts, 89–107, 103.
24 Geoff Dyer, "Who's Afraid of Influence" (Review of *Atonement*), *Guardian*, September 22, 2001, 8.
25 James, *Modernist Futures*, 137, 140.
26 Richard Robinson, "The Modernism of Ian McEwan's *Atonement*," *Modern Fiction Studies* 56.3 (Fall 2010): 479, 480, 481.
27 Ian McEwan, *Atonement*, 33–4. Hereafter abbreviated *A.* and cited parenthetically in the text.
28 Jesse Matz, *Literary Impressionism and Modernist Aesthetics*, 16.
29 Zadie Smith, Interview with Ian McEwan, *The Believer* 26 (August 2005): 50.
30 Matz, *Literary Impressionism*, 1.
31 Virginia Woolf, "Mr. Bennett and Mrs. Brown," in *The Virginia Woolf Reader*, ed. Mitchell A. Leaska, 194; *The Diary of Virginia Woolf, Vol. 2*, ed. Anne Olivier Bell, 248.
32 Robinson, "The Modernism of Ian McEwan's *Atonement*," 477.
33 Ibid., 475.
34 David Lynn, "A Conversation with Ian McEwan," *The Kenyon Review* 29.3 (Summer 2007); rpt. in *Conversations with Ian McEwan*, 153.
35 Qtd. in Brian Finney, "Briony's Stand against Oblivion: Ian McEwan's *Atonement*," *Journal of Modern Literature* 27.3 (2004): 71.
36 James, *Modernist Futures*, 140.
37 See Marcus, "Ian McEwan's Modernist Time," in *Ian McEwan*, ed. Groes, 85.
38 Smith, Interview with Ian McEwan, 50.
39 Robinson, "The Modernism of Ian McEwan's *Atonement*," 479.
40 Fredric Jameson, *The Antinomies of Realism*, 139.
41 Robinson, "The Modernism of Ian McEwan's *Atonement*," 479.
42 Ibid., 479, 480, 481.
43 Matz, *Lasting Impressions*, 228–53.

44 Ibid., 232.
45 Ibid., 26.
46 Ibid., 248, 247.
47 Jeremy Rosen identifies this as an authorial performance of "a more-than-passing familiarity with 'great books,' even if this familiarity manifests itself in a critical stance toward those books," that can "mark literariness" and provide "strategic advantages in a highly competitive literary marketplace" (*Minor Characters Have Their Day*, 30).
48 Another crucial ingredient, one that is especially relevant to *Atonement*, is the film tie-in. Following the 2003 Anchor publication of a trade paperback edition, by 2007 the novel was selling between 1,000 and 2,000 copies per week. Then, just prior to the 2007 release of the film, and accompanied by a new paperback featuring the lead actors' pictures on the cover, sales soared to over 77,000 copies per week and, by early 2008, after the film's release, the novel became number one on the *New York Times* best-seller list. For more thorough data and analysis, see John B. Thompson, *Merchants of Culture: The Publishing Business in the Twenty-First Century*, 281–3.
49 Pierre Bourdieu, *The Rules of Art: Genesis and Structure of the Literary Field*, 167.
50 Sarah Brouillette, *Literature and the Creative Economy*, 50.
51 James Joyce, *A Portrait of the Artist as a Young Man: A Norton Critical Edition*, ed. John Paul Riquelme, 189.
52 Jonathan Goldman, *Modernism Is the Literature of Celebrity*, 62, 64, 65.
53 See Mark Currie, *About Time: Narrative, Fiction, and the Philosophy of Time*; Sebastian Groes, "Ian McEwan and the Modernist Consciousness of the City in *Saturday*," in *Ian McEwan*, ed. Groes, 99–114; and Marcus, "Ian McEwan's Modernist Time," in *Ian McEwan*, ed. Groes, 83–98.
54 On the former approach, see, e.g., John Banville, "A Day in the Life," *New York Review of Books* (May 26, 2005): 8–9; Elizabeth Kowaleski Wallace, "Postcolonial Melancholia in Ian McEwan's *Saturday*," *Studies in the Novel* 39.4 (Winter 2007): 465–80; and Tim Gauthier, "'Selective in Your Mercies': Privilege, Vulnerability, and the Limits of Empathy in Ian McEwan's *Saturday*," *College Literature* 40.2 (Spring 2013): 7–30. Critics questioning McEwan's presentation of Perowne include Molly Clark Hillard, "'When Desert Armies Stand Ready to Fight': Re-reading McEwan's *Saturday* and Arnold's 'Dover Beach,'" *Partial Answers: Journal of Literature and History of Ideas* 6.1 (January 2008): 181–206; and Teresa Winterhalter, "'Plastic Fork in Hand': Reading as a Tool of Ethical Repair in Ian McEwan's *Saturday*," *Journal of Narrative Theory* 40.3 (Fall 2010): 338–63. Sarah Brouillette addresses this somewhat binary critical reception, and shifts attention to the novel's ironic representation of the value of the arts under New Labour; see *Literature and the Creative Economy*, 175–99.

55 Jonathan P. Eburne and Rita Felski, "Introduction: What Is an Avant-Garde," *New Literary History* 41.4 (Autumn 2010): xi.
56 See James, *Modernist Futures*, 147–9.
57 Ian McEwan, *Saturday*, 12.
58 Gauthier, "'Selective in Your Mercies,'" 9, 12.
59 Ian McEwan, "Enduring Fame," interview with Aida Edemariam, *Guardian*, August 18, 2007, https://www.theguardian.com/uk/2007/aug/18/film.aidaedemariam (accessed August 5, 2019).
60 Brouillette, *Literature and the Creative Economy*, 184. As my citation suggests, Brouillette's reading is in many ways parallel to my own. She argues that *Saturday* implicitly performs a kind of confession of literature's complicity in the creative economies of neoliberal governments, a point I extend below in arguing that the novel betrays McEwan's resignation to his role as an elite cultural producer.
61 I draw here on Currie, *About Time*, 132.
62 See especially the essays by Groes and Marcus, in *Ian McEwan*, ed. Groes.
63 Although he does not discuss *Mrs. Dalloway*, Sean Latham has much to say about Woolf's snobbery and its role in her ongoing negotiations with the literary marketplace and modernist aesthetics. See *Am I a Snob? Modernism and the Novel*, 59–117.
64 Virginia Woolf, *Mrs. Dalloway*, 11–12.
65 Jennifer Wicke, "Coterie Consumption: Bloomsbury, Keynes, and Modernism as Marketing," in *Marketing Modernisms: Self-Promotion, Canonization, Rereading*, ed. Kevin J. H. Dettmar and Stephen Watt, 117. See also Carey James Mickalites, *Modernism and Market Fantasy: British Fictions of Capital, 1910–1939*, 133–69.
66 Karl Marx, *Capital: A Critique of Political Economy, Vol. 1*, trans. Samuel Moore and Edward Aveling, 84.
67 Marco Roth, "Rise of the Neuronovel," *n + 1*, September 14, 2009, https://nplusonemag.com/issue-8/essays/the-rise-of-the-neuronovel (accessed August 6, 2019).
68 Brouillette, *Literature and the Creative Economy*, 208.
69 Michael L. Ross offers perhaps the strongest refutation of an easy ameliorative reading: "What the incident primarily establishes is the intruder's ineluctable alienation from Perowne family values—from the community of print wizardry that empowers the family, ratifying their social supremacy" (see "On a Darkling Planet: Ian McEwan's 'Saturday' and the Condition of England," *Twentieth Century Literature* 54.1 (Spring 2008): 87). Others have also questioned this apparent endorsement: see especially Hillard, "'When Desert Armies Stand Ready to Fight,'" 181–206; and Winterhalter, "'Plastic Fork in Hand,'" 338–63.
70 Cited in John Guillory, *Cultural Capital: The Problem of Literary Canon Formation*, 136.
71 Ibid.

72 For a critique of contemporary social resignation to this lack of imagined alternatives, see Mark Fisher, *Capitalist Realism: Is There No Alternative?*
73 Brouillette, *Literature and the Creative Economy*, 199.
74 In interviews McEwan frequently defends this stance. For example, in 1995 he states that "it is at the level of empathy that moral questions begin in fiction"; and ten years later, following the publication of *Saturday*, he says "there's something very entwined about imagination and morals," something that the "elastic, mutable form" of the novel allows us to explore ("An Interview with Ian McEwan," and "Zadie Smith Talks with Ian McEwan," in *Conversations with Ian McEwan*, 70, 112).
75 Here I follow Brouillette's conclusions about the novel, and extend them to argue that *Saturday* demonstrates McEwan's participation in the commodification of modernism as an elite field of reference for generating both cultural authority and economic capital. See Brouillette, *Literature and the Creative Economy*, 199.
76 Pierre Bourdieu, *Distinction: A Social Critique of the Judgment of Taste*, 1; and Bourdieu, *The Logic of Practice*, 50.
77 Pierre Bourdieu, "The Market for Symbolic Goods," *Poetics* 14.1–2 (1985): 16.
78 See Dan Sinykin, "The Conglomerate Era: Publishing, Authorship, and Literary Form, 1965–2007," 470, 486–8.
79 See Paul Crosthwaite, *The Market Logics of Contemporary Fiction*, 24–6.
80 Ian McEwan, *Sweet Tooth*, 228. Hereafter abbreviated *ST* and cited parenthetically in the text.
81 See English, *The Economy of Prestige*, 208.

3 Modernism as Postcolonial Inc.: Authorizing Salman Rushdie

1 "Introduction," *Midnight's Children*, ix, x. Hereafter cited parenthetically in the text as *MC*.
2 Rushdie is merely one especially famous figure within a body of criticism linking postcolonial literature to modernist experiment and political dissent. Simon Gikandi, in fact, makes the rather sweeping claim that the "convergence of political and literary ideologies mark a significant part of the history of modernism and postcolonialism. Indeed, it is my contention that it was primarily—I am tempted to say solely—in the language and structure of modernism that a postcolonial experience came to be articulated and imagined in literary form" ("Preface: Modernism in the World," *Modernism/modernity* 13.3 (September 2006): 420).
3 I take the phrase from the title of Laura Marcus's essay, which addresses the "direct influence" of major modernists on fiction produced since the mid-twentieth

century. See Marcus, "Legacies of Modernism," in *The Cambridge Companion to the Modernist Novel*, ed. Morag Shiach, 82–98.
4 Ibid., 89, 90.
5 Rebecca Walkowitz, *Cosmopolitan Style: Modernism beyond the Nation*, 131, 139.
6 Jean Kane, *Conspicuous Bodies: Provincial Belief and the Making of Joyce and Rushdie*, 44, 68.
7 Robert Eaglestone, "Introduction: Salman Rushdie," in *Salman Rushdie: Contemporary Critical Perspectives*, ed. Robert Eaglestone and Martin McQuillan, 1.
8 See James English, *The Economy of Prestige: Prizes, Awards, and the Circulation of Cultural Value*; and also Pascale Casanova, *The World Republic of Letters*, 15–17.
9 See Aijaz Ahmad, *In Theory: Classes, Nations, Literatures*, 157–8; and Timothy Brennan, *At Home in the World: Cosmopolitanism Now*, 306; and Brennan, *Salman Rushdie and the Third World: Myths of the Nation*, 166, 165.
10 I'm referring specifically to Graham Huggan's "The Postcolonial Exotic," *Transition* 64 (1994): 24, 29, but see also his essay, "Prizing 'Otherness': A Short History of the Booker," *Studies in the Novel* 29.3 (Fall 1997): 412–33; and Huggan, *The Postcolonial Exotic: Marketing the Margins*.
11 See Sarah Brouillette, *Postcolonial Writers in the Global Literary Marketplace*, 82.
12 Ibid., 82, 87, 107.
13 Casanova, *The World Republic of Letters*, 169, 171, 172.
14 This general claim channels the political, cosmopolitan, and materialist readings of Timothy Brennan, Jean Kane, and Graham Huggan, respectively. Writing fairly early in Rushdie's career, Brennan placed his work up through *The Satanic Verses* in a vexed position within Third World literature and politics, arguing that the novel's metafictional frame enacts "an allegory of narrative composition" that uses and explodes Indian myths sacred to nationalist literatures in order to make himself its subversive "culmination." Kane argues that Rushdie follows Joyce in their shared "rejection of national predecessors," adding that he writes a self-consciously "literary" India by attempting to "resolve" the problem of his own distanced identity through Saleem as an "authentic agent." Taking a materialist critical approach to Rushdie's work in the literary market, as I have pointed out, Huggan argues that his fiction manipulates the "commercial codes" of Indian otherness both to exploit them and to critique Western liberal readers' guilty pleasure in consuming "the postcolonial exotic." See Brennan, *Salman Rushdie and the Third World*, 105, 80, 83; Kane, *Conspicuous Bodies*, 44, 43; and Huggan, "The Postcolonial Exotic," 24, 29.
15 Rushdie, *Imaginary Homelands*, 10.
16 Rushdie, *Midnight's Children*, 124–5. Hereafter abbreviated *MC* and cited parenthetically in the text.

17 Bill Ashcroft, *Postcolonial Transformation*, 155.
18 And note that in "Imaginary Homelands" he stresses that he was writing what he calls "my India," one of an infinite variety of possibilities. See *Imaginary Homelands*, 10.
19 Casanova, *The World Republic of Letters*, 86.
20 Brennan, *Salman Rushdie and the Third World*, 105.
21 Roger Y. Clark, *Stranger Gods: Salman Rushdie's Other Worlds*, 14.
22 This brief discussion is a partial summary of Roger Y. Clark's thorough analysis of Rushdie's use of mythic and religious correspondences in the novel. See *Stranger Gods*, 14, 61–99.
23 Brennan, *Salman Rushdie and the Third World*, 80, 101.
24 Michael Kaufman, "Author from Three Countries," *New York Times Book Review*, November 13, 1983; qtd. in Kane, *Conspicuous Bodies*, 44.
25 This is a slight twist on Brennan's sense that it "is not that the entire Indo-English tradition is only a prelude to its culmination in Rushdie, but that Rushdie playfully alludes to earlier moments of Indo-English fiction as though he were its culmination. It is part of his joke" (see *Salman Rushdie and the Third World*, 83). On my reading, Rushdie adapts elements of that Indo-English tradition to a modernist mode of self-fashioning, including a claim to literary autonomy from the predecessors whose work he parodies.
26 For Joyce's own description of his compositional process, see "James Joyce to Frank Budgen, 20 March 1920," in *Letters of James Joyce, Vol. 1*, ed. Stuart Gilbert, 139–40. And I quote here from Goldman, *Modernism Is the Literature of Celebrity*, 62, 7.
27 Pierre Bourdieu, *The Rules of Art: Genesis and Structure of the Literary Field*, 229, 104, 167, 345, 347.
28 Casanova, *The World Republic of Letters*, 169, 171.
29 Brennan, *At Home in the World*, 38; and Brennan, "Cosmopolitans and Celebrities," *Race and Class* 31.1 (1989): 2.
30 See Huggan, "Prizing 'Otherness,'" 424; and Huggan, *The Postcolonial Exotic*, 6, 69–70, 73–3, 94.
31 Brouillette, *Postcolonial Writers*, 69.
32 Kane, *Conspicuous Bodies*, 45, 43.
33 Brennan, *Salman Rushdie and the Third World*, 101, 106.
34 Or, as Anjali Gera Roy argues, "locating the 'marvellous' in the Indian masses, Saleem/Rushdie sidesteps the danger of too facile an identification with the traditional, indigenous, mystical and miracle-laden, which the elite Indian's secular origin denies him unqualified participation in" (see "Fact and Fantasy, Myth and History: The Magic Realist Mode in Salman Rushdie's Fiction," in *Mapping Out the Rushdie Republic: Some Recent Surveys*, ed. Tapan Kumar Ghosh and Prasanta Bhattacharyya, 38).

35 Neil Lazarus, *The Postcolonial Unconscious*, 55.
36 This claim is no doubt influenced by Fredric Jameson's writing on the ideology of the aesthetic generally: "Ideology is not something which informs or invests symbolic production; rather the aesthetic act is itself ideological, and the production of aesthetic or narrative form is to be seen as an ideological act in its own right, with the function of inventing imaginary or formal 'solutions' to unresolvable social contradictions" (*The Political Unconscious*, 79).
37 This is a significant argument in Huggan's "Prizing 'Otherness.'"
38 For a survey of this reception and how its use of marketable terms like "diaspora" and "exile" elide regional Indian realities, see Brouillette, *Postcolonial Writers*, 86–8.
39 For a concise analysis of this bind, see Andrew Wernick, "Authorship and the Supplement of Promotion," in *What Is an Author*, ed. Maurice Biriotti and Nicola Miller, 85–103.
40 Neil ten Kortenaar, "Fearful Symmetry: Salman Rushdie and Prophetic Newness," *Twentieth-Century Literature* 54.3 (Fall 2008): 345.
41 I owe this summary in part to Sarah Brouillette; see *Postcolonial Writers*, 84–5.
42 Lazarus, *The Postcolonial Unconscious*, 31.
43 Salman Rushdie, *The Satanic Verses*, 61. Hereafter abbreviated *SV* and cited parenthetically in the text.
44 Kane, *Conspicuous Bodies*, 108–9.
45 Ibid., 108.
46 The phrase occurs in the novel itself, in one of the earlier passages concerned with Muhammad (*The Satanic Verses*, 95), but in the essay "In Good Faith" Rushdie applies it to the novel's anti-racist intentions more generally. See *Imaginary Homelands*, 402.
47 Kane, *Conspicuous Bodies*, 110.
48 Kane demonstrates how this "dilemma" lies with the novel's use of "simulation as its idiom," with which I agree, but I situate that problem within the market for celebrity that Rushdie inhabits. See *Conspicuous Bodies*, 112.
49 See Brennan, *Salman Rushdie and the Third World*, 164.
50 Alex Knönagel, "*The Satanic Verses*: Narrative Structure and Islamic Doctrine," *International Fiction Review* 18.2 (1991): 71.
51 Brennan, *Salman Rushdie and the Third World*, 152.
52 Clark, *Stranger Gods*, 139.
53 Ibid., 169.
54 Ibid..
55 As Brennan suggests; see *Salman Rushdie and the Third World*, 163.
56 See Kortenaar, "Fearful Symmetry," 350.
57 See Wernick, "Authorship and the Supplement of Promotion," 100–1.
58 See Brouillette, *Literature and the Creative Economy*, 51.

59 See "In Good Faith," in *Imaginary Homelands*, 393–5, 405.
60 Sarah Crichton and Laura Shapiro, "An Exclusive Talk with Salman Rushdie," *Conversations with Salman Rushdie*, 130; and Blake Morrison, "An Interview with Salman Rushdie," in ibid., 136.
61 Martin Paul Eve offers the most concise and persuasive argument on this precedence of the market over academic canonization. As part of the gatekeeping system, academia provides a "*weaker relation*" than that of the publishers, and "the books that academics working on contemporary novels will consider part of the canon of literary fiction must have already been published and, therefore, pre-filtered" (*Literature against Criticism: University English and Contemporary Fiction in Conflict*, 21, 23).
62 See Brouillette, *Postcolonial Writers*, 83, 91–111.
63 For mostly favorable reviews that nevertheless note the novel's tedium, see Hermione Lee, "The Ground beneath Her Feet," *Guardian*, March 28, 1999, https://www.theguardian.com/books/1999/mar/28/fiction.salmanrushdie (accessed July 23, 2019); and the more critical one by Michiko Kakutani, "'The Ground beneath Her Feet': Turning Rock & Roll into Quakes," *New York Times*, April 13, 1999, https://archive.nytimes.com/www.nytimes.com/books/99/04/11/daily/041399rushdie-book-review.html (accessed July 23, 2019).
64 Paul Gray, "Ganja Growing in the Tin," *Time*, Sunday, April 18, 1999, http://content.time.com/time/magazine/article/0,9171,23279,00.html (accessed August 13, 2018).
65 These comments by Mundow and Blythe are extracts found in the front matter of the novel, originally published in *New York Daily News* and *Mirabella*, respectively.
66 Salman Rushdie, *The Ground beneath Her Feet*, 238. Hereafter abbreviated *GBF* and cited parenthetically in the text.
67 Susan Stanford Friedman, *Planetary Modernisms: Provocations on Modernity across Time*, 187–8.
68 Brouillette, *Postcolonial Writers*, 105–6, 190.
69 Salman Rushdie, *Joseph Anton: A Memoir*, 114–15.
70 Zoe Heller, "The Salman Rushdie Case," *New York Review of Books*, December 20, 2012, https://www.nybooks.com/articles/2012/12/20/salman-rushdie-case/ (accessed June 23, 2019).
71 Lazarus, *The Postcolonial Unconscious*, 31.
72 Ibid., 22.
73 *The Golden House* is a possible exception. The novel is set in New York late in 2016 and features a vile Joker-inspired presidential candidate as the target of its satire. It seems that it took the American political crisis of the century, finally, to trump Rushdie's ego.

4 What the Public Wants: Kazuo Ishiguro, Prize Culture, and the Art of Alienation

1 Allan Vorda and Kim Herzinger, "An Interview with Kazuo Ishiguro" (1990), in *Conversations with Kazuo Ishiguro*, ed. Brian W. Shaffer and Cynthia F. Wong, 69.
2 See Graham Huggan, "Prizing 'Otherness': A Short History of the Booker," *Studies in the Novel* 29. 3 (1997): 412–33; and Huggan, *The Postcolonial Exotic: Marketing the Margins*.
3 Several examples focused on *The Remains of the Day* are based on the assumption that Stevens is meant to stand in for the repressed traumas and political failures of the nation over the course of the tumultuous twentieth century. Several readers share an implicitly postmodern assumption about individual and national repression. Richard Bradford blames "Stevens's inability to move beyond his class-based obsessions," while Dominic Head finds in the narrator a "devastating portrait of repressed Englishness and an exploration of those national characteristics that must be expunged before an authentic post-nationalism can emerge"; and Frederick Holmes argues that he and other Ishiguro characters exhibit an "inability to come to terms with the historical traumas of the Second World War." See Bradford, *The Novel Now: Contemporary British Fiction*, 216; Head, *The Cambridge Introduction to Modern British Fiction 1950–2000*, 156; and Holmes, "Realism, Dreams, and the Unconscious in the Novels of Kazuo Ishiguro," in *The Contemporary British Novel since 1980*, ed. James Acheson and Sarah Ross, 12. Numerous others have read the novel in similar terms of individual and national repression and guilt, and perhaps the most convincing of these are Barry Lewis, *Kazuo Ishiguro*; and Brian Shaffer, *Understanding Kazuo Ishiguro*. While I don't wholly dismiss any of these interpretations, I think that they omit problems of professionalism and class during the Thatcher era that the novel is centrally concerned with. James Lang also reads the novel in terms of postmodern historiography, but in a way that provides an important corrective to some of the moral assumptions underpinning the work of these other critics, arguing that the novel works to "interrogate what the differences between public and private memories mean for our understanding of history itself" (James Lang, "Public Memory, Private History: Kazuo Ishiguro's *The Remains of the Day*," *CLIO* 29.2 (2000): 146, 153). Lang applies the narrative theory of Michael André Bernstein that challenges readers' assumptions about "backshadowing"—or applying what we know about the past to the limited agency of historical actors. See *Foregone Conclusions: Against Apocalyptic History*, 16.

The Remains of the Day has also been conveniently slotted into a postcolonial historicism. Susie O'Brien, e.g., rightly acknowledges that the novel explores and explodes a myth of Englishness, but goes on to argue that Stevens's fetishized term, "dignity" functions "like the Empire it served, [and] is predicated on surrendering the dictates of individual conscience and 'natural' human feeling to the authority of a rigidly (if arbitrarily) stratified social hierarchy," a reading that John McCombe tacitly follows in mapping the historical details of that last-ditch effort to preserve the ideology of empire, the Suez crisis, onto the fictional terrain of the novel and to conclude, like so many others, that Stevens is to blame for his "colonialist ideology" and "his belief in the benevolence of the father figure." See Susie O'Brien, "Serving a New World Order: Postcolonial Politics in Kazuo Ishiguro's *The Remains of the Day*," *Modern Fiction Studies* 42.4 (1996): 789, 790; John P. McCombe, "The End of (Anthony) Eden: Ishiguro's *The Remains of the Day* and Midcentury Anglo-American Tensions," *Twentieth Century Literature* 48.1 (Spring 2002): 77–99, 83.

4 Driscoll is centrally concerned with the "evasion" of class in Ishiguro and his contemporaries, and especially in the major critical reception of this work. While he doesn't offer his own sustained reading of *The Remains of the Day*, the Ishiguro novel he addresses, he persuasively exposes the class-oriented blind spots of criticism of that novel. See *Evading Class in Contemporary British Literature*, 55.

5 The key statements of Danius's speech can be found at https://www.nobelprize.org/prizes/literature/2017/summary/ (accessed January 10, 2021).

6 James English, *The Economy of Prestige: Prizes, Awards, and the Circulation of Cultural Value*, 58–60.

7 Ibid., 54, 52, 51.

8 See Neil Lazarus, *The Postcolonial Unconscious*, 31.

9 Allan Vorda and Kim Herzinger, "An Interview with Kazuo Ishiguro," 83–4. Lisa Fluet identifies a thread of specialization running throughout Ishiguro's work, "where a commitment to immaterial labor ultimately makes different forms of knowledge-work irrelevant to each other, inhibiting Ishiguro's hard-working characters from perceiving a life in common with other immaterial laborers" (Fluet, "Immaterial Labors: Ishiguro, Class, and Affect," *Novel* 40.3 (Summer 2007): 271).

10 Kazuo Ishiguro, "Memory Is the Terribly Treacherous Terrain," interview with Graham Swift, *BOMB* 29 (1989): 22–3.

11 Suanne Kelman, "Ishiguro in Toronto," *Conversations with Kazuo Ishiguro*, 48, 50.

12 Ned Rorem, "Fiction in Review," *Yale Review* 84 (1996): 159.

13 James Wood, "Ishiguro in the Underworld," *Guardian*, May 5, 1995, 5.

14 James Walton, "Arts Interview: The Artist Formerly Known as Populist," *Daily Telegraph*, May 6, 1995, AB4.

15 We might note here that a specific problem inhering in these reviews as well as some of the academic reception of the novel is its persistent questioning of the relationship between realism and the dream-like world of the novel, which can clearly be read as a gradually unfolding projection on the part of Ryder. One of

Ishiguro's primary intentions in writing *The Unconsoled* was to move directly away from psychological realism, so when readers look for the temporal and spatial distortions he develops in order to make them affirm some agreed-upon extra-diegetic reality, they miss the point. A. Harris Fairbanks has provided a useful corrective to this tendency, arguing that "the events are not those of a proper dream to be related to some ulterior reality; rather, they belong to a world in which events and the main character's psychological reactions operate as they do in a dream, but which is itself the ultimate reality" (Fairbanks, "Ontology and Narrative Technique in Kazuo Ishiguro's *The Unconsoled*," *Studies in the Novel* 45.4 (Winter 2013): 603–4).

16 For Ishiguro's dismissal of both the "Japanese" element in his fiction and critics' sense of documentary realism, see Gregory Mason, "An Interview with Kazuo Ishiguro," in *Conversations with Kazuo Ishiguro*, ed. Shaffer and Wong, 3–14.

17 For Ishiguro's discussion of these influences, see "Kazuo Ishiguro with Maya Jaggi" [interview, 1995] in *Conversations with Kazuo Ishiguro*, ed. Shaffer and Wong, 113–14.

18 I quote from Natalie Reitano, "The Good Wound: Memory and Community in *The Unconsoled*," *Texas Studies in Literature and Language* 49.4 (Winter 2007): 361. In addition to the critics I cite below, see Barry Lewis's brief summary of these Kafka comparisons in *Kazuo Ishiguro*, 124–5.

19 Robert Lemon, "The Comfort of Strangeness: Correlating the Kafkaesque and the Kafkan in Kazuo Ishiguro's *The Unconsoled*," in *Kafka for the Twenty-First Century*, ed. Stanley Corngold and Ruth V. Gross, 207–8.

20 Pierre François, "The Spectral Return of Depths in Kazuo Ishiguro's *The Unconsoled*," *Commonwealth: Essays and Studies* 26.2 (Spring 2004): 79, 87.

21 Reitano, "The Good Wound," 361. Reitano reads the novel as an allegory for the accelerated pace of our global present, experienced as a traumatic rupture from historical determinants, and argues that the dislocations of time, space, and belonging running throughout the novel strike an appeal for "the urgency of worldly (cosmopolitan) responsibility" (363, 380).

22 Cynthia Quarrie, "Impossible Inheritance: Filiation and Patrimony in Kazuo Ishiguro's *The Unconsoled*," *Critique* 55.2 (2014): 138–9.

23 See Wai-Chew Sim, *Kazuo Ishiguro*, 58.

24 Amit Chaudhuri, "Unlike Kafka," *London Review of Books* 17.11 (June 8, 1995): 30.

25 Ibid., 31.

26 François, "The Spectral Return of Depths," 80.

27 See Shaffer and Wong, *Conversations with Kazuo Ishiguro*, 118–19, 207.

28 Kazuo Ishiguro, *The Unconsoled*, 186, 197. Hereafter abbreviated *U.* and cited parenthetically in the text.

29 Lemon, "The Comfort of Strangeness," 211.

30 See Sim, *Kazuo Ishiguro*, 59.
31 François, "The Spectral Return of Depths," 80.
32 English, *The Economy of Prestige*, 52–3.
33 Linda Simon, "Remains of the Novelist," *Commonweal* 22 (March 1996): 25.
34 See Sim, *Kazuo Ishiguro*, 60.
35 Eric Hayot, *On Literary Worlds*, 44–5.
36 Theodor Adorno, *Aesthetic Theory*, 327.
37 Brouillette, *Literature and the Creative Economy*, 207.
38 Adorno, *Aesthetic Theory*, 336.
39 Nicholas Brown, *Autonomy: The Social Ontology of Art under Capitalism*, 182.
40 Bruce Robbins, "Cruelty Is Bad: Banality and Proximity in *Never Let Me Go*," *Novel* 40.3 (2007): 294.
41 Bruce Robbins, *Upward Mobility and the Common Good: Toward a Literary History of the Welfare State*, 205, 201.
42 Brouillette, *Literature and the Creative Economy*, 204, 200.
43 Kazuo Ishiguro, *Never Let Me Go*, 16, 17. Hereafter abbreviated *NLMG* and cited parenthetically in the text.
44 Shameem Black, "Ishiguro's Inhuman Aesthetics," *Modern Fiction Studies* 55.4 (Winter 2009): 794.
45 Brouillette, *Literature and the Creative Economy*, 201.
46 This is also central to Black's reading, and where I diverge from it; as she puts it: "In critiquing an apparent circulation that masks simple extraction and exploitation, *Never Let Me Go* can be said to offer a metaphor for the inequalities and predations of national and global economic systems. While Kathy and her classmates prefigure a futuristic world of genetic technology, they also reflect an existing late-twentieth- and early-twenty-first-century reality of growing economic imbalances" ("Ishiguro's Inhuman Aesthetics," 796). As I have tried to show, the novel figures the students' aesthetic output and its circulation as integral to the exploitative economy and not as a mask, even if it does serve as a distraction from their full realization or comprehension of their purpose. And while Black's sense that the novel reflects global economic imbalances is compelling, I think it steers away from that specific allegorical function, aiming its ethical and economic questions instead at an increasingly instrumentalized view of the arts and humanities in the context of middle-class education and training.
47 I am summarizing here Brouillette's main line of argument, drawn directly from her title, in *Literature and the Creative Economy*.
48 Stanley Fish (1995), qtd. in Jeffrey Nealon, *Post-Postmodernism, or, The Cultural Logic of Just-in-Time Capitalism*, 185, 186.

49 Cathy Davidson, "Them vs. Us (and Which One of 'Them' Is Me?)," *ADE Bulletin* 125.3 (2000), quoted in Nealon, *Post-Postmodernism, or the Cultural Logic of Just-in-Time Capitalism*, 187.
50 My thinking here owes something to Eric Hayot's notion of "the aperture or bridge that simultaneously unifies and separates [otherworldly fictions] from the world we know." Science fiction and fantasy, for example, often present a "microscosm" that figures as familiar and yet glaringly alternative to the world outside the text. See *On Literary Worlds*, 47.
51 For a sustained study that effectively undermines these binaries, long since canonized in our sense of modernism, see Justus Nieland, *Feeling Modern: The Eccentricities of Public Life*.
52 Hal Foster, *Compulsive Beauty*, 129, 135.
53 Or as Brouillette writes, Ishiguro prefers here "to avoid creating the kind of decorative or ameliorative work that the clones themselves are limited to" (*Literature and the Creative Economy*, 201).
54 Qtd. in Michael D'Arcy and Mathias Nilges, "Introduction," in *The Contemporaneity of Modernism: Literature, Media, Culture*, 5.
55 Ibid.

5 Zadie Smith, Inauthenticity, and Multicultural Modernism

1 On this generational difference, see John Clement Ball, *Imagining London: Postcolonial Fiction and the Transatlantic Metropolis*, 223–6; Dominic Head, *The State of the Novel: Britain and Beyond*, 91–2; and John J. Su, *Imagination and the Contemporary Novel*, 103–6.
2 See Laura Moss, "The Politics of Everyday Hybridity: Zadie Smith's *White Teeth*," *Wasafiri* 18.39 (2003): 39. James Proctor echoes Moss's assertion; see his chapter, "New Ethnicities, the Novel, and the Burden of Representation," in *A Concise Companion to Contemporary British Fiction*, ed. James F. English, 116.
3 I cite Camilla Palmer, who provides a useful survey of Smith's reception and how her work challenges some of the assumptions of multiculturalism and identity that drive its marketing. See "Zadie Smith's 'White Knuckle Ride': From 'Black Woman Writer' to 'Acclaimed Novelist and Critic,'" *Hecate* 41.1–2 (2015): 157.
4 See Claire Squires, *Marketing Literature: The Making of Contemporary Writing in Britain*, 178.

5 Robert McCrum, "If 1900 Was Oysters and Champagne, 2000 Is a Pint of Lager and a Packet of Crisps," *Observer*, December 24, 2000, 19, qtd. in Squires, *Marketing Literature*, 179.
6 Related to this formula, John B. Thompson distinguishes between *"diversity of output"* and *"diversity in the marketplace,"* showing that the early 2000s witnessed an increase overall in the former but a relatively unchanged number of titles actually getting widespread notice in the market. See *Merchants of Culture: The Publishing Business in the Twenty-First Century*, 397. Paul Crosthwaite adds the emphasis that this focus on publishing books that fit a proven formula has tended to squeeze out more experimental or unfamiliar works of fiction. See *The Market Logics of Contemporary Fiction*, 21–3.
7 Anthony Quinn, "The New England," *New York Times*, April 30, 2000, https://archive.nytimes.com/www.nytimes.com/books/00/04/30/reviews/000430.30quinnt.html?_r=1 (accessed August 19, 2020).
8 Squires, *Marketing Literature*, 180.
9 See Palmer, "Zadie Smith's 'White Knuckle Ride,'" 159; and Katarzyna Jakubiak, "Simulated Optimism: The International Marketing of *White Teeth*," in *Zadie Smith: Critical Essays*, ed. Tracy Walters, 210, 202.
10 Tobias A. Wachinger, *Posing In-Between: Postcolonial Englishness and the Commodification of Hybridity*, 194–5. Dominic Head surveys some of these debates as they play out in the reception of Smith and Monica Ali, but comes to a more balanced conclusion about the marketing of their work as an inevitable taint on it. See *The State of the Novel*, 93–4.
11 Brennan asserts this ambivalence through his focus on the United States as a center of cosmopolitan culture in the age of globalization, but the phrase I quote here has strong implications for the Anglo-American market for commercially produced multicultural fiction like Smith's. See *At Home in the World: Cosmopolitanism Now*, 1–2.
12 Proctor, "New Ethnicities, the Novel, and the Burden of Representation," in *A Concise Companion to Contemporary British Fiction*, ed. James F. English, 115–16.
13 Moss, "The Politics of Everyday Hybridity," 39; Proctor, "New Ethnicities, the Novel, and the Burden of Representation," 116; and Jonathan P. A. Sell, "Chance and Gesture in Zadie Smith's *White Teeth* and *The Autograph Man*: A Model for Multicultural Identity?" *Journal of Commonwealth Literature* 41.3 (2006): 27–44, 33.
14 Others have rightly pointed out that it plays on postcolonial tropes but from the perspective of a later, less defensive generation. Jonathan Sell notes several of the novel's obvious postcolonial credentials, including numerous "hybrid" characters, to argue that a litmus test of multiple identities "would rely on an essentialist view of identity which Smith's novels quite plainly reject," and, in *White Teeth*, "the past is there but has lost the crushing weight so manifest in postcolonial fiction." John

Clement Ball places Smith among "the children of 'New Commonwealth' migrants" displaying a "different relation to Britain and the capital" than the previous generation. See Sell, "Chance and Gesture," 28, 29; and Ball, *Imagining London*, 223. Raphael Dalleo provides a compelling model of colonial reversal, arguing that *White Teeth* is a Caribbean novel, creolized and moored in the "contact zone" of London, and that it thus rejects any "essence" of Caribbean culture and identity by digging into "the roots of what too often becomes a dehistoricized hybridity discourse." "Colonization in Reverse: *White Teeth* as Caribbean Novel," in *Zadie Smith: Critical Essays*, ed. Walters, 92–3.

15 Zadie Smith, *White Teeth*, 191, 193–5. Hereafter abbreviated *WT* and cited parenthetically in the text.

16 Lewis McLeod, "Eliminating the Random, Ruling the World: Monologic Hybridity in Zadie Smith's *White Teeth* and Salman Rushdie's *Midnight's Children*," in *Reading Zadie Smith: The First Decade and Beyond*, ed. Philip Tew, 165.

17 Benjamin Bergholtz, "'Certainty in Its Purest Form': Globalization, Fundamentalism, and Narrative in Zadie Smith's *White Teeth*," *Contemporary Literature* 57.4 (Winter 2016): 555.

18 E. San Juan Jr., *Beyond Postcolonial Theory*, 166; and John J. Su, *Imagination and the Contemporary Novel*, 91.

19 As John J. Su puts it in his reading of the novel: "The everydayness of hybridity in this account suggests that social change is an organic process, rather than the result of sustained political activism, and the novel confirms this attitude" (*Imagination and the Contemporary Novel*, 104).

20 John J. Su nicely sums up the sympathetic approach to Smith's representation of hybridity, arguing that "Smith represents a third generation of black British writers who can finally take for granted that the United Kingdom is their home, and this confidence enables them to present hybridity in less controversial and confrontational terms than previous generations could" (*Imagination and the Contemporary Novel*, 103). In this vein, see also Dominic Head, "Zadie Smith's *White Teeth*: Multiculturalism for the Millennium," in *Contemporary British Fiction*, ed. Richard Lane, Rod Mengham, and Philip Tew, 114. For a more critical account of how the novel's celebratory depictions of hybridity play into market demand and, ultimately, into Smith's own celebrity reception, see Jakubiak, "Simulated Optimism."

21 Qtd. in Gretchen Holbrook Gerzina, "Zadie Smith," in *Writing across Worlds: Contemporary Writers Talk*, ed. Susheila Nasta, 271; and Kathleen O'Grady, "White Teeth: A Conversation with Zadie Smith," *Atlantis* 27.1 (September 2002): 106.

22 Paul Gilroy, *Postcolonial Melancholia*, 124, 141.

23 See Bergholtz, "'Certainty in Its Purest Form,'" 559, 565, 560.

24 Mark Stein, *Black British Literature: Novels of Transformation*, 183. More recently, Richard Jean So has documented this problem of lingering inequality in the publishing industry with data-driven evidence. Despite widespread perceptions of increasing representation of Black and other minority authors, data shows that publishing, reviewing, and the distribution of prizes skews toward whiteness. See So, *Redlining Culture: A Data History of Racial Inequality and Postwar Fiction*.

25 Head, "Zadie Smith's *White Teeth*," in *Contemporary British Fiction*, ed. Lane, Mengham, and Tew, 106.

26 Sarah Brouillette, *Literature and the Creative Economy*, 119.

27 See Lexi Stuckey, "Red and Yellow, Black and White: Color-Blindness as Disillusionment in Zadie Smith's 'Hanwell in Hell,'" in *Zadie Smith: Critical Essays*, ed. Walters, 157–69.

28 Qtd. in Philip Tew, *Zadie Smith*, 113.

29 John Mark Eberhardt, "British Author's Novel Reflects the Melting Pot That Is London," *Kansas City Star*, July 5, 2001, F1; and Stuckey, "Red and Yellow, Black and White," 157.

30 See Mathew Paproth, "The Modernist and Postmodernist Zadie Smith," in *Zadie Smith: Critical Essays*, ed. Walters, 10–11.

31 Neil Levi, "How to Do Things with Modernism," *Modernism/modernity* Print Plus 3.4 (2018), https://modernismmodernity.org/forums/posts/how-do-things-modernism (accessed August 15, 2020).

32 For a thorough (and critical) structural comparison, see Lawrence Driscoll, *Evading Class in Contemporary British Literature*, 62–83. See also Philip Tew's brief overview in *Zadie Smith*, 92–5.

33 John Sutherland suggests that there might be "some subtle subversion at work" in Smith's allusions to Forster's novel. See "A Touch of Forster," *New Statesman*, September 12, 2005, 190.

34 See Dorothy J. Hale, "*On Beauty* as Beautiful? The Problem of Novelistic Aesthetics by Way of Zadie Smith," *Contemporary Literature* 53.4 (2012): 818.

35 Zadie Smith, *On Beauty*, 211–12. Hereafter abbreviated *OB* and cited parenthetically in the text.

36 Driscoll, *Evading Class in Contemporary British Literature*, 63.

37 Ibid., 80.

38 Ibid., 73.

39 Ibid.

40 Patrick Herald, "The Anxieties of Authorship: Zadie Smith's *On Beauty*, Fields, and Professional Jurisdiction," *Critique* 60.5 (2019): 611.

41 On engagements with a consolidated model of modernism that help sustain it as a source of cultural and economic capital, see Claire Barber-Stetson, "Modern Insecurities, or, Living on the Edge"; and on metamodernism in its selective,

university-sustained mode, see Alys Moody, "Indifferent and Detached: Modernism and the Aesthetic Affect." Both essays appear in *Modernism/modernity* Print Plus 3.4 (2018).

42 David James, "Wounded Realism," *Contemporary Literature* 54.1 (Spring 2013): 204.
43 Zadie Smith, "Two Directions for the Novel," in *Changing My Mind*, 75, 72, 82, 85, 93.
44 Zadie Smith, *NW*, 3. Hereafter abbreviated *NW* and cited parenthetically in the text.
45 James, "Wounded Realism," 206.
46 Joyce Carol Oates, "Cards of Identity: Zadie Smith's *NW*," *New York Review of Books*, September 27, 2012, https://www.nybooks.com/articles/2012/09/27/cards-identity/ (accessed July 23, 2020).
47 David Marcus, "Post-Hysterics: Zadie Smith and the Fiction of Austerity," *Dissent* 60.2 (Spring 2013): 70.
48 Christian Lorentzen, "Why Am I So Fucked Up?" *London Review of Books* 34.21 (November 8, 2012), https://www.lrb.co.uk/the-paper/v34/n21/christian-lorentzen/why-am-i-so-fucked-up (accessed August 24, 2020).
49 James, "Wounded Realism," 205.
50 Wendy Knepper, "Revisionary Modernism and Postmillennial Experimentation in Zadie Smith's *NW*," in *Reading Zadie Smith: The First Decade and Beyond*, ed. Tew, 117.
51 Oates, "Cards of Identity."
52 Lorentzen, "Why?"
53 On modernist interiority and bourgeois subjectivity, see Carey Mickalites, "*The Good Soldier* and Capital's Interiority Complex," *Studies in the Novel* 38.3 (Fall 2006): 288–303.
54 Wendy Brown, *Undoing the Demos: Neoliberalism's Stealth Revolution*, 36. Tammy Amiel Houser draws on Brown's critique in her reading of *NW* to argue that the novel shows the failure of traditional models of empathy under neoliberal capitalism. See "Zadie Smith's *NW*: Unsettling the Promise of Empathy," *Contemporary Literature* 58.1 (Spring 2017): 116–48.
55 Amiel Houser, "Zadie Smith's *NW*," 139.
56 Elaine Freedgood, *Worlds Enough: The Invention of Realism in the Victorian Novel*, 71.
57 See Moody, "Indifferent and Detached," and Barber-Stetson, "Modern Insecurities, or, Living on the Edge." Both essays appear in *Modernism/modernity* Print Plus 3.4 (2018).
58 Amiel Houser, "Zadie Smith's *NW*," 137.
59 See Andrew Goldstone, *Fictions of Autonomy: Modernism from Wilde to de Man*, 25.
60 Ibid.

61 Tim Woods, "A Complex Legacy: Modernity's Uneasy Discourse of Ethics and Responsibility," in *The Legacies of Modernism: Historicising Postwar and Contemporary Fiction*, ed. David James, 154; and Derek Attridge, *The Singularity of Literature*, 131.

6 Marginal Literary Values, or, How Eimear McBride and Anna Burns Reframe Irish Modernism

1 Paige Reynolds, "Introduction," *Modernist Afterlives in Irish Literature and Culture*, 3.
2 Here I again cite from David James and Urmila Seshagiri, "Metamodernism: Narratives of Continuity and Revolution," 89.
3 David James, "Afterword," in Reynolds, *Modernist Afterlives in Irish Literature and Culture*, 177–8.
4 David Lloyd, *Irish Times: Temporalities of Modernity*, 76.
5 Reynolds, "Introduction," *Modernist Afterlives in Irish Literature and Culture*, 4.
6 Paul Crosthwaite, *The Market Logics of Contemporary Fiction*, 258.
7 Moody contrasts the various market models by which modernism has been revived in contemporary culture with a late-modernist assertion of autonomy that is fundamentally "unfree and anti-social"—figured in the works of Beckett, Auster, and Coetzee (200). As I will show, Burns and McBride each extend the possibilities begun by high modernism, but position their work as a counterpoint to its legacy—as itself a gesture of autonomous commitment—that is more akin to those later modernists' resistance to the market than celebrity writers who redeploy an institutionalized gold standard model of modernism. See Moody, *The Art of Hunger: Aesthetic Autonomy and the Afterlives of Modernism*, 199–205.
8 Pascale Casanova devotes an entire chapter to explaining how Irish modernism became an established and influential model in the movement from national literatures to "the world republic of letters." See *The World Republic of Letters*, 303–23.
9 Ruth Gilligan makes the point about "misery memoirs" and McBride's resistance to the genre. See "Eimear McBride's Ireland: A Case for Periodisation and the Dangers of Marketing Modernism," *English Studies* 99.7 (2018): 785.
10 James and Seshagiri, "Metamodernism," 93.
11 Alice O'Keefe, "Eimear McBride's Daring and Dazzling Novel," review of *A Girl Is a Half-Formed Thing*, by Eimear McBride, *Observer Fiction*, May 18, 2014, https://www.theguardian.com/books/2014/may/18/girl-is-a-half-formed-thing-review-daring-dazzling-eimear-mcbride (accessed November 24, 2020). Justine Jordan similarly positioned McBride "firmly in the Irish modernist tradition of Beckett and Joyce" ("A New Irish Literary Boom: The Post-Crash

Stars of Fiction," *Guardian*, October 17, 2015), https://www.theguardian.com/books/2015/oct/17/new-irish-literary-boom-post-crash-stars-fiction (accessed November 25, 2020).

12 Paige Reynolds, "Trauma, Intimacy, and Modernist Form," *Breac*, September 11, 2014), https://breac.nd.edu/articles/trauma-intimacy-and-modernist-form/ (accessed November 20, 2020).

13 Gilligan, "Eimear McBride's Ireland," 776, 780.

14 Reynolds, "Introduction," *Modernist Afterlives in Irish Literature and Culture*, 4.

15 Reynolds, "Bird Girls: Modernism and Sexual Ethics in Contemporary Irish Fiction," in *Modernism and Close Reading*, ed. David James, 174, 185.

16 Ibid., 175, 186.

17 Gilligan, "Eimear McBride's Ireland," 789, 790.

18 Attridge, "Reading Joyce," in *The Cambridge Companion to James Joyce*, ed. Attridge, 2nd ed., 1; Martha Carpentier, "Introduction," *Joycean Legacies*, 3.

19 Attridge, "Foreword," *Joycean Legacies*, ix.

20 Ibid., xi–xiii.

21 James Joyce, *A Portrait of the Artist as a Young Man*, 276.

22 Eimear McBride, *A Girl Is a Half-Formed Thing*, 4. Subsequent references cited in parentheses as *Girl*.

23 Joyce, *A Portrait of the Artist as a Young Man*, 184–5. Hereafter cited as *Portrait* parenthetically in the text.

24 Sean Latham, "Interruption: 'Cyclops' and 'Nausicaa,'" in *The Cambridge Companion to* Ulysses, ed. Sean Latham, 145.

25 Latham, "Interruption," 145.

26 Reynolds, "Bird Girls," 182.

27 This point builds on Reynolds's similar observation about perspective; see "Bird Girls," 183.

28 Ibid., 174, 186.

29 *Ulysses*, the Corrected Text, ed. Hans Walter Gabler, 644.

30 Ibid., 633.

31 Attridge, "Foreword," *Joycean Legacies*, xviii.

32 Ibid., xv.

33 David Collard, "Interview with Eimear McBride," *The White Review*, May 2014, https://www.thewhitereview.org/feature/interview-with-eimear-mcbride/ (accessed December 1, 2020).

34 See Héctor Ramírez, "A Broken Bildungsroman," *American Book Review* 35.6 (2014): 17.

35 In her argument with Reynolds, Gilligan introduces a similar claim but does not pursue it through a reading of the novel. See "Eimear McBride's Ireland," 780.

36 Moody, *The Art of Hunger*, 1.

37 John Brannigan, "Northern Irish Fiction: Provisionals and Pataphysicians," in *A Concise Companion to Contemporary British Fiction*, ed. James F. English, 142. Related studies include Elmer Kennedy-Andrews, *Fiction and Northern Ireland since 1969: (De-)Constructing the North*; Richard Kirkland, *Literature and Culture in Northern Ireland since 1965: Moments of Danger*; and Eve Patten, "Fiction in Conflict: Northern Ireland's Prodigal Novelists," in *Peripheral Visions: Images of Nationhood in Contemporary British Fiction*, ed. I. A. Bell, 128–48.

38 As Burns has stated in an interview: "Although it is recognisable as this skewed form of Belfast, it's not really Belfast in the 70s. I would like to think it could be seen as any sort of totalitarian, closed society existing in similarly oppressive conditions" (Lisa Allardice, "'It's Nice to Feel I'm Solvent. That's a Huge Gift': Anna Burns on Her Life-Changing Booker Win," interview with Anna Burns, *Guardian*, October 17, 2018), https://www.theguardian.com/books/2018/oct/17/anna-burns-booker-prize-winner-life-changing-interview (accessed December 2, 2020).

39 Qtd. on the cover of the US edition of *Milkman*, from McNamee's review in the *Irish Times*.

40 Brannigan makes a similar point about destabilizing digression in the work of an earlier generation of Northern Irish writers. See "Northern Irish Fiction," 159.

41 *Milkman*, 24. Further references cited parenthetically in the text.

42 Caroline Magennis has written extensively on militant hypermasculinity in Northern Irish fiction set during the Troubles. See *Sons of Ulster: Masculinities in the Contemporary Northern Irish Novel*.

43 Brannigan, "Northern Irish Fiction," 142.

44 Michael North, *Machine-Age Comedy*, 68, 143.

45 See Allardice, "'It's Nice to Feel I'm Solvent. That's a Huge Gift.' Anna Burns on Her Life-Changing Booker Win."

46 Moody, *The Art of Hunger*, 90.

47 Brouillette, *Literature and the Creative Economy*, 14.

48 English, *The Economy of Prestige: Prizes, Awards, and the Circulation of Cultural Value*, 51.

49 On the recent rise of the historical novel to prominence, see Alexander Manshel, "The Rise of the Recent Historical Novel," *Post45* (2017), post45.org/2017/09/the-rise-of-the-recent-historical-novel/ (accessed November 21, 2020). And for a recent empirical survey of how literary prizes affect market trends and sales of new fiction, see Manshel, Laura McGrath, and J. D. Porter, "Who Cares about Literary Prizes," *Public Books*, September 29, 2019, https://www.publicbooks.org/who-cares-about-literary-prizes/ (accessed December 5, 2020).

50 For a sustained study of modernism's challenges to the "epistemological certainty of the nineteenth century" understanding of history and historical narrative, see Seamus O'Malley, *Modernism and Historical Narrative*, 13. Perhaps the first

to argue systematically for this presentist function of historical fiction was Lion Feuchtwanger; see *The House of Desdemona*, 129–63. Margaret Scanlan extends that understanding in her study of contemporary British historical fiction, with a particular emphasis on Northern Irish novels that present the concerns of the Troubles in the guise of the past. See *Traces of Another Time: History and Politics in Postwar British Fiction*, especially Part One.

51 I quote here from Manshel, McGrath, and Porter, "Who Cares about Literary Prizes?" In her *Guardian* interview with Burns, Lisa Allardice mentions the speculative connections between the novel, MeToo, and Brexit.

52 Scanlan observes this disrupted temporality as a modernist inheritance used by postwar British writers. See *Traces of Another Time*, 4–5.

53 See Crosthwaite, *The Market Logics of Contemporary Fiction*, 22–5, 243–4.

54 John B. Thompson, *Merchants of Culture: The Publishing Business in the Twenty-First Century*, 2nd ed., 156.

55 Lee Konstantinou, "Lewis Hyde's Double Economy," *ASAP Journal* 1.1 (2016): 141.

56 Crosthwaite, *The Market Logics of Contemporary Fiction*, 258.

Bibliography

Adorno, Theodor W. *Aesthetic Theory*. Edited by Gretel Adorno and Rolf Tiedemann. Translated by C. Lenhardt. London: Routledge & Kegan Paul, 1984.
Ahmad, Aijaz. *In Theory: Classes, Nations, Literatures*. London: Verso, 1992.
Amis, Martin. *Experience: A Memoir*. New York: Hyperion, 2000.
Amis, Martin. *The Information*. New York: Vintage, 1996.
Amis, Martin. *Money: A Suicide Note*. New York: Penguin, 1986.
Amis, Martin. "The Pros and Cons of Martin Amis." Interview by Graham Fuller. *Interview Magazine* 25, no. 5 (May 1995): 122–5.
Amis, Martin. *The Rub of Time: Bellow, Nabokov, Hitchens, Travolta, Trump: Essays and Reportage, 1994–2017*. New York: Knopf, 2018.
Amis, Martin. *Success*. New York: Vintage, 1991.
Ashcroft, Bill. *Postcolonial Transformation*. New York: Routledge, 2001.
Attridge, Derek. "Foreword: Irish Writing after Joyce." In *Joycean Legacies*, edited by Martha Carpentier, vii–xx. Basingstoke, UK: Palgrave Macmillan, 2015.
Attridge, Derek. *J. M. Coetzee and the Ethics of Reading: Literature in the Event*. Chicago: University of Chicago Press, 2004.
Attridge, Derek. "Reading Joyce." In *The Cambridge Companion to James Joyce*, 2nd ed., edited by Derek Attridge, 1–27. Cambridge: Cambridge University Press, 2004.
Attridge, Derek. *The Singularity of Literature*. London: Routledge, 2004.
Ball, John Clement. *Imagining London: Postcolonial Fiction and the Transatlantic Metropolis*. Toronto: University of Toronto Press, 2004.
Banville, John. "A Day in the Life." Review of *Saturday*, by Ian McEwan. *New York Review of Books*, May 26, 2005. https://www.nybooks.com/articles/2005/05/26/a-day-in-the-life/ (accessed October 30, 2017).
Barber-Stetson, Claire. "Modern Insecurities, or, Living on the Edge." *Modernism/modernity* Print Plus 3, no. 4 (December 11, 2018). https://doi.org/10.26597/mod.0080 (accessed August 14, 2020).
Beckett, Samuel. *Three Novels: Molloy, Malone Dies, The Unnamable*. New York: Grove, 1958.
Begley, Jon. "Satirizing the Carnival of Postmodern Capitalism: The Transatlantic and Dialogic Structure of Martin Amis's Money." *Contemporary Literature* 45, no. 1 (2004): 79–105.
Bényei, Tamás. "The Passion of John Self: Allegory, Economy, and Expenditure in Martin Amis's Money." In *Martin Amis: Postmodernism and Beyond*, edited by Gavin Keulks, 36–54. Basingstoke, UK: Palgrave Macmillan, 2006.

Bergholtz, Benjamin. "'Certainty in Its Purest Form': Globalization, Fundamentalism, and Narrative in Zadie Smith's *White Teeth*." *Contemporary Literature* 57, no. 4 (Winter 2016): 541–68.

Bernard, Catherine. "Under the Dark Sun of Melancholia: Writing and Loss in *The Information*." In *Martin Amis: Postmodernism and Beyond*, edited by Gavin Keulks, 117–36. Basingstoke, UK: Palgrave Macmillan, 2006.

Bernstein, Michael André. *Foregone Conclusions: Against Apocalyptic History*. Berkeley: University of California Press, 1994.

Black, Shameem. "Ishiguro's Inhuman Aesthetics." *Modern Fiction Studies* 55, no. 4 (Winter 2009): 785–807.

Bourdieu, Pierre. *Distinction: A Social Critique of the Judgment of Taste*. Translated by Richard Nice. Cambridge, MA: Harvard University Press, 1984.

Bourdieu, Pierre. *The Field of Cultural Production: Essays on Art and Literature*. New York: Columbia University Press, 1993.

Bourdieu, Pierre. *The Logic of Practice*. Translated by Richard Nice. Stanford: Stanford University Press, 1990.

Bourdieu, Pierre. "The Market for Symbolic Goods." *Poetics* 14, nos. 1–2 (1985): 13–44.

Bourdieu, Pierre. *The Rules of Art: Genesis and Structure of the Literary Field*. Translated by Susan Emanuel. Stanford: Stanford University Press, 1995.

Bradford, Richard. *The Novel Now: Contemporary British Fiction*. Oxford: Blackwell, 2007.

Brannigan, John. "Northern Irish Fiction: Provisionals and Pataphysicians." In *A Concise Companion to Contemporary British Fiction*, edited by James English, 141–63. Malden, MA: Blackwell, 2006.

Brantlinger, Patrick. *Fictions of State: Culture and Credit in Britain, 1694–1994*. Ithaca, NY: Cornell University Press, 1996.

Brennan, Timothy. *At Home in the World: Cosmopolitanism Now*. Cambridge, MA: Harvard University Press, 1997.

Brennan, Timothy. "Cosmopolitans and Celebrities." *Race and Class* 31, no. 1 (1989): 1–19.

Brennan, Timothy. *Salman Rushdie and the Third World: Myths of the Nation*. New York: St. Martin's, 1989.

Brouillette, Sarah. "Impersonality and Institutional Critique." In *The Contemporaneity of Modernism: Literature, Media, Culture*, edited by Michael D'Arcy and Mathias Nilges. New York: Routledge, 2016.

Brouillette, Sarah. *Literature and the Creative Economy*. Stanford: Stanford University Press, 2014.

Brouillette, Sarah. *Postcolonial Writers and the Global Literary Marketplace*. Basingstoke, UK: Palgrave, 2007.

Brown, Nicholas. *Autonomy: The Social Ontology of Art under Capitalism*. Durham, NC: Duke University Press, 2019.

Brown, Wendy. *Undoing the Demos: Neoliberalism's Stealth Revolution*. New York: Zone Books, 2015.

Burns, Anna. "'It's Nice to Feel I'm Solvent. That's a Huge Gift.' Anna Burns on Her Life-Changing Booker Win." Interview by Lisa Allardice. *Guardian*, October 17, 2018. https://www.theguardian.com/books/2018/oct/17/anna-burns-booker-prize-winner-life-changing-interview (accessed December 20, 2020).

Burns, Anna. *Milkman: A Novel*. Minneapolis, MN: Greywolf Press, 2018.

Carpentier, Martha. "Introduction," *Joycean Legacies*, edited by Carpentier, 1–10. Basingstoke, UK: Palgrave, 2015.

Casanova, Pascale. *The World Republic of Letters*. Cambridge, MA: Harvard University Press, 2004.

Chaudhuri, Amit. "Unlike Kafka." Review of *The Unconsoled*, by Kazuo Ishiguro. *London Review of Books* 17, no. 11 (June 8, 1995): 30–1.

Clark, Roger Y. *Stranger Gods: Salman Rushdie's Other Worlds*. Montreal: McGill-Queen's University Press, 2001.

Cooper, John Xiros. *Modernism and the Culture of Market Society*. Cambridge: Cambridge University Press, 2004.

Crosthwaite, Paul. *The Market Logics of Contemporary Fiction*. Cambridge: Cambridge University Press, 2019.

Currie, Mark. *About Time: Narrative, Fiction, and the Philosophy of Time*. Edinburgh: Edinburgh University Press, 2007.

Dalleo, Raphael. "Colonization in Reverse: *White Teeth* as Caribbean Novel." In *Zadie Smith: Critical Essays*, edited by Tracey L. Walters, 91–104. New York: Peter Lang, 2008.

D'Arcy, Michael, and Mathias Nilges. "Introduction," *The Contemporaneity of Modernism: Literature, Media, Culture*, edited by Michael D'Arcy and Mathias Nilges, 1–14. New York: Routledge, 2016.

Davidson, Cathy. "Them vs. Us (and Which One of 'Them' Is Me?)." *ADE Bulletin* 125, no. 3 (2000): 3–8. http://www.mla.org/adefl_bulletin_d_ade_125_3.pdf.

Delany, Paul. *Literature, Money and the Market: From Trollope to Amis*. Basingstoke, UK: Palgrave, 2002.

Detloff, Madelyn. *The Persistence of Modernism: Loss and Mourning in the Twentieth Century*. Cambridge: Cambridge University Press, 2011.

Diedrick, James. *Understanding Martin Amis*. Columbia: University of South Carolina Press, 1995.

Diepeveen, Leonard. "'I Can Have More Than Enough Power to Satisfy Me': T. S. Eliot's Construction of His Audience." In *Marketing Modernisms: Self-Promotion, Canonization, Rereading*, edited by Kevin J. H. Dettmar and Stephen Watt, 37–60. Ann Arbor: University of Michigan Press, 1996.

Doan, Laura. "'Sexy Greedy Is the Late Eighties': Power Systems in Amis's *Money* and Churchill's *Serious Money*," *Minnesota Review* 34, no. 35 (1990): 69–80.

Driscoll, Lawrence. *Evading Class in Contemporary British Literature*. New York: Palgrave, 2009.

Dyer, Geoff. "Who's Afraid of Influence." Review of *Atonement*, by Ian McEwan. *Guardian*, September 22, 2001. https://www.theguardian.com/books/2001/sep/22/fiction.ianmcewan (accessed July 28, 2017).

Eaglestone, Robert. "Introduction: Salman Rushdie." In *Salman Rushdie: Contemporary Critical Perspectives*, edited by Robert Eaglestone and Martin McQuillan, 1–8. London: Bloomsbury, 2013.

Eberhart, John Mark. "British Author's Novel Reflects the Melting Pot That Is London." *Kansas City Star*, July 5, 2001, F1.

Eburne, Jonathan P., and Rita Felski, eds. "Introduction: What Is an Avant-Garde." *New Literary History* 41, no. 4 (2010): v–xv.

Edmondson, Elie. "Martin Amis Writes Postmodern Man." *Critique* 42, no. 2 (2001): 145–54.

Elias, Amy. "Meta-Mimesis? The Problem of British Postmodern Realism," *Restant* 2, no. 9 (1993): 10–31.

Eliot, T. S. *The Complete Poems and Plays, 1909–1950*. New York: Harcourt Brace, 1980.

English, James F. *The Economy of Prestige: Prizes, Awards, and the Circulation of Cultural Value*. Cambridge, MA: Harvard University Press, 2005.

English, James F. "Winning the Culture Game: Prizes, Awards, and the Rules of Art," *New Literary History* 33, no. 1 (2002): 109–35.

English, James F., and John Frow, "Literary Authorship and Celebrity Culture." In *A Concise Companion to Contemporary British Fiction*, edited by James F. English, 39–57. Malden, MA: Blackwell, 2006.

Eve, Martin Paul. *Literature against Criticism: University English and Contemporary Fiction in Conflict*. Cambridge, UK: Open Book, 2016.

Fairbanks, A. Harris. "Ontology and Narrative Technique in Kazuo Ishiguro's *The Unconsoled*." *Studies in the Novel* 45, no. 4 (Winter 2013): 603–19.

Feuchtwanger, Lion. *The House of Desdemona*. Detroit, MI: Wayne State University Press, 1963.

Finney, Brian. "Briony's Stand against Oblivion: Ian McEwan's *Atonement*." *Journal of Modern Literature* 27, no. 3 (2004): 68–82.

Fisher, Mark. *Capitalist Realism: Is There No Alternative?* Winchester: Zero Books, 2008.

Fluet, Lisa. "Immaterial Labors: Ishiguro, Class, and Affect." *Novel* 40, no. 3 (Summer 2007): 265–88.

Foster, Hal. *Compulsive Beauty*. Cambridge, MA: MIT Press, 1995.

François, Pierre. "The Spectral Return of Depths in Kazuo Ishiguro's *The Unconsoled*." *Commonwealth: Essays and Studies* 26, no. 2 (Spring 2004): 77–90.

Freedgood, Elaine. *Worlds Enough: The Invention of Realism in the Victorian Novel*. Princeton, NJ: Princeton University Press, 2019.

Friedman, Susan Stanford. *Planetary Modernisms: Provocations on Modernity across Time*. New York: Columbia University Press, 2015.

Gauthier, Tim. "'Selective in Your Mercies': Privilege, Vulnerability, and the Limits of Empathy in Ian McEwan's *Saturday*." *College Literature* 40, no. 2 (Spring 2013): 7–30.

Gera Roy, Anjali. "Fact and Fantasy, Myth and History: The Magic Realist Mode in Salman Rushdie's Fiction." In *Mapping Out the Rushdie Republic: Some Recent Surveys*, edited by Tapan Kumar Ghosh and Prasanta Bhattacharyya, 34–52. Newcastle upon Tyne: Cambridge Scholars, 2016.

Gerzina, Gretchen Holbrook. "Zadie Smith." In *Writing across Worlds: Contemporary Writers Talk*, edited by Susheila Nasta, 266–78. London: Routledge, 2004.

Gikandi, Simon. "Preface: Modernism in the World." *Modernism/modernity* 13, no. 3 (September 2006): 419–24.

Gildea, Niall, and David Wylot. "The And of Modernism: On New Periodizations." *Modernist Cultures* 14, no. 4 (2019): 446–68.

Gilligan, Ruth. "Eimear McBride's Ireland: A Case for Periodisation and the Dangers of Marketing Modernism." *English Studies* 99, no. 7 (2018): 775–92.

Gilroy, Paul. *Postcolonial Melancholia*. New York: Columbia University Press, 2005.

Glass, Loren. *Authors Inc.: Literary Celebrity in the Modern United States, 1880–1980*. New York: New York University Press, 2004.

Glass, Loren. *Counterculture Colophon: Grove Press, the* Evergreen Review, *and the Incorporation of the Avant-Garde*. Stanford: Stanford University Press, 2013.

Goldman, Jonathan. *Modernism Is the Literature of Celebrity*. Austin: University of Texas Press, 2011.

Goldstone, Andrew. *Fictions of Autonomy: Modernism from Wilde to de Man*. New York: Oxford University Press, 2013.

Gray, Paul. "Ganja Growing in the Tin." *Time*, May 17, 1999. http://content.time.com/time/magazine/article/0,9171,23279,00.html (accessed August 13, 2018).

Gregson, Ian. *Character and Satire in Postwar Fiction*. London: Continuum, 2006.

Groes, Sebastian. "Ian McEwan and the Modernist Consciousness of the City in *Saturday*." In *Ian McEwan: Contemporary Critical Perspectives*, edited by Sebastian Groes, 99–114. London: Bloomsbury, 2013.

Grossman, Lev. "All-TIME 100 Novels: Watchmen." *Time*, January 11, 2010.

Guillory, John. *Cultural Capital: The Problem of Literary Canon Formation*. Chicago: University of Chicago Press, 1993.

Hale, Dorothy J. "*On Beauty* as Beautiful? The Problem of Novelistic Aesthetics by Way of Zadie Smith."*Contemporary Literature* 53, no. 4 (2012): 814–44.

Harris, Donal. *On Company Time: American Modernism in the Big Magazines*. New York: Columbia University Press, 2016.

Hayot, Eric. *On Literary Worlds*. New York: Oxford University Press, 2012.

Head, Dominic. *Ian McEwan*. Manchester: Manchester University Press, 2007.

Head, Dominic. *The Cambridge Introduction to Modern British Fiction 1950–2000*. Cambridge: Cambridge University Press, 2002.

Head, Dominic. *The State of the Novel: Britain and Beyond*. Malden, MA: Blackwell, 2008.

Head, Dominic. "Zadie Smith's *White Teeth*: Multiculturalism for the Millennium." In *Contemporary British Fiction*, edited by Richard Lane, Rod Mengham, and Philip Tew, 106–19. Cambridge, UK: Polity, 2003.

Heller, Zoe. "The Salman Rushdie Case." *New York Review of Books*, December 20, 2012. https://www.nybooks.com/articles/2012/12/20/salman-rushdie-case/ (accessed June 23, 2019).

Herald, Patrick. "The Anxieties of Authorship: Zadie Smith's *On Beauty*, Fields, and Professional Jurisdiction." *Critique* 60, no. 5 (2019): 600–12.

Hillard, Molly Clark. "'When Desert Armies Stand Ready to Fight': Re-reading McEwan's *Saturday* and Arnold's 'Dover Beach.'" *Partial Answers: Journal of Literature and the History of Ideas* 6, no. 1 (2008): 181–206.

Holmes, Frederick M. "Realism, Dreams, and the Unconscious in the Novels of Kazuo Ishiguro." In *The Contemporary British Novel since 1980*, edited by James Acheson and Sarah Ross, 11–22. Edinburgh: Edinburgh University Press, 2005.

Horkheimer, Max, and Theodor Adorno. *Dialectic of Enlightenment: Philosophical Fragments*. Translated by Edmund Jephcott. Stanford: Stanford University Press, 2002.

Houser, Tammy Amiel. "Zadie Smith's *NW*: Unsettling the Promise of Empathy." *Contemporary Literature* 58, no. 1 (2017): 116–48.

Huehls, Mitchum, and Rachel Greenwald Smith, eds. *Neoliberalism and Contemporary Literary Culture*. Baltimore, MD: Johns Hopkins University Press, 2017.

Huggan, Graham. *The Postcolonial Exotic: Marketing the Margins*. London: Routledge, 2001.

Huggan, Graham. "Prizing 'Otherness': A Short History of the Booker." *Studies in the Novel* 29, no. 3 (1997): 412–33.

Huggan, Graham. "The Postcolonial Exotic." *Transition* no. 64 (1994): 22–9.

Huyssen, Andreas. *After the Great Divide: Modernism, Mass Culture, Postmodernism*. Bloomington: Indiana University Press, 1987.

Ishiguro, Kazuo. *Never Let Me Go*. New York: Knopf, 2005.

Ishiguro, Kazuo. "An Interview with Kazuo Ishiguro." Interview by Allan Vorda and Kim Herzinger. *Mississippi Review* 20, nos. 1–2 (1991): 131–54. Reprinted in *Conversations with Kazuo Ishiguro*, edited by Brian W. Shaffer and Cynthia F. Wong, 66–88. Jackson: University Press of Mississippi, 2008.

Ishiguro, Kazuo. "Memory Is the Terribly Treacherous Terrain." Interview with Graham Swift. *BOMB* 29 (1989): 22–3.

Ishiguro, Kazuo. *The Unconsoled*. London: Faber and Faber, 1995.

Jaffe, Aaron. *Modernism and the Culture of Celebrity*. Cambridge: Cambridge University Press, 2005.

Jaggi, Maya. "Kazuo Ishiguro with Maya Jaggi." In *Conversations with Kazuo Ishiguro*, edited by Brian W. Shaffer and Cynthia F. Wong, 110–19. Jackson: University Press of Mississippi, 2008.

Jakubiak, Katarzyna. "Simulated Optimism: The International Marketing of *White Teeth*." In *Zadie Smith: Critical Essays*, edited by Tracy Walters, 201–18. New York: Peter Lang, 2008.

Jaillant, Lise. *Cheap Modernism: Expanding Markets, Publishers' Series and the Avant-Garde*. Edinburgh: Edinburgh University Press, 2017.

James, David. Afterword to *Modernist Afterlives in Irish Literature and Culture*, edited by Paige Reynolds, 175–82. London: Anthem Press, 2019.

James, David, ed. *The Legacies of Modernism: Historicising Postwar and Contemporary Fiction*. New York: Cambridge University Press, 2012.

James, David. *Modernist Futures: Innovation and Inheritance in the Contemporary Novel*. New York: Cambridge University Press, 2012.

James, David. "Wounded Realism." *Contemporary Literature* 54, no. 1 (2013): 204–14.

James, David, and Urmila Seshagiri. "Metamodernism: Narratives of Continuity and Revolution." *PMLA* 129, no. 1 (2014): 87–100.

Jameson, Fredric. *Postmodernism, or, The Cultural Logic of Late Capitalism*. Durham, NC: Duke University Press, [1991] 1999.

Jameson, Fredric. *The Antinomies of Realism*. London: Verso, 2013.

Jordan, Justine. "A New Irish Literary Boom: The Post-Crash Stars of Fiction." *Guardian*, October 17, 2015. https://www.theguardian.com/books/2015/oct/17/new-irish-literary-boom-post-crash-stars-fiction (accessed November 25, 2020).

Joyce, James. *A Portrait of the Artist as a Young Man*. New York: Penguin, 1992.

Joyce, James. *A Portrait of the Artist as a Young Man: A Norton Critical Edition*, edited by John Paul Riquelme. New York: Norton, 2007.

Joyce, James. "James Joyce to Frank Budgen, 20 March 1920." In *Letters of James Joyce, Vol. 1*, edited by Stuart Gilbert. New York: Viking, 1966.

Joyce, James. *Ulysses*, edited by Hans Walter Gabler. New York: Vintage, 1986.

Kane, Jean. *Conspicuous Bodies: Provincial Belief and the Making of Joyce and Rushdie*. Columbus: Ohio State University Press, 2014.

Kaufman, Michael. "Author from Three Countries." *New York Times Book Review*, November 13, 1983. Quoted in Jean Kane, *Conspicuous Bodies: Provincial Belief and the Making of Joyce and Rushdie*, 44. Columbus: Ohio State University Press, 2014.

Kelman, Suanne, "Ishiguro in Toronto." In *Conversations with Kazuo Ishiguro*, edited by Brian W. Shaffer and Cynthia F. Wong, 42–51. Jackson: University Press of Mississippi, 2008.

Kennedy-Andrews, Elmer. *Fiction and Northern Ireland since 1969: (De-)Constructing the North*. Dublin: Four Courts, 2003.

Kermode, Frank. "Point of View." Review of *Atonement*, by Ian McEwan. *London Review of Books* 23, no. 19 (October 4, 2001): 8–9.

Kirkland, Richard. *Literature and Culture in Northern Ireland since 1965: Moments of Danger*. London: Longman, 1996.

Knepper, Wendy. "Revisionary Modernism and Postmillennial Experimentation in Zadie Smith's *NW*." In *Reading Zadie Smith: The First Decade and Beyond*, edited by Philip Tew, 111–26. London: Bloomsbury, 2013.

Knönagel, Alex. "*The Satanic Verses*: Narrative Structure and Islamic Doctrine." *International Fiction Review* 18, no. 2 (1991): 69–75.

Konstantinou, Lee. "Lewis Hyde's Double Economy." *ASAP Journal* 1, no. 1 (2016): 123–49.

Kortenaar, Neil ten. "Fearful Symmetry: Salman Rushdie and Prophetic Newness." *Twentieth Century Literature* 54, no. 3 (2008): 339–61.

Lang, James. "Public Memory, Private History: Kazuo Ishiguro's *The Remains of the Day*." *CLIO* 29, no. 2 (2000): 143–65.

Latham, Sean. *"Am I a Snob?": Modernism and the Novel*. Ithaca, NY: Cornell University Press, 2003.

Latham, Sean. "Interruption: 'Cyclops' and 'Nausicaa.'" In *The Cambridge Companion to Ulysses*, edited by Sean Latham, 140–53. New York: Cambridge University Press, 2014.

Latham, Sean, and Gayle Rogers. *Modernism: Evolution of an Idea*. London: Bloomsbury, 2015.

Lazarus, Neil. *The Postcolonial Unconscious*. Cambridge: Cambridge University Press, 2011.

Lemon, Robert. "The Comfort of Strangeness: Correlating the Kafkaesque and the Kafkan in Kazuo Ishiguro's *The Unconsoled*." In *Kafka for the Twenty-First Century*, edited by Stanley Corngold and Ruth V. Gross, 207–21. Rochester, NY: Camden House, 2011.

Levi, Neil. "How to Do Things with Modernism." *Modernism/modernity* Print Plus 3, no. 4 (December 2018). https://modernismmodernity.org/forums/posts/how-do-things-modernism (accessed August 1, 2020).

Lewis, Barry. *Kazuo Ishiguro*. Manchester: Manchester University Press, 2000.

Lloyd, David. *Irish Times: Temporalities of Modernity (Field Day Files)*. Dublin: University of Notre Dame Press, 2008.

Lorentzen, Christian. "Why Am I So Fucked Up?" Review of *NW*, by Zadie Smith. *London Review of Books* 34, no. 21 (November 8, 2012). https://www.lrb.co.uk/the-paper/v34/n21/christian-lorentzen/why-am-i-so-fucked-up (accessed August 24, 2020).

Lyall, Sarah. "Martin Amis's Big Deal Leaves Literati Fuming." *New York Times*, January 31, 1995, August 14, 2013. http://www.nytimes.com/books/98/02/01/home/amis-bigdeal.html (accessed September 3, 2013).

Lynn, David. "A Conversation with Ian McEwan." *Kenyon Review* 29, no. 3 (Summer 2007): 38–51. Reprinted in *Conversations with Ian McEwan*, edited by Ryan Roberts, 153. Jackson: University of Mississippi Press, 2010.

Magennis, Caroline. *Sons of Ulster: Massculinities in the Contemporary Northern Irish Novel*. Bern: Peter Lang, 2010.

Manshel, Alexander. "The Rise of the Recent Historical Novel." *Post45*, September 29, 2017. post45.org/2017/09/the-rise-of-the-recent-historical-novel/ (accessed November 21, 2020).

Manshel, Alexander, Laura B. McGrath, and J. D. Porter, "Who Cares about Literary Prizes?" *Public Books*, September 3, 2019. https://www.publicbooks.org/who-cares-about-literary-prizes/ (accessed December 5, 2020).

Marcus, David. "Post-Hysterics: Zadie Smith and the Fiction of Austerity." *Dissent* 60, no. 2 (Spring 2013): 67–73.

Marcus, Laura. "Ian McEwan's Modernist Time: *Atonement* and *Saturday*." In *Ian McEwan: Contemporary Critical Perspectives*, edited by Sebastian Groes, 83–98. London: Bloomsbury, 2013.

Marcus, Laura. "Legacies of Modernism." In *The Cambridge Companion to the Modernist Novel*, edited by Morag Shiach, 82–98. Cambridge: Cambridge University Press, 2007.

Marcus, Laura. "Virginia Woolf and the Hogarth Press." In *Modernist Writers and the Marketplace*, edited by Ian Willison, Warwick Gould, and Warren Chernaik, 124–50. New York: St. Martins, 1996.

Marx, Karl. *Capital: A Critique of Political Economy. Vol. 1.* Translated by Samuel Moore and Edward Aveling. New York: Modern Library, 1906.

Marsh, Nicky. "Taking the Maggie: Money, Sovereignty, and Masculinity in British Fiction of the Eighties." *Modern Fiction Studies* 53, no. 4 (2007): 845–66.

Mason, Gregory. "An Interview with Kazuo Ishiguro." In *Conversations with Kazuo Ishiguro*, edited by Brian W. Shaffer and Cynthia F. Wong, 3–14. Jackson: University Press of Mississippi, 2008.

Matz, Jesse. *Lasting Impressions: The Legacies of Impressionism in Contemporary Culture.* New York: Columbia University Press, 2016.

Matz, Jesse. *Literary Impressionism and Modernist Aesthetics.* Cambridge: Cambridge University Press, 2001.

McBride, Eimear. *A Girl Is a Half-Formed Thing.* Minneapolis, MN: Coffee House Press, 2014.

McCombe, John P. "The End of (Anthony) Eden: Ishiguro's *The Remains of the Day* and Midcentury Anglo-American Tensions." *Twentieth Century Literature* 48, no. 1 (Spring 2002): 77–99.

McCrum, Robert. "If 1900 Was Oysters and Champagne, 2000 Is a Pint of Lager and a Packet of Crisps." *Observer*, December 24, 2000, 19. Quoted in Claire Squires, *Marketing Literature: The Making of Contemporary Writing in Britain*, 64. Basingstoke, UK: Palgrave Macmillan, 2007.

McEwan, Ian. *Amsterdam.* London: Jonathan Cape, 1998.

McEwan, Ian. *Atonement.* London: Jonathan Cape, 2001.

McEwan, Ian. *Saturday.* New York: Nan A. Talese, 2005.

McEwan, Ian. *Sweet Tooth.* New York: Anchor, 2013.

McEwan, Ian. "'Enduring Fame': An Interview with Ian McEwan." Interview by Aida Edemariam. *Guardian*, August 18, 2007. http://books.guardian.co.uk/interviews/story/0,,2151430,00.html (accessed August 5, 2019).

McEwan, Ian. "The Art of Fiction CLXXIII." Interview by Adam Begley. *The Paris Review* 44, no. 162 (Summer 2002): 30–60. Reprinted in *Conversations with Ian McEwan*, edited by Ryan Roberts, 89–107, 103. Jackson: University of Mississippi Press, 2010.

McEwan, Ian. "Zadie Smith Talks with Ian McEwan." Interview by Zadie Smith. *The Believer*, August 26, 2005. Reprinted in *Conversations with Ian McEwan*, edited by Ryan Roberts, 108–33. Jackson: University of Mississippi Press, 2010.

McGurl, Mark. *The Program Era: Postwar Fiction and the Rise of Creative Writing*. Cambridge, MA: Harvard University Press, 2009.

McLeod, Lewis. "Eliminating the Random, Ruling the World: Monologic Hybridity in Zadie Smith's *White Teeth* and Salman Rushdie's *Midnight's Children*." In *Reading Zadie Smith: The First Decade and Beyond*, edited by Philip Tew, 155–68. New York: Bloomsbury, 2013.

Menke, Richard. "Mimesis and Informatics in *The Information*." In *Martin Amis: Postmodernism and Beyond*, edited by Gavin Keulks, 137–57. Basingstoke, UK: Palgrave Macmillan, 2006.

Mickalites, Carey James. *Modernism and Market Fantasy: British Fictions of Capital, 1910–1939*. Basingstoke, UK: Palgrave, 2012.

Moody, Alys. *The Art of Hunger: Aesthetic Autonomy and the Afterlives of Modernism*. Oxford: Oxford University Press, 2018.

Moody, Alys. "Indifferent and Detached: Modernism and the Aesthetic Affect." *Modernism/modernity* Print Plus 3, no. 4 (December 2018). https://modernismmodernity.org/forums/posts/indifferent-and-detached (accessed August 15, 2020).

Morrison, Mark S. *The Public Face of Modernism: Little Magazines, Audiences, and Reception, 1905–1920*. Madison: University of Wisconsin Press, 2001.

Moss, Laura. "The Politics of Everyday Hybridity: Zadie Smith's *White Teeth*." *Wasafiri* 18, no. 39 (2003): 11–17.

Murphy, Michael. "'One Hundred Percent Bohemia': Pop Decadence and the Aestheticization of Commodity in the Rise of the Slicks." In *Marketing Modernisms: Self-Promotion, Canonization, Rereading*, edited by Kevin J. H. Dettmar and Stephen Watt, 61–89. Ann Arbor: University of Michigan Press, 1996.

Nealon, Jeffrey. *Post-Postmodernism, or, The Cultural Logic of Just-in-Time Capitalism*. Stanford: Stanford University Press, 2012.

Nieland, Justus. *Feeling Modern: The Eccentricities of Public Life*. Urbana: University of Illinois Press, 2008.

Norman, Will. "Killing the Crime Novel: Martin Amis's *Night Train*, Genre and Literary Fiction." *Journal of Modern Literature* 35, no. 1 (Fall 2011): 37–59.

North, Michael. *Machine-Age Comedy*. Oxford: Oxford University Press, 2009.

Oates, Joyce Carol. "Cards of Identity: Zadie Smith's *NW*." Review of *NW* by Zadie Smith. *New York Review of Books*, September 27, 2012. https://www.nybooks.com/articles/2012/09/27/cards-identity/ (accessed July 23, 2020).

O'Brien, Susie. "Serving a New World Order: Postcolonial Politics in Kazuo Ishiguro's *The Remains of the Day*." *Modern Fiction Studies* 42, no. 4 (1996): 787–806.

O'Grady, Kathleen. "*White Teeth*: A Conversation with Zadie Smith." *Atlantis* 27, no. 1 (September 2002): 105–11.

O'Keefe, Alice. "Eimear McBride's Daring and Dazzling Novel." Review of *A Girl Is a Half-Formed Thing*, by Eimear McBride. *Observer Fiction*, May 18, 2014. https://www.theguardian.com/books/2014/may/18/girl-is-a-half-formed-thing-review-daring-dazzling-eimear-mcbride (accessed November 24, 2020).

O'Malley, Seamus. *Modernism and Historical Narrative*. Oxford University Press, 2015.

O'Reilly, Daragh. "Martin Amis on Marketing." In *Consuming Books: The Marketing and Consumption of Literature*, edited by Stephen Brown, 73–82. London: Routledge, 2006.

Palmer, Camilla. "Zadie Smith's 'White Knuckle Ride': From 'Black Woman Writer' to 'Acclaimed Novelist and Critic.'" *Hecate* 41, nos. 1–2 (2015): 156–65.

Paproth, Mathew. "The Modernist and Postmodernist Zadie Smith." In *Zadie Smith: Critical Essays*, edited by Tracey L. Walters, 9–30. New York: Peter Lang, 2008.

Patten, Eve. "Fiction in Conflict: Northern Ireland's Prodigal Novelists." In *Peripheral Visions: Images of Nationhood in Contemporary British Fiction*, edited by I. A. Bell, 128–48. Cardiff: University of Wales Press, 1995.

Procter, James. "New Ethnicities, the Novel, and the Burden of Representation." In *A Concise Companion to Contemporary British Fiction*, edited by James English, 101–20. Malden, MA: Blackwell, 2006.

Quarrie, Cynthia. "Impossible Inheritance: Filiation and Patrimony in Kazuo Ishiguro's *The Unconsoled*." *Critique* 55, no. 2 (2014): 138–51.

Rainey, Lawrence. *Institutions of Modernism*. New Haven, CT: Yale University Press, 1998.

Ramírez, Héctor. "A Broken Bildungsroman." *American Book Review* 35, no. 6 (2014): 17.

Reitano, Natalie. "The Good Wound: Memory and Community in *The Unconsoled*." *Texas Studies in Literature and Language* 49, no. 4 (Winter 2007): 361–86.

Reynolds, Paige. Introduction to *Modernist Afterlives in Irish Literature and Culture*, edited by Paige Reynolds, 1–8. London: Anthem Press, 2019.

Reynolds, Paige. "Bird Girls: Modernism and Sexual Ethics in Contemporary Irish Fiction." In *Modernism and Close Reading*, edited by David James, 173–90. Oxford: Oxford University Press, 2020.

Reynolds, Paige. "Trauma, Intimacy, and Modernist Form." *Breac*, September 11, 2014. https://breac.nd.edu/articles/trauma-intimacy-and-modernist-form/ (accessed November 20, 2020).

Robbins, Bruce. *Upward Mobility and the Common Good: Toward a Literary History of the Welfare State*. Princeton, NJ: Princeton University Press, 2007.

Robbins, Bruce. "Cruelty Is Bad: Banality and Proximity in *Never Let Me Go*." *Novel* 40, no. 3 (2007): 289–302.

Robinson, Richard. "The Modernism of Ian McEwan's Atonement." *Modern Fiction Studies* 56, no. 3 (2010): 473–95.

Rosen, Jeremy. *Minor Characters Have Their Day: Genre and the Contemporary Literary Marketplace*. New York: Columbia University Press, 2016.

Rosenquist, Rod. *Modernism, the Market and the Institution of the New*. Cambridge: Cambridge University Press, 2009.

Ross, Michael L. "On a Darkling Planet: Ian McEwan's 'Saturday' and the Condition of England." *Twentieth Century Literature* 54, no. 1 (2008): 75–96.

Roth, Marco. "Rise of the Neuronovel." *n + 1* 8, September 14, 2009. https://nplusonemag.com/issue-8/essays/the-rise-of-the-neuronovel (accessed August 6, 2019).

Roy, Anjali Gera. "Fact and Fantasy, Myth and History: The Magic Realist Mode in Salman Rushdie's Fiction." In *Mapping Out the Rushdie Republic: Some Recent Surveys*, edited by Tapan Kumar Ghosh and Prasanta Bhattacharyya, 34–52. Newcastle upon Tyne: Cambridge Scholars Press, 2016.

Rushdie, Salman. *Imaginary Homelands*. London: Granta, 1991.

Rushdie, Salman. Introduction to *Midnight's Children*. The 25th Anniversary Edition, ix–xvi. New York: Random House, 2006.

Rushdie, Salman. *Joseph Anton: A Memoir*. New York: Random House, 2012.

Rushdie, Salman. *Midnight's Children*. New York: Random House, 2006.

Rushdie, Salman. *The Ground beneath Her Feet*. New York: Henry Holt, 1999.

Rushdie, Salman. *The Satanic Verses*. New York: Picador, [1988] 1997.

Rushdie, Salman. "An Exclusive Talk with Salman Rushdie." Interview with Sarah Crichton and Laura Shapiro. *Newsweek* 115, no. 7 (February 12, 1990): 40–4. Reprinted in *Conversations with Salman Rushdie*, edited by Michael Reder, 123–31. Jackson: University of Mississippi Press, 2000.

Rushdie, Salman. "An Interview with Salman Rushdie." Interview by Blake Morrison. *Granta* 31 (Spring 1990): 113–25. Reprinted in *Conversations with Salman Rushdie*, edited by Michael Reder, 132–41. Jackson: University of Mississippi Press, 2000.

Rushdie, Salman. "In Good Faith." In *Imaginary Homelands*, 393–414. London: Granta, 1991.

Ryan, Bill. *Making Capital from Culture: The Corporate Forms of Cultural Production*. Berlin: Walter de Cruyter, 1992.

Ryan, Kiernan. *Ian McEwan*. Plymouth: Northcote House, 1994.

Ryan, Kiernan. "Sex, Violence, and Complicity: Martin Amis and Ian McEwan." In *An Introduction to Contemporary Fiction*, edited by Rod Mengham, 203–18. Cambridge, UK: Polity, 1999.

San Juan Jr., E. *Beyond Postcolonial Theory*. New York: St. Martin's Press, 1998.

Sands, Sarah. "Zadie, the Woman Who Reinvented the Novelist." *Daily Telegraph*, March 24, 2000, 28.

Scanlan, Margaret. *Traces of Another Time: History and Politics in Postwar British Fiction*. Princeton, NJ: Princeton University Press, 1990.

Sell, Jonathan P. A. "Chance and Gesture in Zadie Smith's *White Teeth* and *The Autograph Man*: A Model for Multicultural Identity?" *Journal of Commonwealth Literature* 41, no. 3 (2006): 27–44.

Shaffer, Brian. *Understanding Kazuo Ishiguro*. Columbia: University of South Carolina Press, 1998.

Siegel, Jonah. "Looking at the Limits of Autonomy: Response." *Victorian Studies* 51, no. 3 (Spring 2009): 496–504.

Sim, Wai-Chew. *Kazuo Ishiguro*. London: Routledge, 2010.

Simon, Linda. "Remains of the Novelist." *Commonweal* (March 22, 1996): 25–6.

Sinykin, Dan N. "The Conglomerate Era: Publishing, Authorship, and Literary Form, 1965–2007." *Contemporary Literature* 58, no. 4 (Winter 2017): 462–91.

Smith, Zadie. *Changing My Mind: Occasional Essays*. New York: Penguin, 2009.

Smith, Zadie. *NW*. New York: Penguin, 2012.

Smith, Zadie. *On Beauty*. London: Penguin, 2005.

Smith, Zadie. *White Teeth*. New York: Random House, 2000.

So, Richard Jean. *Redlining Culture: A Data History of Racial Inequality and Postwar Fiction*. New York: Columbia University Press, 2021.

Squires, Claire. *Marketing Literature: The Making of Contemporary Writing in Britain*. Basingstoke, UK: Palgrave Macmillan, 2007.

Squires, Claire. "Novelistic Production and the Publishing Industry in Britain and Ireland." In *A Companion to the British and Irish Novel, 1945–2000*, edited by Brian W. Shaffer, 177–93. Malden, MA: Blackwell, 2005.

Stein, Mark. *Black British Literature: Novels of Transformation*. Columbus: Ohio State University Press, 2004.

Strychacz, Thomas. *Modernism, Mass Culture, and Professionalism*. Cambridge: Cambridge University Press, 1993.

Stuckey, Lexi. "Red and Yellow, Black and White: Color-Blindness as Disillusionment in Zadie Smith's 'Hanwell in Hell.'" In *Zadie Smith: Critical Essays*, edited by Tracey L. Walters, 157–69. New York: Peter Lang, 2008.

Su, John J. *Imagination and the Contemporary Novel*. Cambridge: Cambridge University Press, 2010.

Sutherland, John. "A Touch of Forster." Review of *On Beauty* by Zadie Smith. *New Statesman*, September 12, 2005. https://www.newstatesman.com/node/162810 (accessed September 15, 2020).

Tew, Philip. *The Contemporary British Novel*. London: Continuum, 2004.

Tew, Philip. *Zadie Smith*. Basingstoke, UK: Palgrave, 2010.

Tew, Philip. "Martin Amis and Late-Twentieth Century Working-Class Masculinity: *Money* and *London Fields*." In *Martin Amis: Postmodernism and Beyond*, edited by Gavin Keulks, 71–86. Basingstoke, UK: Palgrave Macmillan, 2006.

The Nobel Prize in Literature 2017. *NobelPrize.org*. https://www.nobelprize.org/prizes/literature/2017/summary/ (accessed January 10, 2021).

Thompson, John B. *Merchants of Culture: The Publishing Business in the Twenty-First Century*. London: Plume, 2012.

Todd, Richard. *Consuming Fictions: The Booker Prize and Fiction in Britain Today*. London: Bloomsbury, 1996.

Todd, Richard. "Literary Fiction and the Book Trade." In *A Concise Companion to Contemporary British Fiction*, edited by James F. English, 19–38. Malden, MA: Blackwell, 2006.

Todd, Richard. "Looking-Glass Worlds in Martin Amis's Early Fiction: Reflectiveness, Mirror Narcissism, and Doubles." In *Martin Amis: Postmodernism and Beyond*, edited by Gavin Keulks, 22–35. Basingstoke, UK: Palgrave Macmillan, 2006.

Turner, Catherine. *Marketing Modernism between the Two World Wars*. Amherst: University of Massachusetts Press, 2003.

Valle Alcalá, Roberto del. "Martin Amis's *Money* and the Crisis of Fordism." *Critique: Studies in Contemporary Fiction* 60, no. 1 (2019): 1–10.

Wachinger, Tobias A. *Posing In-Between: Postcolonial Englishness and the Commodification of Hybridity*. Frankfurt: Peter Lang, 2003.

Walkowitz, Rebecca. *Cosmopolitan Style: Modernism beyond the Nation*. New York: Columbia University Press, 2007.

Wallace, Elizabeth Kowaleski. "Postcolonial Melancholia in Ian McEwan's *Saturday*." *Studies in the Novel* 39, no. 4 (Winter 2007): 465–80.

Waters, Juliet. "The Little Chill: Has the Booker Prize Chosen the Noveau Beaujolais of Fiction?" Cited in Dominic Head, *Ian McEwan*, 144–5. Manchester: Manchester University Press, 2007.

Wernick, Andrew. "Authorship and the Supplement of Promotion." In *What Is an Author*, edited by Maurice Biriotti and Nicola Miller, 85–103. Manchester: Manchester University Press, 1993.

Wicke, Jennifer. "Appreciation, Depreciation: Modernism's Speculative Bubble." *Modernism/modernity* 8, no. 3 (September 2001): 389–403.

Wicke, Jennifer. "Coterie Consumption: Bloomsbury, Keynes, and Modernism as Marketing." In *Marketing Modernisms: Self-Promotion, Canonization, Rereading*, edited by Kevin J. H. Dettmar and Stephen Watt, 109–32. Ann Arbor: University of Michigan Press, 1996.

Winterhalter, Teresa. "'Plastic Fork in Hand': Reading as a Tool of Ethical Repair in Ian McEwan's *Saturday*." *Journal of Narrative Theory* 40, no. 3 (Fall 2010): 338–63.

Woolf, Virginia. *Mrs. Dalloway*. San Diego, CA: Harcourt Brace, [1925] 1997.

Woolf, Virginia. "Mr. Bennett and Mrs. Brown." In *The Virginia Woolf Reader*, edited by Mitchell A. Leaska, 192–212. New York: Harcourt 1984.

Woolf, Virginia. *The Diary of Virginia Woolf, Vol. 2*. Edited by Anne Olivier Bell. New York: Harcourt, 1980.

Woods, Tim. "A Complex Legacy: Modernity's Uneasy Discourse of Ethics and Responsibility." In *The Legacies of Modernism: Historicising Postwar and Contemporary Fiction*, edited by David James, 153–69. New York: Cambridge University Press, 2012.

Zalewski, Daniel. "The Background Hum: Ian McEwan's Art of Unease." *New Yorker*, February 23, 2009. Quoted in David James, *Modernist Futures: Innovation and Inheritance in the Contemporary Novel*, 136. Cambridge: Cambridge University Press, 2012.

Index

Adorno, Theodor 6–8, 27, 122–3, 132–3
aesthetic
   autonomy 1, 4, 6–8, 10, 15, 24, 57, 66, 71,
      77, 80, 82, 100, 124, 132–3, 160, 162,
      165, 168, 171–2, 176, 179, 181, 183
   innovation 153
   medium 8
   sensibilities 148
   values 129
Ahmad, Aijaz 81
Amazon Literary Partnership 184
Amis, Martin 22, 25, 29, 110
   authorial celebrity 30, 32–3
   authorial self-fashioning 31, 44
   brand 30
   commercialization of literature 30
   fictional author 40
   greed storm 29
   Information, The (1995) 29–31, 43–50
   literary celebrity 31
   media scandal 29–31
   modernist literary precursors 35
   Money (1984) 30–1, 37–43, 47
   negotiations with his celebrity status 30
   Night Train (1997) 50
   postmodern satire on social class 31
   satire 30
   self-authorization 31
   self-referentiality 41
   self-reflexive complicity 36, 50
   stylistic affectations 35
   Success (1978) 30–6
   zugzwang 42
Amsterdam (McEwan) 53–5
   Booker Prize 56, 76
   moral critique 56
Anchor Books 75
Anglo-American circles 90
anti-lyrical literary aesthetic 173
anxiety
   of contamination 17
   of Indianness 88

appearance of literariness 82
Arabian Nights, The 85
artistic production 8
Artist of the Floating World, An
   (Ishiguro) 107
Ashcroft, Bill 83
Atonement (McEwan) 53–4, 56–64, 74
   marketing and reception 56
   metafictional conclusion 64
   moral indictment 61
   self-reflexive writerly plot 58
Attridge, Derek 4, 54, 161, 168
author(ial)
   celebrity 11–13, 18, 30, 37
   consciousness 12
   imprimatur 12
   legitimation 75
   self-effacement 12
   self-fashioning 14, 19
autonomy 9–18
   absolute 14
   aesthetic 1, 4, 6–8, 10, 15, 24, 57, 66,
      71, 77, 80, 82, 100, 124, 132–3, 160,
      162, 165, 168, 171–2, 176, 179,
      181, 183
   authorial 3, 94
   creative 54, 64
   cultural 18
   false 179
   formal 28, 139, 143, 210
   literary, 3, 87, 191–192, 207–208
   and market complicity 8
   mythologized 14
   modernism 55
   personal 205
   relative 10, 21, 54, 87
   self-reflexive assertion 54
   stylistic 175

Barber-Stetson, Claire 158
Barnes, Julian 29
Beckett, Samuel 9, 27, 167

Begley, Jon 37
Bergholtz, Benjamin 139, 144
Bernard, Catherine 47
Bertelsmann 19, 29
Bildungsroman 164, 168
Black Dogs (McEwan) 56
Bohemian modernism 44
Bombay talkies 84
Booker Prize
  Amsterdam (1998) 56, 76
  Midnight's Children (1981) 79, 83, 107
  Remains of the Day, The
    (1989) 107, 113
Bourdieu, Pierre 10–11, 13, 15, 64, 82
brand name 18–25
Brannigan, John 175
Brantlinger, Patrick 37
Brennan, Timothy 81, 85, 137
Bretton Woods agreement 38
Brouillette, Sarah 3, 23, 65, 75, 77, 81–2, 96, 102, 113–15, 118, 141, 144, 167, 207
Brown, Nicholas 22, 124
Buddha of Suburbia, The (Kureishi) 136
Bulgakov, Mikhail 26, 96
bureaucratic capitalist modernity 109
Burns, Anna 20, 27–8, 163–5
  experimental aesthetic forms 166
  gendered engagements 165
  Milkman (2018) 28, 164, 175–83

Calder, Liz 91
Cape, Jonathan 29, 91
capitalist
  modernity 8
  promotion 91
Carpentier, Martha 168
Casanova, Pascale 82
celebrities *see also* Amis, Martin; Burns, Anna; Ishiguro, Kazuo; McBride, Eimear; McEwan, Ian; Rushdie, Salman; Smith, Zadie
  contemporary 15
  cultural 112–25
  market promotion of celebrity authors 76
  monopolistic culture of celebrity 3
  promotion 12
  self-promotion 77

Cement Garden, The (McEwan) 53
Cerf, Bennett 17
charismatic ideology 64
Chaudhuri, Amit 115
Child in Time, The (McEwan) 67
Clark, Roger Y. 85
Coetzee, J. M. 4
Coffee House Press 184
collective make-belief 118
Comfort of Strangers, The
  (McEwan) 53, 56
comic allegory 38
comic blasphemy 172
commercialization 82, 119
  complicity 3
  culture 7
  literary market 2
  of literature 29
commodification 8, 11, 30
  of mass cultural production 163
  multiculturalism 137
commodity
  absolute 123–4
  fetishism 23
conglomerate
  finance model 19
  system 29
Connell, Liam 91
Connolly, Cyril 60–1
consumer capitalism 10
consumerist individualism 37
containment strategy 108
contemporary
  capitalism 125
  celebrity 15
  fiction 6, 10
  modernism 4–9
  writing 19
corporate
  production 183
  values 129
corporatization of literary publishing 76
Crosthwaite, Paul 20, 23
cultural production 95
  financialization of 7
  modernist 12
culture(al)
  celebrities 3, 118
  consecration 73

contradiction 71
economy of self-promotion 77
globalization 102
modernity 6

Danius, Sara 108
D'Arcy, Michael 8, 133
Davidson, Cathy 129
Deane, Seamus 175
degree of autonomy 11
Delany, Paul 19
Diedrick, James 40
diegetic convention 114
disinterestedness 14
drama 61
Driscoll, Lawrence 41, 108
Dyer, Geoff 57

Eaglestone, Robert 80
Eberhardt, Mark 145
economic globalization 37
economic instrumentalism 109
economy of prestige 9
Eliot, T. S. 10–11, 35, 86
elitism, social 1
Enduring Love (McEwan) 53
English, James F. 21–2, 108, 126, 137, 159
everyday hybridity 135, 141, 143
experimental writing 2

fashionable multiculturalism 152
fatwa 80
fetishization 127
fictions of autonomy 15
financial deregulation 37
financialization of cultural production 7
Finnegans Wake (Joyce) 85, 94
First Love, Last Rites (McEwan) 53
Ford, Ford Madox 10
Forster, E. M. 1, 5, 160, 168, 169, 171–3
Freedgood, Elaine 158
free-floating exchange market 34
free market deregulation 38

Galley Beggar Press 184
Gandhi, Leela 82
Garcia Marquez, Gabriel 67
Gauthier, Tim 66–7
Gildea, Niall 45

Gilligan, Ruth 167
Gilroy, Paul 143
Girl Is a Half-Formed Thing, A (McBride) 28, 164–75, 184
  academic criticism 167
  split-subjectivity 171
  stream-of-consciousness 172
  transgressive sexual encounters 171
Glass, Loren 12
Goldman, Jonathan 12, 86
Goldstone, Andrew 15, 55
Gollancz, Victor 91
Google Maps 154
Gray, Paul 102
Gregson, Ian 193n11
Greywolf Press 184
Grimus (Rushdie) 79, 91
Ground beneath Her Feet, The (Rushdie) 26, 100–2, 104

Hachette 19
Hamish Hamilton 135
HarperCollins 19, 29, 31, 49
Heart of Darkness (Conrad) 102
historical modernism 9–18
Hodder Headline 19
Hogarth Press 10, 15
Horkheimer, Max 6
Howards End (Forster) 146
Huggan, Graham 81, 107
humanistic inquiry 129
Huyssen, Andreas 16

impressionism 60–4, 70
inauthenticity 151
India, the new myth 83
industrial capitalism 10, 125
Information, The (Amis) 22, 29–31, 43–50
"In Good Faith" (Rushdie) 100
inhuman aesthetic 131–2
Innocent, The (McEwan) 53, 74
institutional diversity 143
institutionalization 3, 55
  of cultural capital 1–2
  modernism 7
instrumentalization of individual identity 111
international book-marketing 136
Irish modernism 165

Ishiguro, Kazuo 9, 26–7, 106–12
  Artist of the Floating World, An
    (1986) 107
  Booker Prize in 1989 107
  Conversations with Kazuo Ishiguro
    (2008) 111
  cultural celebrity 112–25
  literary modernism 114
  literary self-promotion 117
  modernist aesthetic 125–33
  modernist disconsolation 112–25
  Never Let Me Go (Ishiguro) 26–7,
    110, 125–33
  Nobel Prize for literature in
    2017 108, 110
  Pale View of Hills, A (1982) 107
  Remains of the Day, The (1989) 107–8,
    110–11, 113, 116, 125
  Unconsoled, The (1995) 26–7, 112–25
Islamic fundamentalists 139

Jaffe, Aaron 11–12
Jaggi, Maya 113
Jakubiak, Katarzyna 136
James, David 2, 4, 54, 57, 152, 154, 164
James, Henry 26, 54, 66, 68
James Ivory film 110
Jameson, Fredric 6–8, 30 n17, 63
Jonathan Cape 20
Joseph Anton: A memoir
    (Rushdie) 26, 104–5
Joyce, James 11, 26, 41, 54, 66, 80, 85,
    167, 172
Joycean fragmentation 153
Joycean hyperrealism 154
Joycean legacies 168

Kafka, Franz 9, 27, 111–14
Kafkaesque expressionism 120
Kane, Jean 80, 92
Kavanagh, Pat 29
Kelman, Suanne 111
Kermode, Frank 56
Knepper, Wendy 154
Knönagel, Alex 97
Kortenaar, Neil ten 90, 99
Kureishi, Hanif 136

Lady Chatterley's Lover (Lawrence) 105
Latham, Sean 14, 16, 18, 23

Lazarus, Neil 106, 109
legacies of modernism 54
Lemon, Robert 114
Levi, Neil 5, 146, 150
Lewis, Wyndham 30
liberal diversity initiatives 147
literary
  alterity 4
  celebrity 3
  fiction 3, 10
  impressionism 54
  modernism 11
  realism 37
literary autonomy 185
Lloyd, David 165
Lolita (Nabokov) 105
Lorentzen, Christian 153, 155
Lynn, David 61
lyrical realism 62

Madden, Deirdre 175
manufactured multiculturalism 140
Marcus, David 153
Marcus, Laura 54, 80
market
  logics of literary production 23
  metafiction 23
  for modernism 18–25, 116
  promotion of celebrity authors 76
Marriage of Heaven and Hell (Blake) 96
Mars-Jones, Adam 153
mass-market forms of publicity 3
Master and Margarita, The (Bulgakov) 96
Matz, Jesse 26, 55, 58, 63, 158
McBride, Eimear 1, 20, 27, 163–5
  broken bildungsroman 173
  experimental aesthetic forms 166
  gendered engagements 165
  Girl Is a Half-Formed Thing, A
    (2013) 28, 164–75, 184
  life-altering experience 170
  metamodernism 166–75
McCarthy, Tom 151
McEwan, Ian 1, 9, 25, 53–4, 110–11
  aesthetic autonomy 71
  ambivalent metamodernism 65
  Amsterdam (1998) 53–6, 73
  Atonement (2001) 56–64, 74
  authorial legitimation 75

authorial self-fashioning 55, 77
Black Dogs (1992) 56
Cement Garden, The (1978) 53
Child in Time, The (1987) 67
Comfort of Strangers, The (1981) 53, 56
Enduring Love (1997) 53
First Love, Last Rites (1975) 53
impressionism 56–64
Innocent, The (1990) 53, 74
legacies of modernism 54
modernist aesthetics 54–5, 57, 64, 73, 77
neoliberal modernism 65–73
Saturday (2005) 65–7, 71
self-referential fiction 64
Sweet Tooth (McEwan) 53, 71, 74–7
McKibben, Sarah 164
McNamee, Eoin 176
metamodernism 2, 45, 167 *see also* modernism
metamodernist *see also* modernism
appropriations 153
fiction 5, 24
writing 4
Midnight's Children (Rushdie) 26, 79, 87, 136
Best of the Booker in 1993 79
Booker Prize in 1981 79, 83, 107
Indian authenticity 82–3
myth of national optimism 84
Milkman (Burns) 28, 164–5, 175–83
modernism 1–2 *see also* metamodernism
aesthetic autonomy 8
autonomy 55
commercialization of modernism 82
conservative affirmation 5
contemporaneity 8
contemporary 4–9
historical 9–18
institutionalization 7
institutionalized cultural capital 9
Irish modernism 165
legacies of 5, 54
literary 11, 114
literary fiction 10
market for 18–25
mythologized autonomy 14
neoliberal 65–73

modernist *see also* metamodernist
aesthetics 77
authorship 12–14
autonomy 15
myth of autonomy 40
modernist impersonality 155
Money (Amis) 30–1, 37–43, 47
monopolistic culture of celebrity 3
Moody, Alys 5, 181
Morrison, Mark 17
Moss, Laura 135
Mrs. Dalloway (Woolf) 66, 161
multiculturalism 150
authenticity 27
commodities 137
conglomerates 3, 19
millennium 137–8
modernism 27

narrator-artificer 152
Nealon, Jeffrey 129
neoliberal
capitalism 8, 24, 132
deregulation 34
finance 7
modernism 65–73
neoliberal instrumentalization of arts and humanities 125
Net Book Agreement, 1995 19, 29
Never Let Me Go (Ishiguro) 26–7, 110, 125–33
industrial capitalism 125
nonutilitarian authenticity 128
romantic model of expressive subjectivity 128
science-fiction premise 125
training in the arts and humanities 129
Night Train (Amis) 50
Nilges, Mathias 8, 133
nonutilitarian authenticity 128
NW (Smith) 27, 159, 160, 173–180, 186, 184

Oates, Joyce Carol 152
oil crisis, 1973 38
O'Keefe, Alice 167
On Beauty (Smith) 146–51
organic multiculturalism 143

Pale View of Hills, A (Ishiguro) 107
Palmer, Camilla 136
Paradise Lost (Milton) 92, 96
Pearson 19
Picador 20
poetic autonomy 18
political hypocrisy 96
Portrait of the Artist as a Young Man, A (Joyce) 41, 47, 65, 75, 164, 167, 169–70, 173
postcolonialism 138
 literary production 112
 polyphony 145
postmodernism 4 *see also* metamodernism; modernism
 cultural production 7
 as historical antithesis 7
 literary system 19
 metafiction 4, 14
post-Rushdie orthodoxy 139
Pound, Ezra 10
private publishing 12
privatization of literary production 28, 34
pseudo-impressionism 26, 63
psychological realism 62, 113

Quarrie, Cynthia 114

Rainey, Lawrence 11
Random House 17, 29
Reagan-Thatcher economic policy 30
rearticulation 121
Reitano, Natalie 114
Remainder (McCarthy) 151
Remains of the Day, The (Ishiguro) 107, 110–11, 113, 116, 125
 Booker Prize in 1989 107, 113
 tragedy of a life 125
Reynolds, Paige 165, 167–8, 170–1
Robinson, Richard 57
Rogers, Deborah 91
Rogers, Gayle 18
romantic model of expressive subjectivity 128
Rorem, Ned 113
Rosen, Jeremy 5, 24
Roth, Marco 71
Rushdie, Salman 1, 25–7, 67, 79, 110, 136
 as ad-writer 79, 92

authorial autonomy 80
Best of the Booker in 1993 79
Booker Prize in 1981 79, 83, 107
encyclopedic formal experiment 80
fatwa 80, 97, 100–6
Grimus (1975) 79, 91
Ground beneath Her Feet (1999) 26, 100–2, 104
"In Good Faith" (1990) 100
Joseph Anton: A memoir (2012) 26, 104–5
legacies of modernism 80
Midnight's Children (1981) 26, 79, 87, 136
modernist cosmopolitanism 80–1
multinational branding 80
postcolonial modernism 80, 87
postcolonial writing 80
progressive cosmopolitan style 81
Satanic Verses, The (1988) 26, 90–100, 105, 138
self-reflexive pose of authenticity 89–90

Satanic Verses, The (Rushdie) 26, 90–100, 138
 censorship of 105
Saturday (McEwan) 65–7, 71
self-authorization 26, 31, 82
self-consciousness 58
self-legislating style 152
self-promotion 3
self-referential aesthetic effect 152
self-reflexive
 authorial references 34
 fictional space 42
 metamodernist strategies 2
 strategies 87
 sympathies 91
Seshagiri, Urmila 2
sexual fantasies 59
Shaffer, Brian 111
shameless self promotion 12
Sim, Wai-chew 114
Simon, Linda 120
simulated optimism 136
Sinykin, Dan 21
Smith, Zadie 1, 20, 24, 27, 106, 135–8
 On Beauty (2005) 146–51
 commercial fashioning 137

and literary industry for
multiculturalism 136
market for multicultural fiction 138–46
metamodernism 153
modernism and
multiculturalism 146–62
NW (2012) 27, 159, 160, 173–180,
186, 184
White Teeth (2000) 27, 135, 138,
140, 144–5
social elitism 1
social inequality 6
social transformation 7
Squires, Claire 19, 136
stream-of-consciousness 152, 155, 164,
175, 178, 180, 183
structural integrity 85
stylistic evocation of Kafka 114
Success (Amis) 30–6
Sweet Tooth (McEwan) 53, 74–7
self-perpetuating system 71

Tamás Bényei 37
Target 184
Thompson, John B. 21
Time Warner 29
Todd, Richard 29
Tóibín, Colm 64
totalitarianism 176
transnational identities 80
Trial, The (Kafka) 113
Turner, Catherine 190 n.48

Ulysses (Joyce) 11, 17, 65–6, 85, 102, 105,
155, 172

Unconsoled, The (Ishiguro) 26–7,
110, 112–25
unKafkaesque 115, 121
utopian pluralism 143

Vanity Fair 17
Viking 20
Vogue 17

Wachinger, Tobias 136–7
Walkowitz, Rebecca 80
Walton, James 113
Waugh, Evelyn 35
Waves, The (Woolf) 59–60
Wells Fargo 184
White Teeth (Smith) 27, 135
hybrid models of multiculturalism 138
literary economy 140
multicultural British society 135
multicultural marketing 144
publications of 145
Wicke, Jennifer 70
Wilson, Robert McLiam 175
Wong, Cynthia 111
Wood, James 113
Woods, Tim 4
Woolf, Leonard 10–11, 15, 26, 57
Woolf, Virginia 10–11, 15, 54, 66, 69
Woolfian impressionism 5, 9, 60–1, 63
Wylie, Andrew 29, 91

zugzwang 42